D0204261

Spenserian Poetics

Spenserian Poetics

Idolatry, Iconoclasm, and Magic

Kenneth Gross

Cornell University Press
Ithaca and London

First published 1985 by Cornell University Press.

International Standard Book Number 0-8014-1805-4
Library of Congress Catalog Card Number 85-47701
Printed in the United States of America
Librarians: Library of Congress cataloging information appears on the last page of the book.

The paper in this book is acid-free and meets the guidelines for permanence and durability of the Committee on Production Guidelines for Book Longevity of the Council on Library Resources.

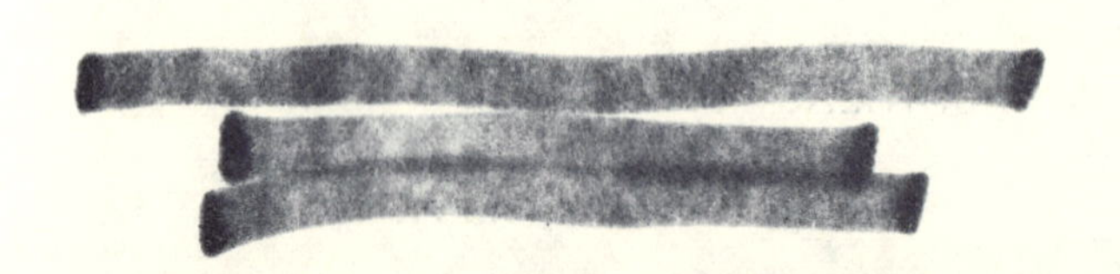

For WW and JMG

A false doctor is not a kind of doctor,
but a false god is a kind of god.

Iris Murdoch

Contents

Preface

The following pages describe a problem and essay a mode of commentary. They examine the work of a poet who both embraces and fears mythology, whose visionary quests come into conflict with a manifold skepticism of vision. Such a conflict has (in part) been described before. But I want here to reevaluate its stakes and to develop a more adequate language by which we might make sense of it. My main text is Edmund Spenser's *The Faerie Queene*, and my initial route into that poem is through a study of idolatry and iconoclasm, that is, a study of ideas about true and false gods, about their potent or empty images, and about the violence that might be worked against them. Though taken over from the narratives of a religious tradition, notions of idolatry and iconoclasm allow me to construct a conceptual grammar that can illuminate a variety of political, artistic, and erotic themes. Indeed, I have tried to juxtapose my own readings of that tradition against Spenser's allegorical imagemaking in ways that raise fresh questions for the larger theory of poetic expression. I have looked at Spenserian romance in terms of its concern with error and illusion, and with their problematic cures; strangely enough, the poet emerges as one for whom idolatry may be something as much to be courted as attacked.

My analysis focuses on episodes of *The Faerie Queene* which present unsettling, sometimes violent encounters with divinity, phantasm, or artifice, but I have tried to do justice to as wide as possible a range of Spenser's modes, voices, and masks. I am not certain, however, how recognizable will be the face of the poet revealed in this study. Spenser the propagandist for empire, the literary pictorialist, the intricate (if playful) moralist, the hieratic cosmologist, the apocalyptic visionary, the humanist educator—all of these labels I want at once to honor and rethink. My own Spenser may at first glance appear to be a strongly Protestant poet, though here the use of such a rubric depends more on my showing his links to strategies of biblical writing than on his ties to the literature of any contemporary religious movement. An even more accurate name for that poet's stance, however, might be found in the displaced, diffused, demystified, ironic, and hyperbolized Protestantism we have learned to call Romanticism. The likeness is far from exact, of course, but the Romantic element in Spenser is stronger than many of his scholars have been willing to admit. The reader should at least be aware that I describe a poet whom I think Blake or Keats or Ruskin could have taken seriously as a master, and who might have posed formal and intellectual questions that could trouble even a Freud or a Stevens. Admitting the risks of distortion, I think this Spenser might tell us something important about our own romanticisms and modernisms, for he is one of their notable forerunners. Such a figure is hardly visible even in much of the best Spenser criticism, and it seems to me an urgent and not merely anachronistic exercise to see what his lineaments might be.

That Spenser remains very much a Renaissance poet seems needless to assert or deny at the outset. My way of situating the poet's work in literary, religious, and political history will at times appear idiosyncratic, especially since my emphases tend to shift in line with the changing, pragmatic burdens of my commentary. The difficulties here derive not so much from lack of commitment to the field and facts of history as from the peculiar requirements of my analysis, and from the radical eclecticism of Spenser's poetry. In order to compose a properly *conceptual* grammar, ideas of idolatry, iconoclasm, and (as I shall explain later) magic must help us to stretch our notions of literary *conceivability*, as well as to fix the boundaries of certain analytic concepts. Their usefulness in my commentary depends precisely on *not* assigning them any automatic philosophical or historical limitations. The ideas, images, and gestures I have studied develop within a complex tradition that diverse sects can put to diverse uses: each iconoclast will define idolatry in his or her own way and will often propose a mode of iconoclasm which an opponent would take as the purest idolatry. Spenser, indeed, is peculiarly sensitive to the way that gestures of iconoclasm can themselves turn into or conceal idolatry. This mobility in ideas of idolatry and iconoclasm which Spenser both exposes and expands is something that I in turn have tried to maintain, for it is their mobility which makes these concepts such powerful tools for investigating the shape of the poet's dramatic allegories. They point to stresses and questions in *The Faerie Queene* too easily glossed over by other modes of analysis; though partly ahistorical, such an approach may keep us from oversimplifying Spenser's dialogue with both his own period and ours.

Having said this, I must touch on one broadly historical issue before I start. To co-opt for my own uses so loaded and nowadays clichéd a term as "iconoclasm" is itself a risk, especially in the generalized way that I have done. And though I have tried to restore some of the word's religious force, my analysis slights the immediate, material aspects of iconoclasm in the sixteenth century. We need to remind ourselves of the degree to which such forms of physical destruction involved complex acts of imagination: the breaking down of a crucifix, the tearing up of a brass tomb relief, the dismantling of a mural of Purgatory, the whitewashing of saints' portraits—all of these acts were bound up in a dense web of words, ideas, and myths, both in what they turned away from and in what they turned toward. However much acts of iconoclasm might seem imitations of prophetic gestures, the motives for violence against the symbolic fabric of medieval church architecture could vary from simple greed and desire for political revenge to a deep, almost physiological horror, a sense of demonic contagion inhering in every stone of a church, a hatred that could resolve itself not in the simple removal but in the degradation of formerly sacred shapes. To break an image is not necessarily to break away from images. Hence a complete grammar of iconoclasm would also teach us to look closely at the partial survivals of and substitutions for images, at the forms or fragments left behind and at what was raised up in their place: the desanctified pulpit or communion table set on the spot where the fixed holy altar had stood, the royal coat of arms erected in the place of a holy rood or a mural of Purgatory, the iconic texts from Scripture lettered over the blanked-out panels of a triptych. Even minor relics of iconoclasm can be instructive in this context. For example: hanging on my wall is a rubbing taken from the brass tomb of one of Henry VIII's knights. A reformer's chisel has struck some odd, random blows across the face and torso of the armored figure, and then excised with great care the last phrases of the Latin epitaph—probably a prayer that sounded too much like a magical spell or rejected liturgical formula. The empirical or aesthetic loss is minimal. But the scars and erasures inscribe a radically altered interpretation on the image; thus disfigured, it becomes at once a potential and partly cured idol. Though certainly ambiguous, such historical traces as are left on the brass ("old dints" and "cruell markes") nevertheless define a poetry and a pathos to which Spenser was witness and that might in some ways provide excellent commentary on his own scenes of iconoclasm and disenchantment.

A book about such things, however, is not the one that I have been able to write. Spenser seems to me so to expand upon the myths and poetic ideas that fed iconoclasm that he might really serve better to interpret the physical evidence than that evidence serves to interpret him. Furthermore, while *The Faerie Queene* turns iconoclasm more fully into parable, looking at its corruptions as well as its clarifications, it also interweaves images of iconoclasm with forms of action to which they would seem unrelated in historical life. Which means that we may have to consider the complex, paradoxical disenchantments of the poem in isolation from the material archeology of iconoclasm, at least until we have found the remains of a church in which idols were made and broken at the same instant.

"To read means to borrow; to create out of one's readings is paying off one's debts." Yet some things owed must be acknowledged more plainly. Throughout the long process of composition, John Hollander offered both parables and practical advice. Paolo Valesio reminded me of what a difficult business it is to speak about magic. And Angus Fletcher, whose own books were with me from the beginning of the project, toward the end helped me to work through a crucial revision. The essays of Harry Berger, Jr., first showed me the "secret discipline" of reading Spenser's poetry. Of those friends whose words I have found myself most urgently answering or stealing, I must thank in particular John Guillory and Herbert Marks. Elizabeth Calihan and Tenney Nathanson worried the text with me at length; I owe them a better understanding of a book which I thought I knew. A myriad of helpful ideas, questions, and echoes have come from others, including Harold Bloom, Donald Cheney, Joan Dayan, Calvin Edwards, Margaret Ferguson, Carla Freccero, Thomas Hyde, Bernhard Kendler, Jill Robbins, and Joseph Anthony Wittreich, Jr. My family I owe much for their steady kindness. I must thank as well my friends and colleagues at the University of Rochester, whose interest and support have made the completing of this book a saner and more engaged task than it might otherwise have been.

I am grateful for permission to use the following: material from Oxford Standard Authors Edition of *Spenser: Poetical Works*, edited by J. C. Smith and E. de Selincourt (1912) and from Spenser's *A View of the Present State of Ireland*, edited by W. L. Renwick (1970), reprinted by permission of Oxford University Press; lines from "Notes toward a Supreme Fiction," from *The Collected Poems of Wallace Stevens* (copyright 1942 by Wallace Stevens), reprinted by permission of Alfred A. Knopf; lines from "A Dialogue of Self and Soul," from *Collected Poems of W. B. Yeats* (copyright 1933 by Macmillan Publishing Company, renewed 1961 by Bertha Georgie Yeats), reprinted by permission of Michael B. Yeats, Macmillan London, Ltd, and Macmillan Publishing Company.

KENNETH GROSS

Rochester, New York

Introduction

The quests of *The Faerie Queene* often culminate in the breaking of images, in the abandonment or putting off of expected fulfillment, in the incursion of some chaotic mode of representation. The endings of the books are sites of disenchantment, however heroic, and of loss, however necessary, while the most potent visions of harmony and restitution—the Garden of Adonis, the Marriage of Rivers, the dream in Isis Church—stand tenuously "in the middest of things." They intersect the quests only obliquely, and we often encounter them by way of excursus or excursion, allusion or illusion; nor are these crucial passages themselves without some internal disharmony. I am speaking of the broad shapes of Spenser's narratives, but the violence that seems to fulfill the quest and the tentativeness even in the ideal visions reflect tendencies that show up on every level of the poet's writing. "All metaphor breaks down somewhere," said Robert Frost; "that is the beauty of it." This evasive charm is something that the poem is always tracing, even as it struggles with an equally disturbing truth: some metaphors refuse to break down, and that is the beauty and danger of them.

The strenuous play of Spenser's writing involves more than working out a redemptive iconography or syncretistic plenitude of symbolic meanings. Spenser always multiplies and opposes perspectives in his poem, always sets one mode of imagination against another—not for the sake of rhetorical display but to keep his ideals from turning into idols, his tropes into traps. The poem tries to keep its hieratic icons from becoming reductive types, ideologically determined vehicles for propaganda, or a mere home for private obsession. Spenser, indeed, comes to us as a paradox; he is a skeptical visionary, a demythologizing mythmaker, an iconoclastic iconographer. His writing inevitably develops a highly figured, wholly nonmimetic surface, as if the allegorical argument depended on images with an almost magical power to elevate and entrance the mind. And yet there is also a simultaneous tendency for such powerful images to evade determinate shape. Or rather, theirs is a determinacy and a centrality that transcend the fixed attractions of simple rhetorical patterning, freeing imagination and desire where they might otherwise threaten to bind. Spenser's allegories, as Shelley wrote of poetry in general, "enlarge the circumference of the imagination by replenishing it with thoughts of ever new delight, which have the power of attracting and assimilating to their own nature all other thoughts, and which form new intervals and interstices whose void for ever craves fresh food."

This double valence of the imaginative work, its mingling of tyranny and freedom, is something that the poem confronts with a certain anxiety and that it tries both to accommodate and contain. Within the narrative proper, the poet seems to work through such conflicts by the nearly obsessive repetition of scenes in which icons, statues, phantasms, illusions, and so on are first elaborately described and then summarily transgressed, broken, dissolved. Such narratives I will examine in greater detail later, but at the outset it may help to see a similar conflict unfolding at the level of the poet's concern with allegorical language, especially in his desire to achieve a formal or conceptual closure within an allegory whose hermeneutic openness seems at different times to be useful, inevitable, and uncomfortable. The terms of such a struggle emerge in Spenser's letter to Sir Walter Raleigh, which was printed as a preface to the 1590 text of *The Faerie Queene*. As is well known, he sets forth in that epistle the orderly scheme of twelve public and private virtues on which the moral fabric of his poem was allegedly to be based, but what I want to concentrate on is rather the letter's peculiar opening movement: "Knowing how doubtfully all Allegories may be construed, and this booke of mine . . . being a continued Allegory, or darke conceit, I have thought good as well for avoyding of gealous opinions and misconstructions, as also for your better light in reading thereof . . . to discover unto you the general intention and meaning, which in the whole course thereof I have fashioned. . . ." Here it seems that the double meaning of allegory makes the poem potentially available not only to enlightening irony but to a more troubling kind of duplicity. Indeed, it is as if allegory's vulnerability to the work of "gealous opinions" were the most pressing thing to note about such a darkened mode of discourse.

Doubtless allegory is traditionally treated as a form of literary defense, a means of enclosing sacred truth or political messages which protects them from the investigations of the vulgar or profane. Spenser's letter, however, suggests that the necessary hiddenness of meaning in the poem is the very thing that leaves it open to the threat of violation by willful or slanderous misinterpreters. The business of fashioning a reader "in vertuous and gentle discipline" thus begins with the poet's marking out a subtle doubt of both the poem and its readers; he situates the imaginative work in a field of threat, so that mere semantic uncertainty becomes something potentially more dangerous. The anxiety of this opening is sketchy and perhaps self-dramatizing at best, but it does suggest that we might view the rest of the letter less as an authoritative, a priori conceptual order around which the entire poem is hung, and more as a partly retrospective attempt to contain and defend from violation the proliferating suggestions that the poem opens up.

Spenser's writing, of course, may be said to feed on certain species of doubt. An original uncertainty or sense of distance from secure centers of meaning may initiate the quest-narrative, just as the darkness of the poet's allegorical conceits should stir the interpreter to move beyond the blind surface of the imagery in search of "higher significances." But in every expansive progression toward a stable center, in every attempt to achieve something like a visionary identification with a sacred emblem, the fear of fixation or of subsequent misreading haunts the literary quest like a demon. The achieved magical sign seems either ready to collapse into an idol, a moral fetish, or else reveals such a mass of unfixed meanings as to leave it open to the deforming power of "gealous opinions." The poem, as Angus Fletcher suggests, seems to accept as a working principle something like the archaic idea of magical contagion, as if only this could ground the poem's strange, superlogical strategies of mythic analogy and narrative movement; and yet, the allegory is nonetheless sickened throughout by the indefinite power that such a rhetorical magic generates (*Allegory*, 207). If this sort of internal conflict accounts for the poem's dissatisfaction with any illusion of closure, it may also suggest the oddly therapeutic function of the poem's willful, even arbitrary overdeterminings of its allegorical patterns, the fragmentation and redundancy of its allusions—all of which complicate our reading of either the poem's ideological simplicity or its polysemy. The poem continues to spin, intertwine, and cut off its narrative threads, as if one form of wandering or error could cast out another, defeating our often catastrophic illusions of clarity by its refinements of ambivalence. Its intricate structural design, rather than being simply a mirror of ethical or cosmic orders, at once contains and reinforces that wandering; that design gives shape to chaos even as it wards off the equal threat of a violent, reductive order.

Yet for all of the poet's free inventiveness, *The Faerie Queene* unfolds beneath a shadow; it moves "with mazie error under pendant shades," as Milton says of the river in his ambiguous Eden. The shadow, shade, or burden is not easy to name. Spenser's sense of the liabilities of allegorical writing is one of its aspects but not necessarily its ultimate source. Unlike his Romantic followers, Spenser in his quest-romance never constructs or confronts an image of his own literal death (nor, for that matter, an image of his possible immortality, as does Dante)—and yet he does give radical figurative shape to what one might call the death of his art and imagination, and shows us violent images of art and imagination turned demonic. We may identify the danger in such cases with idolatry—the threat of the empty, blank, and yet infectious image—or with literalistic reading; we may trace the shadow back to the strange, alienating animations and fixations of sexuality, or speak plainly of black magic and spiritual enchantment. But it is nearly impossible to name the thing precisely, especially if we are honest about the incapacity of most of our analytic vocabularies and interpretive perspectives to compass the difficult inflections of metaphor in Spenser's poem—a work that indeed teaches us how literalistic are our definitions of metaphor, how metaphorical our definitions of the literal. No dogmatic insistence on interpretive openness, no ghostly model of a Renaissance "world view," will be of great help here, since the discipline of the poem teaches us that we cannot take such concepts for granted. What we can say, perhaps, is that the evasiveness of the burden is itself a part of the burden; the shadow lengthens because defining what is false is as difficult as refining what is true. Many of the poem's heroes quest for an idol to destroy rather than for a prize to recover or redeem (as in Book II, where the enemy is a corrupt simulacrum of Eden rather than a dragon that infects that fallen kingdom). But if the isolation, accusation, and casting out of idolatry are, as in biblical prophecy, stages of the road to vision, we must admit that this process may beget further stumbling blocks as well as a sense of renewed imaginative freedom. For just as he evades any final image of truth, so the poet will not claim any pure power of demystification, nor any mode of iconoclasm free from the possibility of error. By the end of the poem, in fact, iconoclasm itself becomes just as much of a threat as idolatry. The quests of Book I may center on the overturning of false religious mystery and idol worship.

But, as I shall argue in a crucial section of Chapter 6, the Blatant Beast that rages through the world at the end of Spenser's last completed book is an all but apocalyptic image of an iconoclasm that itself engenders corruption and sacrilegious mystery; it is the type of a violent faithlessness—full of "gealous opinions and misconstructions"—that feeds upon and re-creates the idolatry it ostensibly breaks down (even as it blocks all but the most meager and politic mythologizings of the poet's world). Furthermore, insofar as the poet's own allegorical methods and gestures are partly implicated in the evil that the Beast represents, we cannot easily identify that creature with any earlier mythic monster or debased moral concept. Despite the availability of the fixed types of divine and demonic in Christian tradition, no certain revelation gives a final shape to the poet's narratives of the fight between idolatry and iconoclasm. If there is a redemptive vision wandering between these dialectical poles, we may discover in the end that it is only a finer form of idolatry, or a subtler repetition of magic.

The business of the present study is to consider the dynamic interrelations of idolatry, iconoclasm, and magic in Spenser's poem. The most important structural feature to note at the outset is the double introductory movement of Part One. The first chapter, "A Poetics of Idolatry," develops a conceptual framework for later readings, based largely around the analysis of biblical and a few postbiblical texts. My central argument is that the idea of the idol offers us something like a limiting case for the study of human imagemaking; it gives shape to the awareness that invented figures for divinity, however much they may seem to be the vessels of power and knowledge, may become empty, dead, or reductive. The idol defines in strangely figurative terms the anxieties of the biblical tradition about the dangers of figurative discourse and the forms of religious revelation, describing a condition against which such discourse and revelation must always defend themselves. Given this dilemma, however, I want to argue that iconoclasm itself remains entangled in the very sorts of symbolic action that may issue in idolatry.

The chapter also examines the ways in which the struggle against idolatry finds for itself a textual or hermeneutic locus. Especially within Christian tradition, definitions of proper allegorical or typological reading are clothed in the imagery of a sacred iconoclasm; likewise, certain forms of allegorical reading or fablemaking are seen as potentially idolatrous. Such valuations are unstable of course, especially in a century like Spenser's own when ideas of mystification and revelation are continually exchanging places. Hence we may find in Spenser's time few normative terms for critical analysis. Nevertheless, even such partial, polemical theories of reading as fill contemporary religious debates will help reinforce my broad application of the metaphor of idolatry to more purely rhetorical and narrative structures in Spenser's poem, and clarify some of the issues that are at stake even in many of the poet's most complex scenes of visionary enchantment and disenchantment.

I should say here that I do not want to align Spenser with any particular religious or political camp; nor am I comfortable with the work of recent critics who have tried to make English Renaissance literature into a predominantly Protestant or Calvinist phenomenon. What is radical in Spenser's poetry, at least, is not so easily labeled. And though I think that Spenser is, in many ways, a religious poet, *The Faerie Queene* hugely complicates the question of what religion might or can mean to us. I have occasion in this study to refer to a wide range of religious controversies, but my only extended attempt to give a firmer historical locus to the problems opened up in my ahistorical and speculative first chapter will be found in a detailed commentary on Spenser's prose dialogue, *A View of the Present State of Ireland* (1596)—a commentary that constitutes the facing half of my opening diptych. This dialogue emerges from a realm of great physical and cultural violence, one in which Spenser spent most of his adult life; it also reveals the poet's skeptical fascination with certain forms of mythic, religious, or political imagination. As both an ironic mirror to the abstracted discourse of Chapter 1 and an anticipation of my later reflections on Spenser's poetry, the second chapter explores how the dialogue attacks the idols or myths embedded in Irish law, custom, worship, and folklore; it also looks at Spenser's comments on the propaganda, repressive nostalgia, and reductive legalism that compromised the often catastrophic English efforts at rule and reform. My intention here is not simply to suggest how Spenser's poetry might reflect religious or political history, however; it is as much the reverse, namely, to show the poet's sense of how history shapes itself as a battleground of poetry and poetic ideas, though often of a debased sort. Only in this form does history become material for the poet. I want to suggest in Chapter 2 the imaginative stress of Spenser's encounter with the antiutopia of Ireland, and to make more palpable the risks of the allegory that composes his own ideal Fairyland.

The questions opened up in these earlier chapters are explored more fully in Part Two, which comprises four essays in commentary on major episodes of *The Faerie Queene*, including Arthur's fight with

the giant Orgoglio (I.vii–viii); Britomart's encounter with the magic mirror of Merlin and her rescue of Amoret from the House of Busyrane (III.ii and III.xi–xii), as well as her dream in Isis Church (V.vii); the Garden of Adonis (III.vi); Calidore's vision of nymphs and Graces on Mount Acidale (VI.x); the Blatant Beast (especially in VI.xii); and the Mutabilitie Cantos, with special attention to the Faunus episode. I will attempt no summary here, beyond what has already been hinted at above. The main thing to say is that my approach is that of an exploratory essay, one that is both analytic and theoretical but nonsystematic, pragmatic but also re-creative. The discourse shifts, at times quite abruptly, among close reading, philosophical reflection, and literary-historical collage. Since I am both reading Spenser and trying to explore a mode of criticism which I think he teaches, I have tried to develop an idiom capacious and mobile enough to do justice to his own. Despite the expanded field of allusion in the commentary, however, scholarly annotation has been kept to a minimum. Often I have pointed to what is a less than central source-text in order to put Spenser's problematic strategies starkly in perspective. I have also at times paid more attention to so-called secondary sources—though less as substitutes for the primary sources than as occasions for critical reflection in their own right. Insofar as I can explain my motives here, I should say that I have tried to constellate various critics within my own commentary in ways that both bring out their seriousness and turn us back to unresolved problems in the text. To cite a hypothetical instance: in trying to make sense of how critics have viewed the relative opacity or transparency of Spenser's secular scripture, I might find it useful and plausible to describe Paul Alpers as a radically Protestant exegete, an avatar of the "literal" text, whereas James Nohrnberg, for whom the text is almost infinitely permeable to analogy, strikes me more as a Scholastic or Catholic interpreter. Such rubrics are partial at best and court all of sorts of uncertain value judgments. But they are worth the risk for a critic if they suggest how the poet writing in the sixteenth century may have been responding in his text to imaginative stances that we are still working through today, and perhaps with no more clear success.

I close with just a few comments on the third key word of this book's very un-dialectical subtitle. "Magic," I shall be suggesting, points to a horizon of poetic and religious discourse that is crucially related to definitions of idolatry and iconoclasm. Magic can often be called idolatry, among other reasons because it seems to depend upon an autonomous power being granted to the blind gesture or sign (hence the derogatory use of the word "magic," like "myth," to refer to ritualized slogans or calcified institutions). In this form magic is something that one may wish to renounce, although it may possess aspects that the artist may seek to appropriate or purify. For there are also forms of magic that may emerge through less reductive gestures or structures, forms of magic that contain comic as well as tragic potential. As it appears in *The Faerie Queene*, at least, such a clarifying or liberating magic is not necessarily located in a single character, place, or object; its locus may in fact shift among several figures or places within a particular episode. Furthermore, such a power may show itself only as a paradoxical wish, and then only at moments of disenchantment, where it will appear mainly as a subtler countermagic that serves to extend the labor of iconoclasm—the kind of magic found, for example, in the complex mythic shield that Arthur uses to defeat the inflated Orgoglio, or in the ambiguous strategies by which Britomart frees Amoret from Busyrane's vicious allegorical theater. Variously human and divine, natural and supernatural, black and white, this magic becomes the focus for some of the poet's most troubling questions about the nature of his imaginative work.

Magic, then, in both the poem and my commentary, ends up being something of a surd; the term may indeed sound unusually anomalous in what I tend to think of as a skeptical and de-idealizing approach to Spenser. So it may clarify my strategy to set it in relation to the reading of magic in two other scholars of the period.

Frances Yates, as in all of her studies of forgotten disciplines, is eager to show the intellectual seriousness of Renaissance interest in Hermetic magic. To this end, she always brings out the rhetorical self-consciousness of such thinkers as Marsilio Ficino and Giordano Bruno, as well as their clear sense of the place of human memory and imagination in magical work. She also never forgets the religious politics that affect the study of magic. Perhaps more than any other student of the period, she has shown how much Humanist and Neo-Platonist interest in magic is in agreement with the strongly antimagical bias of Protestant Reformers, all of whom shared in the attempt to break away from what they took to be the reductive enchantments of the medieval church. In these areas my own approach to the dialectics of magical agency in Spenser derives strongly from Yates (although not quite in the fashion of commentators who take Yates's readings of noncanonical, occult traditions and make them the core of all Renaissance drama and poetry). Hence I find myself particularly disturbed when, after one of her subtle disquisitions on the art of divination by magical statues in the writings of Pico, she is moved to suggest that "the operative Magi of the Renaissance were the artists, and it was a

Donatello or a Michelangelo who knew how to infuse divine life into statues through their art" (*Giordano Bruno and the Hermetic Tradition*, 104). Such a surmise is necessary, possibly profound, but also oddly trivial. Yates converts magic into so bland and easy a metaphor that it might as well be literal. It may be gratifying to have the artist exalted and the magician demystified and diminished, but to make the latter into a mere trope for the former may beg the important question of just what an artist is in the first place, and how his or her magic may differ from other forms or myths of enchantment. It may be simply that Yates does not properly "believe" in magic, but in any case the result of her phrasing is to coarsen our sense of what may really be at stake in the representation of both magic *and* art.

Such nuances of taxonomy may be relatively unimportant in Yates's historical studies, but they are crucial if we are to come to terms with a literary romance like *The Faerie Queene*. A more useful foil for my own approach might be found in A. Bartlett Giamatti's important essay, "Proteus Unbound" (in his *Exile and Change*, 115–50). Focusing on the shifting iconography of the sea god in the Renaissance, Giamatti is able to bring out the period's deep ambivalence about the idea and power of magic. While a figure like Spenser's Archimago may reveal in his similarity to Proteus aspects of the god's power to enchant and change which are clearly evil (*FQ* I.ii.10), various alternate interpretations of Proteus leave his moral coloring much more vague. In Spenser and others, he can represent all the anarchic, lustful, or greedy powers of the human mind; he can also figure the imagination's capacity to impose changing images on reality and so to call into question the stability of human icons, orders, institutions, and ideologies. As such he can be the object of considerable anxiety, hardly to be distinguished from Archimago himself. And yet it is the very amorality of the metamorphic power represented by Proteus that makes this demigod, mage, and sometime prophet so fascinating an image for Renaissance poets and politicians. He comes to represent, among other things, the urgent human need to adapt action and speech to the shifting contingencies of the secular world, especially in the light of the period's somewhat destabilized sense of metaphysical authority. Giamatti thus defines a central concern of this study, and yet there are at least two aspects of his account of Proteus's magic (typical of other Renaissance scholars) from which I must differ. Giamatti offers a fine account of the period's ambivalence about magic in its connection with the mutability of human desire, judgment, and power. And yet one discerns in his argument too exclusive (if not quite defensive) an emphasis on the contaminated manifestations of change, and a perhaps simplistic account of the demonic forces of chaos against which the opposing category of "order"—whether cosmic, civil, or spiritual—can by contrast appear as relatively unproblematic. In addition, the order of human politics and the order of human art end up as all but identified. By contrast, my own analysis points to the ways in which order, or the will to order, may itself become an object of anxiety in Spenser, a source of false enchantment that may be strangely at odds with the revelations of art.

A more immediately relevant difference is that Giamatti invariably takes magic as a trope for processes that are discretely rhetorical, psychological, or political. Such a demystification is inescapable in places, especially to the degree that it serves the work of iconoclasm. Yet I have tried at times to hover over passages in *The Faerie Queene* where we must at least delay the translation of magic into metaphor. This is not to say that Spenser was in any sense an operative magus like Ficino, Bruno, or John Dee. Even the occult Spenser is never mystagogic, and yet there may be a subtler idolatry in too quickly demystifying or rationalizing the more uncanny gestures of Spenser's writing. Hence, there are moments in the following pages when, in order to refresh available critical categories, I have taken the poet's fictions of disenchantment almost literally, or at least tried to suggest that "magic" may be as adequate a term as "metaphor," "language," "love," or "miracle" to describe the forces and states of being that play a part in *The Faerie Queene*. "Magic" in this sense is no escape clause but an attempt to name what is most difficult, mysterious, and necessary in Spenser's romance.

PART ONE

Two Opening Essays

1

A Poetics of Idolatry

Nothing upon the earth is interesting except religions.
Baudelaire

A proper poetics of idolatry would place us at a threshold. To find the idea of the idol in all of its seriousness means seeing in it a category that cuts across many of our conventional distinctions between the sacred and the profane, the divine and the demonic, the aesthetic and the religious, the subjective and the objective, the figurative and the literal. The figure of the idol haunts Western tradition in its quests after both vision and disenchantment, for the empty, blind, petrified sign, the dead or never living idol that is no-thing, is also the vessel of the freedom, the violence, and the stress of the human imagination in search of its gods.[1] The idol is the mocking ghost, the fantastic and recalcitrant limit of what we call representation; it is the blank interior of our myths of revelation, the place where our questions about divinity and authority receive their most severe test. The idol may be the emphatic lie taken for truth, but it is also the truth that has collapsed into a lie, the urgent, mythopoeic cipher converted into a vacant myth. The idol may be the originally secular or profane image invested with an almost sacred trust. It can also be the sacred, hierophantic image reduced to mechanism, a mystery become a temporal institution subject to the rule of a selfish priesthood. "Idolatry" thus implies the blockage or betrayal of vision, and yet it may also be

1. The description of the idol as "no-thing" depends on the Hebrew use of the word *'elil,* "nonentity," "worthlessness," to refer to idolatrous images. The word appears among other places in Leviticus 19.4, Psalms 96.5, Isaiah 2.8, 18, 20, and Ezekiel 30.13. Its pejorative sense is often reinforced in these texts by its ironic proximity to the words *'el* or *'elohim,* generic titles for the Hebrew god. On the variety of Hebrew epithets for "idol" or "graven image," see George Buttrick et al., *Interpreter's Dictionary of the Bible,* 2:673–74.

the name by which a troubled orthodoxy slanders the visionary work of the poet, magician, or prophet. Nor is that name the worst banner under which such laborers might enlist, not only because one person's idolatry is another's orthodoxy, but because it is as often the scholiasts of illusion as the purveyors of revelation who have most to teach us about human religion and human imagination. W. H. Auden advises: "Recognizing idols for what they are does not break their enchantment." And yet to embrace, even in ambivalence, a conscious idolatry may help put off the blindness of a greater one.

Such words as "idolatry," "iconoclasm," and "magic" must be more than fossilized metaphors. The following remarks, mostly on biblical texts, will suggest that they are complex names and conceptual tropes for forms of imaginative conflict which still have no perfectly adequate taxonomy. The idol, for instance, is a thing that presses upon us the central questions of what a religious discourse might be, even as it denies to our speculations the abstract refuge commonly provided by appeals to "belief." For the tradition that invents for itself the idea of a revelation that must somehow transcend all falsifications of image should make us realize all the more strongly how much any means of worship may constitute or mar the object of that worship, how much belief may be bound by its formal vehicles. That the creations of the human imagination may impinge on, even create a God is an idea that did not have to wait until the Reformation; the texts of the Bible register, even in a sometimes repressed or crudely mythic way, the stresses of that realization. What emerges in response to it is a mode of religious writing which obsessively dramatizes its own conflict with other myths, authorities, and divinities, one in which revelation emerges through the violent attack on what is taken to be idolatry or illusion.

This chapter breaks into three interlocking sections. The first attempts to locate the complex range of meanings and ironies in the idea of idolatry itself; the second studies a number of narratives that not only represent but in a sense help to enact the ambivalent work of iconoclasm; the third places idolatry and iconoclasm within a theory of allegory. One of the difficulties in separating out these concerns, especially those of the first and second sections, is that the very idea of the idol tends, at its most urgent, to be bound up with the mythology of the iconoclast, rather than with that of the one accused of idolatry. And while the identification and elimination of an idol can register a certain critical consciousness about the limitations of any image, curative acts of iconoclasm may still entail a continuing, though more ironic and dialectical process of imagemaking. Iconoclasm may call itself demystification, but it remains demystification under the aspect of the sacred, and possesses none of the rationalized purity of a negative theology. It is as much a symbolic, even a magical act as idolatry itself, though it may give rise to a more complex dynamic of violence and substitution. As Francis Bacon notes, there may be "a superstition in avoiding superstition" (*Works*, 6:416). Hence an enlightened or philosophical consciousness may fear the unstable power mobilized in acts of iconoclasm as much as it does idolatry. But a study of the myths of idolatry and iconoclasm has this advantage: while it provides a focus for skeptical impulses in discussing problems of sacred and secular representation, it may remind us how much a philosophical skepticism about images may be merely an intellectualization of a more primary ambivalence and, furthermore, how liable that skepticism is to become bound by its own philosophical idols or myths.

My reticence about an epistemological approach to the problem of idolatry may at least excuse this chapter's neglect of the Platonic account of human illusion—the ground covered in any case by Eric Havelock in his *Preface to Plato* and by Jacques Derrida in "Plato's Pharmacy" (*Dissemination*, 61–171). The Greek philosopher's efforts to invent a mode of discourse which might overcome the skeptical deceptions of Sophistic rhetoric, his hate and love of mythology, his attack on the falsehoods of dramatic and mimetic art—all of these find powerful analogues in Spenser's poem. And the central Platonic fable of the cave in *The Republic*—the progressive turning of the mind from shadows on a wall to their sculpted sources and again to the originary sunlight outside, as well as the difficult task of turning again to enlighten those left behind—might frame a discussion of error in quest-romance as well as my own focus on questions of idolatry and iconoclasm.[2] No doubt Plato's account of this place of human illusion underlies many episodes of fantastic descent in Spenser, such as the Cave of Mammon or the House of Busyrane. We should also recall that our word "idol" has, after all, a Platonic as well as a Hebraic genealogy. Although its use to render the biblical idea of a graven image has determined the word's common use, Bacon's four "idols," for instance, depend at least as much on the original Greek sense of *eidolon*—which could mean "mental image," "likeness," "fantasy," "shadow," or "ghost." The word is aligned with its more ambiguous root *eidos*, "form," "type," "idea" (deriving from a Greek verb mean-

2. Eric Havelock's *Preface to Plato*, in particular, studies the philosopher's attack on poetic representation in a way that would bring it into line with the biblical attack on idolatry, especially in Havelock's use of the term "identification" to describe the binding, limiting absorption of Greek mind, culture, and moral behavior by the forms of Homeric poetry which so disturbed Plato.

ing "to see"), as well as being associated with *eikon*, "image," "similitude," "reflection."[3] This vocabulary obviously conditions Christian philosophical debate about the function and limitations of the image up through the Renaissance, and certain of its terms will inevitably enter into my later discussions. Nevertheless, the biblical tradition proper provides at least three special emphases that are not quite so strong in Platonic thought: (1) The biblical fight against idolatry is more continuously dramatic; it urges and sanctifies the breaking of idols as much as the intellectual turning away from them, giving its narrative figurations of demystifying violence a much starker and more ambivalent shape.[4] (2) While, for Plato, representations fall short because they are subject to the flux of time and opinion, the historicizing emphasis of the Bible suggests that it is the very delusive stillness and fixity of the idolatrous image or word which betray both the flux of human imagination and divine revelation. Idolatry as a diachronic rather than a synchronic phenomenon means that even a divinely instituted form of sacred figuration (e.g., the Brazen Serpent) can collapse into the condition of an idol if it is taken as final or complete, as sacred in and of itself, or if it binds revelation within delusively stable or merely anterior forms. (3) From this argument follows the extension of iconoclasm to attacks on ritual, legalism, syncretistic mythology, false prophecy—and finally to the crucial identification of idolatry with false forms of reading and writing. In such a situation, the work of iconoclasm must also extend itself into the realm of interpretation, often founding a radical hermeneutic of suspicion as well as making use of the literary resources of irony, parody, and revisionary narrative.

Before proceeding, it must be said that this chapter is not about Spenser; rather it opens up toward his work at every point. I mention *The Faerie Queene* only at intervals, but that poem is the beginning and end of my investigations. I am interested in showing how deeply embedded in Judeo-Christian tradition are those conflicts about the nature of myth and image which I examine in Spenser, but I do not

3. The most complex Christian use of this Platonic vocabulary, and of its later Neo-Platonic elaborations, can be found in the controversies surrounding the sacred image in the Byzantine church (whence also the coinage, "iconoclasm"). On this subject, see Ernst Kitzinger, "The Cult of Images in the Age before Iconoclasm," and Gerhart Ladner, "The Concept of the Image in the Greek Fathers."

4. Cf. Gerhard von Rad, *Old Testament Theology*, 1:218: "The relentless shattering of cherished concepts of God which occupied the pre-Exilic prophets stands in a theological relationship which is perhaps hidden, but which is, in actual fact, very close to the commandment forbidding images."

mean to identify the poet with one particular branch of that tradition. Indeed Spenser's poem (though not necessarily the historical person of the poet, who seems to have been a staunch supporter of the Elizabethan settlement) holds in suspension and sometimes sets in subtle conflict both Catholic and Protestant attitudes toward the image. At the same time, his poem displaces the problem of idolatry into secular—political, erotic, and aesthetic—realms with a freedom that no ascetically theological discourse could allow itself. I have not tried to reconstruct "Spenserian" readings of biblical texts. Nevertheless, I have found in the poet's skeptical inventions a model for my own decenterings and complicatings of questions about the poetic image. Spenser is only a single representative of the problematic tradition mapped out below; but he is also, if not its guiding spirit, then its implicit cartographer.

Idolatry

The heavens declare the glory of God;
  and the firmament sheweth his handywork.
Day unto day uttereth speech,
  and night unto night sheweth knowledge.
There is no speech nor language,
  where their voice is not heard.
Their line is gone out through all the earth,
  and their words to the end of the world.
In them hath he set a tabernacle for the sun,
  which is as a bridegroom coming out of his chamber,
  and rejoiceth as a strong man to run a race.
His going forth is from the end of the heaven,
  and his circuit unto the ends of it:
  and there is nothing hid from the heat thereof.
(Ps. 19.1–6)

But our God is in the heavens:
  he hath done whatsoever he hath pleased.
Their idols are silver and gold,
  the work of men's hands.
They have mouths, but they speak not:
  eyes have they, but they see not:
They have ears, but they hear not:
  noses have they, but they smell not:
They have hands, but they handle not:
  feet have they, but they walk not:

neither speak they through their throat.
They that make them are like unto them;
so is every one that trusteth in them.
(Ps. 115.3–8)[5]

In the first of these texts the divinity is present in and proclaimed by his creation, but he is not contained or restricted by the elements that manifest him. Beyond nature, he is yet not located in a rationalized myth of an eternal realm, any more than he is to be found in a river, a tree, or a mountain. The very antithetical status of this God indeed seems to be that which generates the strange power of the text's "natural" imagery, something we may feel in the sublime paradoxes of God's absent and present voice, or in the disenchanted anthropomorphisms that describe the sun (and, by displacement, its creator) by joining figures of sexual exuberance and physical competition. The elliptical quality of both of these examples suggests how much the text manages to avoid anything like the tendency of mythological thought to collapse its gods or god into nature and creation, to naturalize divinity even as it divinizes both nature and its own cultural institutions.[6] Such an identification of nature, culture, and divinity, as such scholars as Henri Frankfort and Yehezekel Kaufmann have argued, perpetuates itself in the blank worship of fixed images (whether mimetic or nonmimetic), and in prescriptive rituals that both enshrine the cyclical movements of nature and reinforce the binding power of established, state-centered religions, embedding divinity within forms of presence which are ultimately under human control.[7] The Hebrew God, however, seems necessarily to transcend both creation and cult;

5. Unless otherwise indicated, all biblical quotations in this chapter are taken from the Authorized King James Version. In later chapters, when pointing to specific biblical echoes in Spenser, I have cited the sixteenth-century Geneva Version with which the poet himself seems to have been most familiar.

6. It is in this context that we should understand the Decalogue's double injunction against worshiping "other gods" and making "graven images" or "likenesses" of earthly or heavenly phenomena (Exodus 20.3–4). The words do not refer to the epistemological error of mimesis as recognized in Platonic tradition. It is rather that, in religions in which nature is divinized or in which nature and divinity are one, any such "imitations" or "likenesses" must be seen from the perspective of Israelite religion as idolatry, the creation of rival witnesses to the more complex manifestations of the antinatural god of Israel. For further discussion, see Brevard Childs, *Book of Exodus: A Critical, Theological Commentary*, 404–9.

7. My extremely summary account of the Hebrew Bible's attitude toward mythic religion, and its peculiar use and misuse of mythological narrative, is especially indebted to the work of Martin Buber, *The Prophetic Faith*; Brevard Childs, *Myth and Reality in the Old Testament*; Henri Frankfort et al., *The Intellectual Adventure of Ancient Man*; Paul Ricoeur, *The Symbolism of Evil*; and Herbert Schneidau, *Sacred Discontent: The Bible and Western Tradition.*

his original house is not a fixed temple, but a tabernacle and a portable ark; his Word not only sets down the stable orders of reality but also continually breaks in upon them in a way that both reorients one's view of past contingencies or forms and imposes a fatal or freshening future upon them.[8]

Psalm 115, then, provides a dark parody of mythological religion seen from the perspective of Hebraic faith. It stresses the emphatic emptiness and negativity of the idol, the product of a human labor whose paradoxes of being—eyes that see not, ears that hear not—are at best a mockery of the sublime ironies of Psalm 19. It suggests that the devotion to sensuous images of divinity can become a death of the senses as well as a death of the spirit; it reveals idolatry as a binding fascination that is entrapment rather than covenant, reductive identification rather than salvific atonement. The aggressive rhetoric of this picture of idolatry actually makes the text of the psalm a kind of exorcism, a mocking litany that raises the specter of spiritual vacancy in what is otherwise an indifferent statue. Finally, in fact, to read the psalm in all of its urgency we must recognize how strange is the story that the poem tells itself and see that the idea of the idol as lie is in part a lie imposed on pagan religion, a polemical reduction that feeds the antithetical mythmaking of Israelite religion.

An axiom of modern scholarship is that biblical narrative is skeptical, historicizing, and demythologizing. It offers us a vision of a people's sacred origins within rather than beyond time, and leaves unfixed the future forms of both God's manifestations and the human response to them. In the Bible, all ritualized cycles of mythic time give way to the ever shifting accidents of "history," which has become a realm of both blessing and curse, freedom and alienation, power and burden. It is exactly this situation that makes the Hebrew poets so sensitive to the fragility and false permanence of the pagan idol, although their sense of being caught in time may also generate a certain anxiety as to their alienation from established temporal orders, an anxiety mastered by the Bible's invention of its own and its God's uniqueness and originality. Whether or not this contention is plausible, the important point is that the business of historicizing or de-

8. The Hebrew idea of God's Word, *davar*, thus differs considerably from the Greek concept of *logos*. The former refers to Yahweh's creative and destructive manifestations in time; it is an effective word, a bearer of power and judgment, whereas *logos* tends to compass the stable, unified, rational orders of mind and cosmos. Even as a power within creation the *logos* is something to be known rather than something to be uttered or answered. See Thorleif Boman, *Hebrew Thought Compared with Greek*, 58–69, for further discussion of this contrast (one that admittedly breaks down in later Christian and apocalyptic writing).

mythologizing pagan myth must be seen as an ongoing, dialectical process, one that may in the end leave us with what is after all only a more obscure or ironic mythology (as Paul Ricoeur emphasizes repeatedly in his *Symbolism of Evil*). We can leave aside for now the question of whether Yahweh himself, the iconoclastic god of historical revelation, is not in some ways simply a more exalted, uncanny idol than the gods of pagan myth—a solution to the problem of religious origins embraced in different ways by the Gnostics, Saint Paul, and the philosophers of the Enlightenment. The matter of the blindness or lie in Psalm 115's picture of idolatry can, however, be clarified by Kaufmann's account of how thoroughly the Hebrew Bible reduces the complex forms of pagan mythology to the level of absurdity. For while the writers of the Bible impute the darkest motives to both pagans and backsliding Israelites for their "whoring after strange gods," they are at the same time "utterly unaware of the nature and meaning of pagan religion" (*Religion of Israel,* 7).

The prophet looks at foreign cults and sees only statues—the dead work of human hands, figures made from the same stone with which a worker might erect a house or the same wood that might be used to build a fire (a fire whose ashes in Isaiah 47.14 become an emblem for the idolater's false spiritual nourishment). The attack on idolatry is grounded in the trivializing of pagan religion into a system of fetishism, by the wholesale refusal to recognize it as a structure of religious beliefs in any way comparable to those that characterize the religion of Yahweh. Paganism read as idolatry in this sense is not a religion at all. The extremity and blankness of such a refusal comes through clearly in what might otherwise seem to be ironic assertions of Kaufmann: "[The Hebrew Bible] is entirely ignorant of the close relationship between magic and the gods; it knows nothing of the cosmic-mythological basis of the pagan cult; it has no appreciation of the symbolic value of images" (20). The idolater is represented as one who has taken the image or sacred object as the god itself—a mistake that, as Gerhard von Rad points out, is hardly credible even in the most primitive cultures observed by modern anthropologists and certainly not in the cults with which Israel came into contact (*Old Testament Theology*, 1:214), and, as Edwyn Bevan shows, is found hardly anywhere in classical accounts of magical statuary (*Holy Images,* 82–83). One may want to ask, "Which is the idolater here, and which the Jew?"—since it is the Hebrew iconoclast who identifies the idol *as* an idol and who creates the new myth of imagistic emptiness.

The conceptual violence of such "demystifications," however, may yet help us construct a more flexible, a more dialectical notion of magical figuration. We can say first that the biblical myth of the idol constitutes a limiting case, and a critique, of the idea that the cultic image is, if not the god itself, then a true revelation of the god, a means of making it present, and the medium through which worshipers may feel a center of energy in themselves identified with one located in and beyond the created image. In idolatry, Owen Barfield argues, we see rather the "effective tendency to abstract the sense-content from the whole representation and seek that for its own sake, transmuting the admired image into a desired object" (*Saving the Appearances*, 111).[9] The idea of the idol then tells us that an image may not so much stand for or contain a god as usurp that god's place; it becomes a blank and blind signifier preempting the manifestation of the sought-after divinity, replacing a revealed otherness with a palpably human creation that is yet not quite recognized as such. Insofar as one does not seek beyond it, or one makes it over into agent instead of image, the idol becomes at once restricted and unbound, full and empty, all of the god and yet none of the god. Such a "distorted" (primally distorted) image will seem to limit the worshiper's knowledge of its represented divinity. Yet by that very limitation it ministers to an expanded sense of the worshiper's ability to manipulate divinity through the reductive signs of that divinity's presence—hence the fear that the idol, instead of being the consecrated medium of a sacred communion or "*at-onement*," allows only the narcissistic *identification* or parodic atonement of a worshiper and the god he has made of and for himself. Though the idol may be empty of knowledge, it is nonetheless the agent of both power and pleasure, especially insofar as it is embedded in a fixed, nonreflexive ritual praxis, available to the shifting motives of history and religious politics.[10] The use of the idol thus feeds that system of magical symbolism by which, as Kaufmann argues, mythological religion removes "any fixed bounds between [the gods] and the world of men and other creatures" (*Religion of Israel*, 35)—the idolatrous element in magical rites consisting not so much in trafficking with evil gods or demons as in assuming an autonomous power to control or communicate in human work, imagery, and action.

Reductive as it may appear, the Bible's stark view of the idol as a blind, pragmatic lie can be linked to that assertive negativity noted in primitive magic by its greatest modern scholar, Bronislaw Malinowski:

9. On this tendency of the sacred image to wander into the state of an idol, see Richard Bernheimer, *The Nature of Representation: A Phenomenological Inquiry*, 149–50.

10. Cf. Paul Ricoeur's discussion of the metamorphic capacities of ritual *praxis* in *The Symbolism of Evil*, 94–95.

"I think that if we stripped all magical speech to its essentials, we would find simply this fact: a man believed to have mystical power faces a clear blue sky and repeats: 'It rains; dark clouds forgather; torrents burst forth and drench the parched soil.' Or else he would be facing a black sky and repeat: 'The sun breaks through the clouds; the sun shines.' . . . The essence of verbal magic, then, consists in a statement which is untrue, which stands in direct opposition to the context of reality" (*The Language of Magic and Gardening*, 238–39). The anthropologist goes on to insist that it is the organized social belief in magic, or in the magician, which inspires the conviction that the untrue may become true. And yet one may wonder whether it is not the empirical groundlessness and empty self-identity of the magical sign which allow it to accommodate such beliefs, and which give it the power so to mobilize human desires for changing nature, resisting accident or death, and for making present desire's gods. As it is released within the shifting motivations of the historical world, the flexible negativity of the magical sign or idol might indeed account for the double fear of idolatry's demonic, disruptive influence and its tremendously conservative, deceptively natural force—an irony reflected in the Bible's paradoxical way of associating the rebellious, chaotic powers of nature and the human imagination with the idolatrous images that are the outward signs of religious, political, and social order.

Mircea Eliade has argued that any manifestation of the divine, any "hierophany" effected by means of image or natural object, will be inescapably paradoxical to the degree that it appropriates the profane in order to reveal the sacred, the hierophany being located at the overdetermined threshold between sacred and profane, between the image considered as object and as representation of a power other than itself (*Patterns in Comparative Religion*, 12–14). Now I would argue that the idol, the godless statue, continues to possess such a threshold status and attracts a similar uncertainty about the destructive and redemptive power of the *sacer*. But the primary ambivalence surrounding the powers of the sacred image or presence is complicated in biblical writing by an attack on sacred mimesis as such; the helpful and harmful poles of divinity are translated into true and false, purer and more corrupt forms of representation. Moreover, while it is apparently the manmade nature of the idol which accounts for its danger, the idol is rejected with a sacred horror that belies more than a simple perception of ontological emptiness. Indeed, despite its rationalistic mockery of fetishists and dreamers, the strength of the Bible's iconoclastic rhetoric (especially in the prophets) arises from its way of mythologizing idolatry and spiritual error as forms of supernatural entrapment, seduction, and whoredom. Hence a fear of sacred pollution, and the elaborate machinery of ritual separation it produces continue to complicate the attack on false gods. Given the need for radical, accusatory definitions of error and evil, the desire to posit autonomous mythological enemies continues to haunt the discourse of a religion in which ideally, as Buber puts it, "no god was in a position to displace YHVH, saving only His own distorted image" (*Prophetic Faith*, 121).

The complexly dialectical nature of the attack on idols and the continuing ambiguity about the locus of the idol's power will concern me more in the next section. The confusing sense of spiritual threat in the empty idol may be rationalized, as in Augustine's dogmatic distinction between the manmade statue and the supernatural demons that inhabit or use it—a distinction partly anticipated in Deuteronomy's careful separation of "likenesses" from "other gods." But even in that case, as I will argue, the idol and demon share an uncanny life together within the space of their redundancy. The two may be ever more emphatically distinguished by anxious theologians, but they may also collapse back together in the stark tropes of apocalyptic personification, where the forms of natural and supernatural error are concentrated into a few ultimate symbols—Beast, Whore, Antichrist. Even within a largely demystified, skeptical discourse on idolatry, one that reflects no apparent belief in literal demons, some residue of a more primitive ambivalence tends to reassert itself. The problem is apparent in Spenser, certainly, all of whose idols (good *or* bad) tend to be difficult composites of human and beast emblems, the latter usually serpents or dragons of the sort most often linked to the realm of the daemonic. Or else, as in the case of the idol of Geryon in Book v, the dead statue of a tyrant finds a horrific, living, and cannibalistic monster hidden beneath its base. The frequent animation of such idols in fantasy or dream, besides dramatically exposing the secondary sense of "idol" as "specter" and "phantasm," suggests yet again the surplus energy that hovers about the figure of the idol, as does the fact that Spenser allows no single act of iconoclasm ever finally to cut off the proliferating magical error of idolatry.

Let me return to my earlier definition of idolatry as a reductive, usurping identification of man and god, god and image. It may clarify what is at stake in this definition, and also in my discussion of what I would call the iconoclast's ambivalent romance with idolatry, to adduce by comparison Giambattista Vico's idea of "divination." To set this excursus in context, recall first that idols are seen in Scripture as man's attempt not only to oppose a creator but also to overcome a situation of anxiety, to perpetuate a benign and rationalized order in the face of an unknown future. Recall also the image of idolaters and false prophets as those who "walk after the imaginations and deceits of their own hearts" (to conflate Jeremiah 23.17 and 26). Vico similarly sees the fierce Gentile gods as splendid lies originating in propaedeutic acts of imagination, traces of the primitive mind's fearful identification with, and warding off of, the abyss of impotence and ignorance in its experience of the world. In a crucial passage of *The New Science*, Vico opposes his "poetic theology" to a Baconian or Cartesian view of knowledge as mastering and mirroring the outside world: "As rational metaphysics teaches that man becomes all things by understanding them *(homo intelligendo fit omnia),* this imaginative metaphysics shows that man becomes all things by *not* understanding them *(homo non intelligendo fit omnia);* and perhaps the latter proposition is truer than the former, for when man understands he extends his mind and takes in the things, but when he does not understand them he makes the things out of himself and becomes them by transforming himself into them" (II.2.ii, par. 405). This is indeed the sin of backsliding Israel, to have worshiped images of divinity "which ye made to yourselves" (Amos 5.26), "gods whom they knew not" (Deut. 29.26), idols wrought out of the "blindness of the heart" and out of apparent ignorance of true divinity.

The power of idolatry, then, is a version of what Erich Auerbach called "the terrible cruelty" of primitive man's "magical formalism" ("Vico and Aesthetic Historism," *Scenes from the Drama of European Literature*, 193). Because he writes within a Christian, though also a rationalist context, Vico always carefully distinguishes the orders of the Gentile gods from the God of Scripture. But he simultaneously discerns a subtler idolatry in the inability of contemporary thinkers to recognize the force of the original Gentile idolatry, despite appeal to rationalized abstractions like "Sympathetic Nature" as a way of explaining primitive superstitions about an animated cosmos. Indeed, he can complain with a sublime humor that "it is naturally beyond our power to form the vast image of this mistress called 'Sympathetic Nature.' Men shape the phrase with their lips but have nothing in their minds; *for what they have in mind is falsehood, which is nothing; and their imagination no longer avails to form a vast false image*" (II.1.i, par. 378; emphasis mine). I would even risk suggesting that the traditional Judeo-Christian polemic against idolatrous imagination is a primary, if ironic source for the enlightened Vico's theorizing about poetic history[11]—ironic because, by the sheer weight of his attention to the Gentile gods, one tends to see divination, and hence idolatry, emerging as master tropes for all forms of religion. Under this reading, the explicit attempt to destroy "idolatry" becomes a means both to repress the consciousness of one's own continuing involvement with image and imagination, and yet perhaps, over and against the rationalized superstitions of an established cult, to restore a fresher, more severe, and more harassing lie.

If we are to keep this identification of idolatry, religion, and divination from being itself merely a callous reduction, one qualification must be kept in mind. Man's making of gods *for* himself is not at all far from his making a god *of* himself, something that may limit or destroy as well as exalt the human subject. Hence Jeremiah says of idolaters, "every man is brutish by his knowledge; every founder is confounded by the graven image: for his molten image is falsehood, and there is no breath in them" (51.17); or Augustine, "it is easier for a man to cease to be a man, by worshipping as gods things of his own creation, than it is for things of man's own creation to become gods as a result of his worship" (*City of God* VIII. 23). If idols (do we call them fetishes? works of art? cultural myths?) give form to and deify the shifting desires and fears of human beings, the Bible superadds the darker suspicion that those who create or depend upon idols will become victims by assimilation:

> They have mouths, but they speak not:
> eyes have they, but they see not:
> . . . neither speak they through their throat.
> *They that make them are like unto them;*
> *so is every one that trusteth in them.* (emphasis mine)

This text is first of all a rebuke to our myths of magical animation. The maker who seeks to give divine life to statues here becomes no more than the parodic cousin of Yahweh or Prometheus, who created men in their own likenesses. The psalm makes the idolater a disenchanted Pygmalion; in the light of the text's *dis*trust, the miraculous animation of this sculptor's statue becomes less of a mythic hope than a

11. Vico himself confirms this association of idolatry and divination in *The New Science*, II.i.1, par. 382: "Thus it was fear which created gods in the world; not fear awakened by men in other men, but fear awakened in men by themselves. *Along with this origin of idolatry is demonstrated likewise the origin of divination, which was brought into the world at the same birth*" (emphasis mine).

metaphor for the wandering, unassimilable element of idolatrous *eros* which inhabits aesthetic creation (this same animation being read by medieval mythographers as a pathological illusion). But above all of these reflections, the lines from Psalm 115 remind us that, while the idol can hardly escape being a static entity, in making an idol man opens up a space for his *own* metamorphosis. He "transforms himself into" his ignorant images of things, to use Vico's phrase. Finally, I would say that the created idol here turns into the mirror of Narcissus, possessed only of that magic inhabiting the face of Medusa, which turns all who look at it to stone: "They that make them are like unto them; so is every one that trusteth in them."

It is this disturbing sense of the idol's power to transform its viewer (not always distinguishable from the worshiper's hope of a *redemptive* magic in the sacred image) which seems to me to create so much tension in those Spenserian scenes where a quester must confront the graven image of a god, whether Cupid, Venus, or Isis. Even the iconoclast may be subject to human ambivalences before manifestations of deity, however false. Furthermore, this apparent power of the idol to change or petrify has an ironic twin in the capacity of the human eye itself (whether in attitudes of love or fear) to turn men and women into statues, to subject a life *other* than its own to the reductions of idolatry. In Spenser we can see this happening when the triumphant and envious Britomart stares an embracing couple into the ambiguous figure of a marble hermaphrodite (*FQ* III.xii.46 [1590]); or when a lost, denuded Serena is metamorphosed all at once into an erotic icon, a military trophy, an altar, and a sacrificial victim under the gazes of cannibalistic savages that mingle hunger, lust, and religious awe (VI. viii. 41–43).[12] The uneasy symbiosis of idol and idolater thus becomes

12. It is worth quoting Spenser's description in full:

> Her yvorie necke, her alablaster brest,
> Her paps, which like white silken pillowes were,
> For love in soft delight thereon to rest;
> Her tender sides, her bellie white and clere,
> Which like an Altar did it selfe uprere,
> To offer sacrifice divine thereon;
> Her goodly thighes, whose glorie did appeare
> Like a triumphall Arch, and thereupon
> The spoiles of Princes hang'd, which were in battel won.
> (VI.viii.42)

It might be argued that Spenser wants to suggest how much the sophisticated, hieratic language of the narrator is at odds with the "loose lascivious sight" and superstitious vision of the cannibals. But Spenser's poetic anthropology also indicates how much the "early" forms of aggression and idolatry continue to infect the "later" imperial and ceremonial imagery.

for Spenser the material for a remarkable kind of visionary poetry in which psychological, religious, and aesthetic categories are difficult to distinguish.

The Plot of Iconoclasm

If the idol is the medium of mythological religion's sacred identification of man, god, and nature, Psalm 115 warns that without any purifying alienation between humanity, creation, and divinity, without the continual questioning of inherited images of God, human worship and human work issue only in divisive confrontations of the self with its most reductive images—mythological self-expression becoming over time an idolatrous self-enslavement. To adapt Buber's language, this would be the meeting not of an I and a Thou but of an I and a Me. Or rather, since it is the nature of the Thou which partly shapes the being of the I, one would have a situation in which I and Me become merely It and It, a subject and an object which by their relation are turned blind, deaf, and voiceless.

I mean neither to be cynical about Buber's formula nor to overestimate its anthropological validity; it is enough if, together with Psalm 115, it clarifies the peculiar structure of idolatry. From this standpoint, however, we need to look more closely at some of the dynamics of iconoclasm, especially the ways in which iconoclasm is itself entangled with the invention of idolatry. To break an image is, again, a necessarily symbolic act, as much a movement of substitution as of demystification. The violences of the iconoclast may seek to expose the violence or violations hidden under the lie of idolatry; they may help us to recover a difficult power, a revelation, an otherness, an openness, in the face of blockage, reification, and reduction. But even if iconoclasm avoids simply raising up one idol in the place of the old, the desacralizing act may have to defend itself against becoming a dead ritual of desecration, or an empty iconoclasm based merely on the illusion of freedom. This, it seems to me, is the lesson of Franz Kafka's disenchanting parable about transgressions of the sacred: "Leopards break into the temple and drink the sacrificial chalices dry; this occurs repeatedly, again and again: finally it can be reckoned upon beforehand and becomes a part of the ceremony" (*Great Wall of China,* 282).

We do not know if the leopards serve prophets or demons, whether the temple is Hebrew or pagan, whether the chalices of sacrifice contain literal blood (animal? human?) or symbolic wine (the vehicle of a real or a metaphorical presence?). We cannot easily prefer the original violence or the restored ceremony, or decide which violates the other more. The parable instead complicates the forms of sacredness and sacrilege by a hallucinatory pattern where the dialectical poles of idolatry and iconoclasm seem to merge. Still, Kafka keeps the tense, dreamlike conflict of violence and ceremony from falling into a static opposition by casting the terms so insistently into such a stark narrative form—itself almost a parody of some unknown etiological fable intended to justify a ritual or cult, but here mocking the tales of both priest and iconoclast. Despite his insistent suspension of partisanship, Kafka nevertheless serves to point up some of the resources of the older and somewhat more immediately polemical texts examined below. For in these too, the tales told about idolatry and iconoclasm suggest pressures that cannot quite be contained by any neutral theological categories, and in which the violent designs of the iconoclast find yet a subtler subversiveness in story. These texts, insofar as they feed on the sacred slander of the cultic image as idol, also reinscribe the violence turned against images within narratives that complicate or ironize that violence; they establish a kind of countermagic that attempts at once to coopt and to overcome the liabilities of magic, divination, and idolatry.

Before going on to my first biblical example—the Tower of Babel—I want to cite a text in which the narrative transformation of idolatry and iconoclasm works at a fairly modest level. This is the well-known midrash, in which the young Abraham, whose father Terah is said to be quite literally a maker of idols, first mocks his father's customers and then proceeds to break all but the biggest of the statues in Terah's shop. Placing a great stick in the hands of that figure, he later explains to his father that a controversy had arisen among the statues about an offering of grain left by a customer, and that in the end the largest of the "gods" had risen up and broken all of the others. Such a fantastic tale serves first parabolically to extend the merely literal act of iconoclasm by mocking the narratives of mythological religion—especially any such theomachic fable as might suggest that a true god's power over other deities resulted from the primordial defeat of one by another, rather than from the fact that such a god (like Yahweh) inhabits an entirely different order of being. More crucially, perhaps, at the local level of the midrash Abraham's lie tricks the patriarch's natural father into a confession of his own irrational idolatry. The story repeated, Terah cries to Abraham "Why do you mock me? Have they any knowledge?"—to which the father of monotheism replies, "Should not your ears listen to what your mouth is saying?"[13]

The midrash—a lesson about a lesson—suggests something of the iconoclastic resources in fable and lie even within the context of the grave, rationalistic critique of idol worship such as we find in Rabbinic tradition. In a biblical context, however, we may expect to find the plot of iconoclasm put to more extreme uses, articulating conflicts of faith and authority that do not resolve themselves quite so charmingly as in the text just cited. Let me quote at length from Genesis 11.1-9:

> And the whole earth was of one language, and of one speech. And it came to pass, as they journeyed from the east, that they found a plain in the land of Shinar; and they dwelt there. And they said to one another, Go to, let us make brick, and burn them throughly. And they had brick for stone, and slime had they for mortar. And they said, Go to, let us build us a city and a tower, whose top may reach unto heaven; and let us make us a name, lest we be scattered abroad upon the face of the whole earth.
>
> And the Lord came down to see the city and the tower, which the children of men builded. And the Lord said, Behold, the people is one, and they have all one language; and this they begin to do: and now nothing will be restrained from them, which they have imagined to do. Go to, let us go down, and there confound their language, that they may not understand one another's speech. So the Lord scattered them abroad from thence upon the face of all the earth: and they left off to build the city. Therefore is the name of it called Bab-el; because the Lord did there confound the language of all the earth: and from thence did the Lord scatter them abroad upon the face of all the earth.

The building of the city and tower is a kind of second, parodic creation, doubly so perhaps because of the degraded substitution of slime for mortar and brick for stone. The basic thing to observe is that the impulse of men to make a name for themselves is more than a search for temporal fame; the romance of building and self-naming is interpreted as an act of both aggression and defense, and, moreover, one that Yahweh seems to perceive as more than an empty threat. As Buber points out, the men strive "to establish a mighty name-magic against the Lord of the lightning, in order to prevent His 'scattering'

13. The full text of the story can be found in the *Midrash Rabbah*, "Genesis," XXXVIII.13 (Freedman and Simon translation, 1:310–11).

them over the face of the whole earth" (*Prophetic Faith,* 92). Not surprisingly, the rabbis identified this assumption of autonomy and stability as idolatry—a reading strangely literalized in one interpretation, which indicates that the builders wanted to place an armed statue on the top of the tower to wage war with God, as if their idolatry extended to the illusion of a literal power to animate dead matter.[14] We may also note that the builders' wish to make a name for themselves links them to the "giants and men of renown" (literally "men with a name") in Genesis 6.1–4, born of the union of the sons of God and the daughters of men (Speiser, *Genesis,* 45).

But instead of naming themselves like Vichian giants or primitives, these builders are in the end named by another; against their aggressive "magic" Yahweh poses a sacred force that is at once revelation and decreation, unnaming and renaming. This is a magic that converts the prior unification of human work and speech into an ironic figure for what, from the stance of Yahweh, is a radical confusion of the powers of God and man, or an overestimation of man's power to unify society and speech. The patterned narration shows the deity at once repeating, answering, enacting the words of those below, responding mockingly to their "let us build" with his "let us go down," and accomplishing just that "scattering" of language and identity which they had earlier feared. In lieu of the "name" that they sought to create for themselves is the God-given name for the uncompleted, abandoned city: Babel, interpreted as "confusion." Yahweh's sovereign act is to institute the incompleteness of human work, the fragmentation and multiplicity of human speech; the act of parodic creation issues only in a second Fall, or a return to chaos.

The persuasiveness of such a text lies in its deliberately ironic heightening of both human pathos and divine power, and in its way of embedding iconoclastic violence within the structures of narration and address. One crucial historical irony is that the story demonstrates the power of Yahweh—or that assumed by his author—over the inherited and seemingly natural meanings of words. As Buber argues, "it must not be supposed that the narrator did not know the [etymological] derivation of Bab-ilu, gate of god; but it is over against this that he sets his story of the name, as the *true* sense" (*Prophetic Faith,* 93). That "truth," however, though it lies partly in the historical authority of the scriptural text itself, is a function of a canny, rhetorical

14. This detail can be found in the Targum Pseudo-Jonathan, Genesis 11, reproduced along with related midrashic readings in John Bowker's *The Targums and Rabbinic Literature: An Introduction to Jewish Interpretations of Scripture,* 182–85.

exuberance, of a local, antithetical force in the divinity's pun; that is to say, it lies in a *rhetorical* authority which cannot quite be measured by any organized mystery or system of doctrinal truths (such, perhaps, as would constitute our own modern version of the Tower of Babel).[15] The narrative force of that renaming is further reinforced by the evidence that this parody of biblical creation simultaneously parodies a central Mesopotamian foundation myth, which told that the Ziggurat of Ur (the probable model for the tower, and the focus of a cosmologically ordered religious and political hierarchy) was originally a sacred *omphalos* first erected by the gods.[16] The Genesis etiology thus mocks the myth of the tower's divine origins by showing it to be clearly a human structure, even while it projects the "presumptuousness" and idolatry of the older fable onto the builders themselves.

The continuity between the problems I have been discussing and the sort of referential and narrative ironies which condition typological allegory will help me show how the radical poetics of the Babel myth might become relevant for Spenser. But the bridge thrown between the Hebrew Bible and *The Faerie Queene* will be a speculative one. It is likely that Spenser's own sophisticated, subversive, and recreative parodies of the mythic mode are modeled more on the philosophical fables of Plato or the metamorphic myths of Ovid, not to mention Ariosto. The main advantage of the Genesis analogy here is that it shows the process of parody sacralized; as a portion of a total scripture, the tale's demythologizing tendencies feed a still mythic and magical vision, one in which a divine, iconoclastic chaos restructures the illusory, defensive orders of human work and human naming. (Nor do the lessons of Babel preclude the tale of a single hero gaining a new name by wrestling all night with an "angel," or dreaming not of a parodic *omphalos* but a blessed stairway on which supernatural beings descend and ascend.) "Magic," like "myth," is no

15. It seems wholly characteristic of the Yahwist so to posit unnatural, figurative, or redundant etymologies for the names of persons and places in his stories, names whose complex meanings are wrought out of the immediate pragmatic crisis of the sacred narrative rather than being sanctioned by any single "proper" etymology or fixed cultic name. Speiser points out many of these etymological puns throughout his commentary on Genesis, as does Herbert Marks, in "The Double Cave: Biblical Naming and Poetic Etymology."

16. As Eliade notes, in mythological cultures "the founding of a new town repeats the creation of the world. . . . Every eastern city stood at the center of the world. Babylon was a *Bab-ilani*, a 'door of the gods,' for it was there that the gods came down to earth. The Mesopotamian ziqqurat was, properly speaking, a cosmic mountain" (*Patterns*, 374, 376)—that is, a cultural artifact that has become a portion of the divinized natural world. For more specific comments on the background of the Genesis text, see Buber, *Prophetic Faith*, 92–93, and Speiser, *Genesis*, 75–76.

single thing in a text like the Tower of Babel. It is a serious but usefully fluid category that emerges at the point of conflict between opposing powers. The only danger for us as critics is if we try to locate some rationalized *belief* about magic in the biblical narrative, a liability that holds as well in the case of my next example, the Brazen Serpent.

This "representative anecdote" (as Burke would call it) centers around a more literal act of iconoclasm, one that occurs within the context of Israelite worship itself. The Brazen Serpent, which stood by the altar of Yahweh in the first temple, remained for both Jewish and Christian authors the focus of many troubling questions about the nature of sacred representation. Reputed to be a magical relic of the Exodus, the serpent seems to have fallen over time from a momentary miracle to a fixed cultic symbol and finally to an object of idolatrous worship and sacrifice in its own right—which is not to say that the serpent was taken as an autonomous god but that it appeared idolatrous insofar as it led to the worship and address of Yahweh under the forms of mythological religion, dangerously muddling the difference between the false and the true. As such it was "broken in pieces" during the reign of King Hezekiah (2 Kings 18.4) in a reformation that also swept away high places, images, and "groves." In this case the act of iconoclasm, to the degree that it levels the serpent with idols outside the cult, has the effect of simultaneously raising and quelling the specter of an idolatrous syncretism, as indeed any act of iconoclasm is in some way responsible for both marking and unmaking idolatry. Yet what can be said about the historical crisis in the Israelite cult is less immediately interesting (or accessible) than the ways in which the simultaneous fascination with and reticence about the function of the serpent survive even in those scriptural texts that seek to justify the serpent's power.

The primary narrative of Numbers 21 is, it has been argued, a carefully constructed priestly etiology, a retrospective fable intended as an *apologia* for the awkward presence of an image by the altar of the imageless God and, perhaps, as a defense against the possibility of its idolization. The text reports that at a crisis in the Israelites' journey through the wilderness, Yahweh sends "fiery serpents" to sting those Jews who long for a return to the magical, idolatrous land of Egypt and cry out against their elect leader. When that leader prays for a means to avert the punishment, "the Lord said unto Moses, Make thee a fiery serpent [literally, "a fiery," *saraph*], and set it upon a pole: and it shall come to pass, that every one that is bitten, when he looketh upon it, shall live. And Moses made a serpent of brass, and put it upon a pole, and it came to pass, that if a serpent had bitten any man, when he beheld the serpent of brass, he lived" (Num. 21.8–9). As a phase in the larger narrative of sacred questing, this is a deeply problematic text. It first seems to describe a very primitive sort of image magic, a homeopathic healing by means of a mimetic talisman in which like cures like, and in which the difference between curse and cure begins to collapse. (It may point up the ambivalence to note in passing that the root *saraph* can be used in a later biblical text like Isaiah to refer to *both* the poisonous inhabitants of the prophesied wasteland and the angels, or *seraphim*, who sing at the Throne of God.)[17] The patterned narration's close repetition of God's words of command in the account of miraculous healing reinforces the peculiar sense of magical efficacy, but we should also note how carefully the text wards off any suggestions of a crudely mechanical or shamanistic magic, as well as any impression that the history entails the institution of a ritual.[18] The curative serpent is itself not a miracle but clearly a made thing, commanded by God for this one particular crisis, and its effect depends on the people turning to the image of their own accord. Still, such a demythologizing interpretation of the episode may grant too much to contemporary apologetics, unless one is prepared to recognize some of the less rationalizable ironies and dislocations of agency (from God, to Moses, to the Brazen Serpent) which here render uncanny both the nature of God's judgment and the means of human atonement.

Such uncertainties about the place of magic also become a problem when examining the later texts on the Brazen Serpent. The serpent figure surfaces again in the Hellenistic Book of Wisdom, with its impermanence as a vehicle of Grace quite emphatically marked, likewise its function as covenantal reminder rather than magical talisman. Indeed, the author seems so anxious to empty the snake of enchantment that he in effect suppresses the image: "When . . . they were perishing from the bites of writhing snakes, your wrath did not continue to the end. . . . for they had *a saving token* to remind them of the commandment of your Law. Whoever turned to it was saved, not by what he looked at, but by you, the universal saviour" (Wis. 16.5–7, Jerusalem Version; emphasis mine). The later author here decontaminates the ambiguous magic of the earlier text by converting it to doctrinal metaphor. Even this pious abstraction, however, does not fully close off the

17. See Buttrick et al., *Interpreter's Dictionary of the Bible,* 3:289–90.

18. Cf. Martin Noth, *Numbers: A Commentary,* 157: "Release from the fatal effects of the serpent bites is linked to a test of obedience set by Yahweh in his free judgment, a test which, at the same time, bears witness to the sovereign power of Yahweh even over the dangerous and sinister character of the desert."

channels of suggestion in the text. The Snake of Brass undergoes another metamorphosis in John 3.14–18, where it is read as a type of the redemptive power of the crucified Christ. Even later, along with a great many other of the trials and miracles of the Exodus, exegetes could take the Serpent to prefigure the power of the established church and its sacraments—as if the breaking of the original image were the best evidence that the tale of the Serpent was intended to prefigure later mysteries.[19]

I reserve more detailed treatment of idolatry and typology until the final section of this chapter. Still, in those texts I have been citing we can see a foreshadowing of the complex debates about the relation of scriptural interpretation and liturgical practice such as characterized the period of Spenser's writing; we may also get a sense of the impasse that led Donne to worry that "to adore, or scorn an image, or protest / May all be bad." The temple of the true God always threatens to become the home of the false, and the violence of King Hezekiah against the ornaments of that temple finds echoes in the work of those reformers anxious and radical enough to tear down the visible images of the crucified God they so strenuously preached—regarding such forms neither as sacred vessels, symbols, nor even as aesthetic objects, but only as sacrilege.[20] The texts from Wisdom and John help show furthermore how much the defense against idolatry may involve, in addition to physical destruction, the coopting of stories told about the image, recreating that image as an abstract conceptual metaphor or else translating it (under the aegis of demystification) into another symbolic language, one that is purportedly more complete, authoritative, and efficacious. We must learn, however, not to take such transformations for granted but to measure their persuasiveness and their stakes (just as we must study the mixed motives of iconoclasm). We must remind ourselves that, however powerful the later readings of the Brazen Serpent are in their reordering and sublimation of sacred categories, to translate the Serpent wholly into a cipher of faith may blind us to the eloquent magic of the original text. Likewise we should be wary of transforming an obscure exchange of power into a merely

19. On the patristic discovery of a sacramental typology in Exodus, see Jean Daniélou, *From Shadows to Reality: Studies in the Biblical Typology of the Fathers*, 153–201.

20. For an excellent discussion of iconoclasm in sixteenth-century England see John Phillips, *The Reformation of Images: Destruction of Art in England, 1535–1660*, 41–101. Phillips steadfastly refuses to sort out a single guiding motive for iconoclasm; rather, he points to the difficult overlapping of spiritual, political, and economic forces at work, the frequent gaps between ideal desire and pragmatic possibility in the efforts of Reformers to rid the church of images, as well as the sometimes rationalistic, sometimes mythic rhetoric of the iconoclasts themselves.

allegorical or "spiritual" category, or of making the Serpent into the emptied vehicle of religious polemic.[21]

Brooding over the later history of the Serpent, one may be reminded of the situation of a reformer such as Martin Luther. His early writings reject with some horror the mechanical magic of medieval ritual, with its apparent power to deceive human desire and conscience. And yet Luther became even more severe with the demystified sacramentalism of reformers like Ulrich Zwingli, who would have turned Christ's words instituting the Eucharist—"This is my body"—into the institution of a communal metaphor. Luther took his stand on the divine literalness of that "is," despite his own emphasis on the Eucharist as fundamentally promise and testament, as a vehicle of the Word which could neither magically do anything for others nor offer anything to God.[22] We need not now consider the theological debates surrounding this issue, nor the ways in which the definition of the Eucharist became a crux both for theories of scriptural exegesis and for the pragmatics of liturgy.[23] At the moment we need only witness the urgency of one reformer's attempt to hold on to a miracle while stripping it of superstition. He sought, as the texts we have been reading seek, to recover for religion a more obscure and strenuous magic, a mode of supernatural presence that could feed a hunger for the uncanny without collapsing into either materialistic or rationalistic idolatry, the automatically efficacious or the vacantly figurative sign.

Such a precarious situation might help explain why so ardently decentered a Protestant as Spenser would project his own rendering of a sacramental moment into an allegorical narrative which contains, however, no clear types of church, formal ritual, or priesthood, and which evades the possible reductions of rationalizable metaphor or strict historical typology.[24] Likewise, the simultaneous need for and

21. One should remember that, despite what doctrinal tradition claims, to read an Old Testament miracle as a type of the Grace offered by the incarnation and crucifixion of Christ is crucially different from reading it as a shadow of a ritual performed by a church that is that savior's earthly "Body."

22. Cf. Francis Clark, *The Eucharistic Sacrifice and the Reformation*, 106–7.

23. For a detailed account of Luther's exegeses of New Testament texts concerning the Lord's Supper viewed in relation to both traditional Catholic theology and other Protestant interpretations, see Jaroslav Pelikan, *Luther the Expositor*, 137–204.

24. As Northrop Frye observes, the balm-giving tree and the living well that restore Redcrosse Knight during his three-day battle with the dragon of the fallen world (*FQ* I.xi) probably represent the two sacraments, Eucharist and Baptism, accepted by the Reformed church (*Anatomy of Criticism*, 194). But Spenser's visionary translation of the sacraments stalls any doctrinal questions as to whether these convey a real or a metaphorical presence. The narrative is figurative, of course, but not in any rationalizable, Zwinglian fashion; the allegorical images of the text point to no theological abstraction

danger of demystification might suggest why the poet endlessly rehearses the intricate trials of idolatry and iconoclasm in both sacred and secular loci, and yet directly depicts the stripping or defiling of a *church* only when the agents are quite clearly evil. Such strategies leave the ideological and metaphorical dimensions of Spenser's ritualized or iconoclastic narratives in considerable flux. The result is that his tales of vision, struggle, and purification often approach more clearly the ambivalent strangeness of a text like Numbers 21 than they do the determined sublimations of Wisdom or the Gospel of John. Indeed, as an eclectic, belated author, Spenser may come even closer to the bizarre inflections of my final anecdote of iconoclasm—a generic hodgepodge of folktale, parable, and intellectual satire wholly outside of normative tradition. This story is both more schematic and more esoteric than either the Tower of Babel or the Brazen Serpent, yet more useful than any other I know in what it suggests about the interanimation of certain dilemmas of language with those of magic, idolatry, and iconoclasm.

My example centers on the figure called the Golem, a magically created being whose name derives from the Hebrew word used by Talmudic authors to describe the clay body of Adam into which God breathed life.[25] A creature of Jewish Kabbalistic mythology, the Golem, like the alchemical homunculus, is the end-product of the scholar's study of the secret orders of creation. It is often not so much a made thing as it is an ideal that reflects the mage's ecstatic apprehension of the God who made man in his own image. Still, this being also has analogues in that Hermetic tradition where the Promethean work of the magician was literally to "make gods" and animate dead statues. The Golem himself is animated by the inscribed or uttered Word of God, but it usually lacks the power of speech. In some legends it was created as a helper and defender of the embattled communities of the Diaspora, thus a kind of millennial savior, but it was also represented as an ambivalent, unruly monster that could run amok and have to be

---

but to the radical, mythic types of Genesis, the Gospels, and Revelation. And even these allusions are so layered within the complex narrative that no single type can be said to form the absolute ground of the allegory. Spenser "represents" the Eucharistic mystery again in his personification of Faith in the House of Holiness (I.x.13), a figure who carries both a book "signd and seald with blood" (the locus of the sacramental word of promise) and a sacramental cup of wine and water "in which a Serpent did himselfe enfold." Whatever else that last image does, it suggests some ambivalent, supernatural presence in the physical chalice which is unavailable to the simplifications of theological allegory, a presence aligned with but by no means equivalent to that symbolized by the unnamed book.

25. My discussion of the Golem legend and its sources is indebted particularly to Gershom Scholem, *Kabbalah*, 352–55.

destroyed. In all of this, the fascination and poignancy of the myth within the anti-iconic context of Judaism have to do with the fact that the Golem inhabits an uncertain middle ground between god and idol, man and demon, blasphemy and miracle.

The following passage, taken from Gershom Scholem's paraphrase of a sixteenth-century Kabbalistic text, contains a Golem who is strangely able to speak—but only so that he may tell and enact a parable about his ambiguous condition of being:

> The prophet Jeremiah was busying himself alone with the *Sefer Yetzirah* ("The Book of Creation") when a heavenly voice went forth and said: "Take a companion." Jeremiah, obeying, chose his son Sira, and they studied the book together for three years. Afterward, they set about combining the alphabets in accordance with the Kabbalistic principles of combination, grouping, and word formation, and a man was created to them, on whose forehead stood the letters, *YHWH Elohim Emet*, meaning: God the Lord is Truth. But this newly created man had a knife in his hand, with which he erased the letter *alef* from the word *emet* ("truth"); there remained the word *met* ("dead"). Then Jeremiah rent his garments (because of the blasphemy, God is dead, now implied by the inscription) and said: "Why have you erased the *alef* from *emet*?" He replied: "I will tell you a parable."

The parable describes two men who, having learned the secrets of a master architect, break with him and become builders in their own right. But because they charge less for a commission than their master, the people honor the renegade pupils instead of him.

> "So God has made you in His image and in His shape and form. But now that you have created a man like Him, people will say: There is no God in the world beside these two!" Then Jeremiah said: "What solution is there?" He said: "Write the alphabets backward with intense concentration on the earth. Only do not meditate in the sense of building up, as you did before, but the other way around." So they did, and the man became dust and ashes before their eyes. (*The Messianic Idea in Judaism*, 337–38)

Scholem adds, "It is indeed significant that Nietzsche's famous cry, 'God is dead,' should have gone up first in a Kabbalistic text warning against the making of a Golem and linking the death of God to the realization of the idea of the Golem" (338).

The Golem's tale sounds like a dry revision of the Tower of Babel, but more interesting is the magical theory of language underlying the scene. Kabbalistic thought, against anything like an Augustinian skepticism of language, found in human speech and writing the means of a potentially direct access to the central orders of divine creation. What made this possible was a conception of the physical and metaphysical cosmos, but more particularly of the sacred text of the Hebrew Bible, as vehicles of God's self-naming and self-expression. Hence even the individual letters of the biblical text, insofar as they unfolded the powers and meanings of that Name, could become not just a conceptual and mythic map of divinity but a way of repossessing divine creativity, a means of gaining operative power as well as intellectual insight.[26] At its best, the Kabbalistic science of letter combination and numerological interpretation extended more fully the Jewish tradition's massive cathexis in the text of Torah as the container of all meaning and could win back from the often indifferent or merely historical reference of the Book of God a higher sense of mystical potency. The more literary, interpretive labor, however, slid easily into the magical; so-called practical Kabbalah could indeed collapse into naive demonology or crude talismanic magic. But the quest for the Name might also extend to a sanctified repetition of original creation, even to the making of a second man.

The above fable, however, locates an irony, a transgression latent in this most sacred magic; it points to the idolatry—the structure of identification, usurpation, and negation—infecting even a divinely enjoined act of repetition. What is crucial here is not so much the pious warning about the limits of magical speech as the fact that it is the Golem, the breathing idol, who alone confesses the dark implications of his making; he is a creature, a son, turning against both himself and his human father. The sanctioned quest for knowing does issue in a transgression or sacrilege, but also in a moment when (as Nathaniel Hawthorne says of his animated scarecrow, Feathertop) an illusion sees and fully recognizes itself. It is as if the Tower of Babel could name itself Confusion. The unexpected violence of the Golem's response is really a sacred blasphemy that exposes the death in that truth and the truth in that death. Again, however, we must hold onto the irreducible sense of mystery, the residue of some autonomous magical force that survives such a stark demystification, a magic that is in some ways more persuasive, if more ironic than that which we find at work in the initial fiction of achieved animation. For the shift or fall that spreads itself through the successive movements of erasure, parable, and counterspell is more than a dramatic emblem of how human magic decays into idolatry and death. That movement is also a pre-

26. Cf. Scholem, *Major Trends in Jewish Mysticism,* 17, and *Kabbalah,* 170.

emptive defense against that decay, as well as a way of keeping hold on an efficacious magic that combines radical naming and radical unnaming, radical enchantment and radical disenchantment. The clay man is the vessel of a form of knowing which negotiates the metaphysical and temporal threshold between creation and idolatry, truth and death; it is a magic that encompasses the means by which magic undoes itself, even lives in the death of magic.

The Golem fable may serve to frame some of the basic intuitions of my poetics of idolatry. It shows us a figure of divinity, a divine man, and a divine magic, all haunted by the ghosts of their own dissolution; it presents a sacred hermeneutic or magical mimesis dangerously on the verge of parody, illusion, and lie; it tells of the making of animate icons that must be saved from the frigid shadows of human will and cultural system, and yet in which any breaking of magic still proceeds under the burden of magical agency.

In the most general terms, I might offer "Golem," and by extension "idol," as metaphors or transferred names for a poem, a myth, a text, an idea—for all of those things in the human world which cause us so much labor and pleasure. More specifically, I would argue that Spenser's own most powerful scenes of disenchantment—Arthur's unveiling of his antithetical, metamorphic shield; Britomart's dissolving of the masque of Busyrane; Calidore's idolatrous transgression of Colin Clout's idyllic vision of dancing goddesses—all frame the work of magic in the same problematic fashion as the Golem narrative. The peculiar usefulness of that fable, however, may be clearer after a survey of the allegorical tradition in which Spenser might more directly have discovered his origins.

Allegory and Idolatry

To recapitulate some earlier points in too simple a fashion: the Hebrew Bible debunks the gods of other cultures, empties the ceremonial magic of pagan religion of its efficacy, and exposes the self-deceptiveness of divination. Though it presents us with fiery serpents, dragons, monsters of land and sea, true and false celestial messengers, and so on, it elaborates no cosmic hierarchies of angels, demons, or astral spirits. Magic remains a hugely ambiguous presence, but the fight against idolatry tends to locate itself in a world emptied of all supernatural forces save those of Yahweh himself. Hence, turning to the following text from the Epistle to the Ephesians—one that is crucial for Spenser—we may seem to be in an entirely different world:

> Finally my brethren, be strong in the Lord, and in the power of his might. Put on the whole armour of God, that ye may be able to stand against the wiles of the devil. For we wrestle not against flesh and blood, but against principalities, against powers, against the rulers of the darkness of this world, against spiritual wickedness in high places. (6.10–12)

> . . . against the Sovereignties and the Powers who originate the darkness in this world, the spiritual army of evil in the heavens. (Jerusalem Version)

Here Paul maps out a spiritual battleground somewhat in the mode of late apocalyptic and Gnostic writers; the text reflects their sometimes primitive, sometimes sophisticated and rationalized demonology and angelology, their transformation of contemporary religious politics into a cosmic battle between sharply divided powers of good and evil.[27] What the writer emphasizes, in this passage and in what follows, is the stance of defense, a stern readiness (combining awe and aggression) in the face of an otherworldly enemy always ready to reconstitute itself along other lines, both political and spiritual.[28] The text thus does not go to the extreme limit of eschatological rhetoric and claim to possess a vision of the end of all idolatry, a vision of the concentration of spiritual error into a single creature or set of creatures to be overthrown by a final revelation of divine power. For though the degree to which such aggressive mythic dualisms tend to support universalizing, deterministic cosmologies is what makes apocalyptic so tempting a mode for revolutionary political and religious movements, it also makes the apocalyptic a liability for any prophetic author who refuses to exclude either man or God from the ongoing processes of choice and change. Hence it may be that the text from Ephesians maintains, along with its vision of cosmic antagonism, a subtler sense of unresolved tension between the human and supernatural realms.

One may agree with such scholars as Rudolf Bultmann, then, that Paul does not naively appeal to a dualistic or specifically Gnostic cosmology; he neither preaches the objective existence of evil spirits nor projects his "mental fight" wholly into a mythic time beyond time. The battle is within history, as well as in the sky. And yet I do not

27. See *Theology of the New Testament,* 1:164–83, for Bultmann's discussion of Gnostic elements in the writings of Paul.

28. See Jean Starobinski, "The Struggle with Legion: A Literary Analysis of Mark 5:1–20," for an exemplary analysis of such defensive and oppositional strategies in another New Testament narrative. On the more broadly political and sociological implications of the apocalyptic stance, see Norman Cohn, *The Pursuit of the Millennium: Revolutionary Millenarians and Mystical Anarchists of the Middle Ages,* 13–36, and passim.

think it sufficient to say that Paul employs the idea of apocalyptic adversaries merely as demythologized metaphor, as just a sharp way of characterizing the falsity of human imagination or corrupt religious and political traditions (governments, principalities, and powers).[29] Paul's writing never completely undermines its own mythological rhetoric. We cannot preemptively divide the supernatural world from the earthly, for the mutual contamination of human and supernatural forces in the passage is part of its force. One might even say that the Pauline text gains its spiritual urgency at the risk of idolatry, since it suggests the nearly autonomous, supernatural scope of powers and institutions which are not only human in their origin but also problematic precisely insofar as they have been subject to a prior act of idolization or divination.

There is in this text an uneasy symbiosis between the living demon and the demystified idol which also emerges in such Pauline concepts as the Flesh, Sin, Law, or the Letter (all of which in a sense overlap). "Flesh," for instance, is neither a wholly physiological nor metaphysical category, but a radical trope of the spirit which cuts across the dualism of body and spirit, a demonic figure for the deadness of literal reading. The Flesh can be an agent, a space, an age, a mode of thought, just as Sin can be a king, a slave-master, a murderer, a being that can both die and revive, and as Law can appear to be a living, corruptive force in a spiritual cosmos.[30] This is more than simply demythologized metaphor. Insofar as Paul assigns to them a double genealogy—as entities constituted by the self-deceived work of fallen man in creation, and as beings within an objective order created by God—the Law, the Flesh, and Sin become at once more abstract and more threatening. These dead things come to possess an unnatural life, the darkest paradox of their double origin being that man

29. Markus Barth's notes to his translation of Ephesians betray a telling nervousness about the scope of Pauline eschatology: "The 'principalities and powers' are at the same time intangible spiritual entities and concrete historical, social, or psychic structures or institutions of *all created* things and *all created* life. They represent a certain order in God's *creation—though their idolization by man has often resulted in chaotic conditions.* It was stated that on exegetical grounds it is as yet impossible to identify exactly the several groups mentioned by Paul or to sketch the hierarchy among them. Their many names indicate their diversity, and listing them sometimes expresses the desire either to secure their help or to ward off their interference" (*Ephesians,* 800–801; emphasis mine). I would only insist here that the "chaotic conditions" this critic mentions are generated and sustained by the Pauline rhetoric itself. Barth, for all his pious insistence on the "createdness" of the demons, both admits their confusing relation to the eschatological hierarchy and ends by describing the text's personifications in terms appropriate to more ambivalent strategies of magical invocation and defense.

30. On Paul's mobile personifications of sin, see Bultmann, *Theology of the New Testament,* 1:245.

turns out to be responsible for the world that possesses him; he inherits and is mastered by a demonic world he himself seems to fabricate.

The kind of personifications I have been examining may suggest a general rule for allegory, one that is especially relevant in the light of earlier arguments: any mode of religious rhetoric which seeks to dramatize a spiritual, conceptual, or political conflict by giving independent mythic existence to a negative term so that it may be symbolically simplified, slandered, and cast out always risks creating a verbal figure suspended between the states of demon and idol. Such a figure both stems from and constitutes the allegorical agon; it is the creature of a discourse that seeks to attack what it sees as human illusion but—rather than opposing any putatively rational mode of knowledge or expression—reserves for itself some access to a magical form of speech, a potent form of the Word which must serve the purposes of iconoclasm and revelation. Allegory thus tends to sustain even as it empties out the realm of the demonic and the idolatrous.[31]

The euhemeristic and philosophical allegorism of late antiquity, not to mention the period's often satirical and half-ironic use of mythic fable, seems insistent on demystifying the gods. And yet even for a later classical writer like Plutarch, eager to avoid both blind superstition and proud disbelief, the use of allegory allowed him to give the gods a shadowy life as *daimones*, and (as in Plato's *Symposium* 202e) to make them the mediating agencies of prayer, divination, and magic.[32] Early Christianity's demystification of paganism proceeds more aggressively by splitting the ambiguous, articulate realm of classical daemons into distinct worlds of demons and angels—refiguring but still not

31. Walter Benjamin in fact argues that the original impulse of Western allegory feeds on the projection of the antique gods into an alien world and on their conversion into evil, fallen demons. Freed from their living cultic and mythological contexts, the all but empty emblems, attire, and names of the gods become the vehicles of new contents which are predisposed to allegorical representation: "The deadness of the figures and the abstraction of the concepts are therefore the precondition for the allegorical metamorphosis of the pantheon into a world of magical, conceptual creatures" (*Origin of German Tragic Drama*, 226).

32. Cf. Anne Hersman, *Studies in Greek Allegorical Interpretation*, 25–39. Plato's derivation of *daimon* from the Greek *daēmonas*, one who is learned or knowing (*Cratylus* 398b), however well it fits the function of such beings in the work of prophecy and magic, nevertheless seems to be a false etymology; the more likely derivation is from *daiomai*, to distribute or divide (Schneweis, *Angels and Demons*, 82). This etymology suggests, as Fletcher notes (*Allegory*, 59), the work of daemons as distributors of individual fates and characters. But the etymology may also indicate that the mythic idea of daemons is generated by systems of hierarchy and the situations of conflict or contradiction which they may control, institutionalize, or conceal. It may also suggest how much the idea of daemonic agency, or of daemonic enemies, is generated by the desire to clarify or dramatize a difficult conflict by riving apart ambivalent or antagonistic positions within the simplified scheme of an embattled eschatology.

disbanding the older pantheon. Furthermore, in Augustine and others we also find the constitutive ambiguity of demon and idol in Pauline references to the evil realm transformed into a studied redundancy: pagan cults become a structure of empty idols, their images and rituals the debased vehicles of human cupidity and hunger for mystery; and yet, this empty structure is inhabited and sustained by a huge, objectively real race of demons, beings themselves beset by human passions and idolatrous instincts.[33] The old gods are thus granted a disturbing and morbid new life, the perceived reality of the demonic world being necessary to reinforce the church's sense of its own magical, iconoclastic authority. (Priests can not be exorcists unless there are devils.) This reading of idolatry as in part the work of demons has interesting parallels in those Gnostic writings that mock the Hebrew Bible by reinventing its mythic genealogy, making that text into the revelation of an evil demiurge and the created universe into an astral cage that is both an imposed illusion and a degraded imitation of the true heaven.[34] Even in Spenser, for whom the psychological and moral dimensions of the fight against idolatry are primary, the defensive rhetoric of allegory keeps moving merely psychomachic personifications into a mythic or apocalyptic dimension. If Spenser insistently complicates the threshold between the two, it is because he knows that the blind mythifying of psychic categories into autonomous, supernatural creatures can itself be a delusive response to experience—projecting visionary dualisms in the service of antinomian or authoritarian stances. The poet's obsessively contrived verbal and allusive polyvalence keeps the narrative from being cast into a single, apocalyptic framework, just as it keeps the reader from literalizing the always duplicitous tropes of eschatological myth.

It is possible that most allegorists recognize some of the complex liabilities of their mode. At least it seems to me that there is some implicit recognition of allegory's rhetorical illusions in the fact that the allegorical enemy—whether demon or idol—tends only to be defeated by what is itself a starker form of allegorical representation, a more ambivalent, if more urgent moral magic. Such is the case in the disenchanting work of Arthur and Britomart which I will be looking at in later chapters, and even in the case of Redcrosse—who becomes by the end of Book I a more complex personification as well as a "better

33. Cf. Peter Brown, *Augustine of Hippo*, 311: "With Augustine . . . the nexus between men and demons was purely psychological. Like was drawn to like. Men got the demons they deserved; the demons, for their part, perpetuated this likeness by suggesting to the masses immoral and anarchic gods as symbols of divine power."

34. Cf. Hans Jonas, *The Gnostic Religion*, 43.

person," and who must learn after his early defeat of a monster labeled "Errour" that the forces of error tend to exceed any limiting names that culture or poetry might find to contain them. The crises of the allegorical battle can also be exemplified in a schematic way by a somewhat earlier Renaissance text such as Giordano Bruno's *Expulsion of the Triumphant Beast.* In this work, half Hermetic apocalypse and half Lucianic dialogue, a council of Olympian gods undertakes a moral reformation of images, casting out what they see as the vice-infested grotesques of the ancient zodiac (hidden manifestation of the universal, biblical Beast), and replacing them with fresher, heroic personifications of virtue. Indeed, Bruno's vision of astral and psychological purification recalls strongly the more archaic lineaments of the Pauline text that follows the passage quoted at the outset of this section, where the author opposes to the "principalities" and "powers" not a single divine entity but a series of more ambiguous, tense, and internalized tropes:

> Wherefore take unto you the whole armour of God, that ye may be able to withstand in the evil day, and having done all, to stand. Stand therefore, having your loins girt about with truth, and having on the breastplate of righteousness; and your feet shod with the preparation of the gospel of peace; above all, taking the shield of faith, wherewith ye shall be able to quench all the fiery darts of the wicked. And take the helmet of salvation, and the sword of the Spirit, which is the word of God. (Eph. 6.13–17)

The earlier passage's strong realignment of hierarchies, its remapping of the wonted battlefield—not "flesh and blood" but "spiritual wickedness in high places"—had been the first move of the battle itself. In what follows, rather than just talking about allegorical armor, we might do better to say that the allegory itself *is* the armor, the battle, and the weapons (the word become sword), at least insofar as it is the words which mark out the attitudes of aggression and defense into which readers must throw themselves so as to recognize the enemy under a new guise. The contrast between the idea of a "whole armour" and the fragmented, metaphorical body may point to the divisive, possibly self-wounding quality of such attitudes. And yet in assembling or reassembling such a complex allegorical stance, it is the very isolation of each image and, even more, the stiff separation of each "concrete" figure from its spiritual abstraction which account for the text's power. The images and the abstractions react upon each other in such a way that each in turn becomes less natural and more obscure, more emptied of stable categories of meaning and more possessed by or available to the apprehension of daemonic energy.

In metamorphosing the conceptual and the figurative into such a magical field, one of the verbal hinges is the preposition "of."[35] This, in Greek as well as English, makes it possible to read a phrase like "the sword of the Spirit" as either "spiritual sword" or "sword wielded by the Spirit"—the reference to "spirit" thus wandering between a generalized faculty and a more explicit mythological personification, just as "sword" is both a rationalizable metaphor (a figure for the radically figurative Word), and a more uncanny, tropic weapon, indeed the only "active" weapon in the catalogue. From such a web of figures does Spenser begin to construct his own vision of Redcrosse, the Christian Knight, as he notes in the letter to Raleigh. Of course, by the sixteenth century each Pauline image must have carried with it a considerable weight of doctrinal interpretation, complicated by later developments of the spiritual soldier in medieval romance or Reformation propaganda. But it is not in order to define some idealized origin that I am pointing back to the Ephesians text. Rather, the ambiguous, poetic, and moral lure of that text may suggest the urgency of Spenser's attempt to cast it back into his own intricate narrative, repossessing and reanimating for further allegorical battle what might otherwise remain only a cumbersome armor of inherited words and worn-out chivalric figures.

My last comments raise a more general problem for the discussion of allegory. Up until now I have examined mainly the synchronic structure of allegorical rhetoric. But matters such as the unstable relation of demon and idol in allegory, or what I have called allegory's "aggressivity," tend to involve a diachronic problematic. Some of the strangeness of a text's allegorical tropes may derive from the text's reflection on its own mythological language, or from a wholesale transfiguration of contemporary religious politics. But the characteristics I have described so far may also be determined by the author's reflection on an earlier text or dramatize the writer's belated act of reading. As my comments on the Brazen Serpent, Paul's figure of the Law, or Augustine's treatment of the pagan gods may suggest, the ambiguous magic of allegory is often a product of the effort to reduce, transform, repossess, or overgo earlier mythologies or allegories. There is more at stake in such retrospective revisions than the simple shuffling around of old and new images; for the allegorical struggle grows out

35. On the problematic grammar of the Greek phrase, *machaira tou pneumatos* ("sword of the Spirit"), see Barth, *Ephesians,* 776. The same author provides detailed speculations on the historical and mythological sources of the Pauline imagery on 764–77 and 787–800. We should recall that the metaphor of the word as sword is given an apocalyptic literalism in the description of the "Son of Man" in Revelation 1.16, "And out of his mouth went a sharp twoedged sword."

of a continuing tension between an attachment to the power and authority of an older set of images and the need to find a continuity (even an illusory one) between those images and present life, or the riskier desire for a new and more complete revelation. What determines the importance of this dilemma for my larger argument is that in this case the allegorist takes the place of the iconoclast by undoing any idolatrous overestimation of anterior revelation.

This displacement of an iconoclastic concern into a hermeneutic dimension is visible particularly in Christian interpretations of Scripture, and in the doctrinal myths that support those interpretations.[36] The same kind of distortion is involved here as in the use of the word "idolatry" to refer to prebiblical mythology. For instance, when the Hebrew Bible is reinvented as the polemically named "Old" Testament, its narratives are often emptied of their original meanings and ambiguities—or, rather, the retrospective act of interpretation may impose on the pious reader a certain blindness to their significance. Reading a text allegorically means reshaping both our desire for and perception of its meanings. Often the interpreter, in attempting to reappropriate the earlier text's imagery, must discover or invent a mystery where before there was none. The text may thus become a seductive, even a corrupt revelation that only the allegorist can expose, or else a rationally determined covering for doctrinal truths. The act of interpretation may claim to resolve the absurdities or overcome the scandals of the earlier text, pointing, for instance, to those "hidden" senses in Scripture which only become apparent through Christ and his church. And yet, however much they claim to demystify, the readers who discover such truths will tend to bear the burden of further mystification and secrecy (no matter whether the deciphered significance of the Old Testament narrative turns out to be another historical event or a theological abstraction). In this light, one can note the shrewd logic of those rhetoricians who give to the figure of *allegoria* names like *dissimulatio* or "false semblaunt," or classify it as a form of the tropes *ironia* and *illusio*.[37] For allegorical writing—whether in exe-

36. In addition to those studies mentioned in the text, my discussion of allegory and typology is indebted to Edwin Honig's *Dark Conceit: The Making of Allegory*, 57–62, and passim, particularly for ideas on the ways that allegorical texts can reinvent the authority and referentiality of their "sources," and both consume and exceed inherited symbolic patterns.

37. Quintilian (*Institutio oratoria* VIII.vi.54) links allegory to irony and *illusio*. See also Fletcher, *Allegory*, 229–33 and 340–41, for more detailed comments, and 328–31 for a shrewd analysis of Puttenham's ironic account of allegory as "the figure of false semblaunt." A further sidelight on this situation can be provided by Auerbach's history of the word *figura*. Though traditionally used by Christian interpreters to refer to the

getical or literary contexts—works in the space of illusion, and often aggressive illusion at that. Allegory will create for itself the irony, the gap, the mystery in the prior text which it presumes to interpret; it will lie about that text in order to tell its truths. Like the ambivalent Golem, an allegorical reading both wounds and heals the sacred words, idolizes texts, and breaks that idolatry, or creates a wholly mythic separation between true and false readers. Indeed, one can say of allegory what Karl Kraus said of psychoanalysis, that it is itself the disease of which it purports to be the cure.

In this reading, by the way, we must shift the grounds on which we distinguish formal allegory from typology. Philo's discovery of an abstract, Platonic psychology hidden below the narratives of Scripture does seem to compromise the centrality of that text's historical presence, or project the sources of its highest meaning outside of time. Typology, on the other hand, seems firmly bound to history. As Auerbach reminds us, in typological interpretation the two poles of a figure (e.g., the Brazen Serpent and the crucified Christ) are separate, "but both, being real events or figures, are within time, within the stream of historical life" ("Figura," in *Scenes from the Drama*, 53). Still, we must also remember that the typological situation is likely to turn on a primarily textual locus or occupy a moment of present time haunted by atemporal, mythic claims. Moreover, the two poles of such a figural reading are not just set in analogical correspondence. Rather, the aggressive transpositions of typology involve a "radical actualization, a drastic evacuation of the past into the present, which 'strikes' indirectly at the priority" of the earlier text (Marks, "Pauline Typology and Revisionary Criticism," 79)—the later reading becoming a raiding of meaning, power, and authority. There is something both shadowy and violent in typology: "events are considered not in their unbroken relation to one another, but torn apart, individually, each in relation to something other that is promised and not yet present" ("Figura," 59). Insofar as typology does appropriate the reader's own historical moment as the dramatic middle point of the hermeneutic relation, it is mainly so as to achieve a subtler means of defense against the anxieties of being dislocated in time and tradition or alienated from earlier centers of divine influence. Typology is thus as dehistoricizing as it is historicizing. Its difference from allegory lies not so much in its greater historical truth as in its more powerful illusion

"true shadows" of New Testament events in the narratives of the Old, the word, thanks to its roots in pre-Christian rhetorical tradition, could also refer to rhetorical circumlocutions that might conceal, transform, or evade a truth (*Scenes from the Drama of European Literature*, 45–46).

of truth, not just in its greater legitimacy but in its greater power to legitimate.

As a pendant to my earlier analysis of Ephesians 6, we can see a crucial and beautifully schematic example of the allegorist's situation in Paul's account of the Letter-Spirit dichotomy in 2 Corinthians 3.[38] This text presents not so much a typology of Christ as a typology of Christian reading, a mythicized, theoretical defense of intertestamentary allegory—one whose power depends, moreover, on Paul's startling reorientation of the Hebrew Bible's imagery of idolatry and iconoclasm.

Paul declares the congregation at Corinth is "an epistle written in our hearts . . . the epistle of Christ ministered by us, written not with ink, but with the Spirit of the living God; not in tables of stone, but in fleshy tables of the heart" (3.2–3). He defines himself as a minister "of the new testament; not of the letter, but of the spirit: for the letter killeth, but the spirit giveth life" (3.6). At this point begins Paul's crucial revision or misremembrance:

> But if the ministration of death, written and engraven in stones, was glorious, so that the children of Israel could not stedfastly behold the face of Moses for the glory of his countenance; which glory was to be done away: How shall not the ministration of the spirit be rather glorious? For if the ministration of condemnation be glory, much more doth the ministration of righteousness exceed in glory. . . .
>
> Seeing then that we have such hope, we use great plainness of speech: and not as Moses, which put a vail over his face, that the children of Israel could not stedfastly look to the end of that which is abolished: But their minds were blinded: for until this day remaineth the same vail untaken away in the reading of the old testament; which vail is done away in Christ. But even unto this day, when Moses is read, the vail is upon their heart. Nevertheless when it shall turn to the Lord, the vail shall be taken away. Now the Lord is that Spirit: and where the Spirit of the Lord is, there is liberty. But we all, with open [RSV: "unveiled"] face beholding as in a glass the glory of the Lord, are changed into the same image from glory to glory even as by the Spirit of the Lord. (3.7–18)

The imagery of inscription, hearts, and stones in verses 2 and 3 interweaves figures from Jeremiah 31.33 and Ezekiel 11.19, both of which speak (though in more prospective terms) of a new internal covenant that will replace the old, a heart of flesh that will supplant a frigid heart

38. My analysis of 2 Corinthians 3 is much indebted to Marks's essay, "Pauline Typology and Revisionary Criticism."

of stone. Up to this point, despite the inventiveness of Paul's tropes, one is inclined to emphasize the relative continuity between Old and New Testaments, even in their prophetic tropes of newness. By further relating the image of stony writing to the graven tablets of the Law handed down on Mount Sinai, however, Paul prepares for a more radical transformation. The deep "trick" here is that he describes as a surface of idolatrous brightness that veil which in Exodus 34.29–35 had served mainly to shield the Israelites from the glory of God shining in Moses' face. That is, Paul revises the scene by identifying the blinding light of divine revelation with the veil that originally just mediated it. But having done this, he goes further, and by a marvelous metonymy of face and author for text—in his phrase "when Moses is read"—Paul refigures that brightness into something that serves mainly to cover a revelation that has totally faded away, or (by a further metonymic displacement) to cover the hearts of those who read or trust in that revelation. Though he admits the early glory of "the ministration of death"—Paul's figure for the Torah as "law" or "legal code"—he suggests that the veil now conceals an absence rather than mitigates a presence.

Auerbach allows that Paul's writing "eminently combined practical politics with creative poetic faith" ("Figura," 51). Nietzsche, more darkly, thought the saint "one of the most ambitious and importunate souls [with] . . . a mind as superstitious as it was cunning" (*Daybreak*, aphorism 68—"superstition" not always being easy to distinguish from "poetic faith"). The above text illuminates such remarks, for in it Paul's retrospective reduction of Mosaic revelation to a glorious idolatry serves largely to support the dramatic, apologetic image of Christ and Paul himself as iconoclastically stripping away the veil from the earlier text. The imagery of veiling and unveiling is thus itself a fictive veil, though an enabling one, that the New Testament author draws over his subtle mis-taking of the Hebrew text. What makes that imagery all the more powerful is its extreme mobility; for if the veil image is originally employed in a distorted allusion to discredit Moses, Paul can elsewhere (with a kind of dream logic) allow the veil to reassume some of its salvific power as a textual medium, displacing the veiled splendor of the Mosaic covenant with the veiled "light of the glorious gospel of Christ" (2 Cor. 4.4; cf. Marks, "Pauline Typology," 85). At the close of the passage quoted above, he can even conjure up the image of the unveiled worshiper beholding "as in a glass the glory of the Lord, and changed into that same image from glory to glory"—the mediating mirror replacing the veil in a redemptive version of that assimilation of worshiper and image which characterizes idolatry.[39] To say that Paul somehow fulfills the hidden sense of the earlier text is at best an idealization. His manipulation of the veil image in order to convert a moment of theophany into the institution of idolatry suggests instead that his message emerges out of a radical will to discontinuity—something that might justify, for Paul at least, the infamous Marcionite version of Christ's words in Matthew 5.17: "I have not come to fulfill the law but to abolish it."[40]

The figure of the blinding veil, deployed secretly or openly within the narratives of vision, seems often to have haunted Spenser as an emblem of what was most problematic in his own allegorical enterprise, as I will suggest below. In Paul, too, it is the burden of interpretation itself which seems to create the ambiguous boundary between veiling and revelation, idolatry and iconoclasm, lie and truth. I am not unaware that 2 Corinthians 3 was used by later authors to justify a more harmonious view of the relation between the Hebrew Bible and the New Testament, and yet it seems to me that even the main line of Christian interpretation can hardly evade the ironies and discontinuities that are at work in Paul's use of typology. These problems may be concealed by pious fictions like the notion of typological "fulfillment," but they tend to emerge again as an aspect of other ideologies or anxieties generated by the need to devise a stable theory of scriptural reading. We can see this occurring even in the more orthodox and conceptually generalized hermeneutics of Augustine.

I do not want to approach Augustine's theory of language proper, although there is much in it that is relevant to my general arguments, especially its peculiar mixture of skepticism and idealism: on the one hand, the sense of a linguistic dimension divided from but desiring direct knowledge, a fallen speech that is coextensive with the world of sin, labor, error, time, and loss; on the other hand, a faith not in some superlinguistic revelation but in an internal, paradoxically wordless speech, a potent and articulate silence, or else in the sublimated myth of a Word that might serve as the hidden and revealed mediator of all authentic discourse.[41] More relevant for my developing scheme are certain questions that emerge in Augustine's pragmatic account of allegorical reading in his *On Christian Doctrine*, especially as allegory

39. On the mimetic tradition of spiritual reformation and the complex theology concerning the soul's relation to the image of God, see Ladner, *The Idea of Reform: Its Impact on Christian Thought and Action in the Age of the Fathers,* 83–106 and 185–203.

40. Cf. Pelikan, *Emergence of the Catholic Tradition,* 76.

41. On Augustine's theory of language and its relation to his theology of the Word, see Burke, *Rhetoric of Religion: Studies in Logology,* 43–171, and Markus, "St. Augustine on Signs." Also Brown, *Augustine of Hippo,* 259–69.

there becomes a discipline for healing the split imposed on human consciousness by time, sin, and speech.

Augustine's book splits the act of reading along the axis of love. True reading uses words to minister to the ends of spiritual truth and Grace, especially the teaching of *caritas*—the rule localized in that text which tells man to love his neighbor but which is also the ontological essence of divinity. Such a use of signs is indeed itself a manifestation of *caritas* (a god-term that functions in this work somewhat as "Christ" does in the theological writings). Augustine contrasts it to the reading ensnared in idolatrous *cupiditas*, which enjoys instead of uses words that should by rights point to higher things more worthy of love. *Caritas* should properly overcome this "carnal servitude to signs" by forcing upon us a sense that words do not mean what they seem to mean; the true reader thus does not rest on the blind or gorgeous surface of a text but breaks through the verbal "husk" to get at the spiritual food inside. He is likewise able to expose the empty husk, that which "shakes sounding pebbles inside its sweet shell, but . . . is not food for men but for swine" (III.7).[42] The spiritual stresses of reading arise from the paradox that although the inescapable uncertainty of textual signs is, like the temptation of *cupiditas*, bound up with the effects of the fall, it is the adept of *caritas* who can embrace the otherness of words and measure the fatal distance between the sign and its referent. Scripture itself seems furthermore to compound the given problems of language; it forces the allegorical move upon the reader by the layered incommensurabilities, scandals, and snares of its narratives, which both motivate and humble the reader who might have thought to master the text's complexities at a single sitting.[43]

The sense of sacred difficulty, of the need to abide the labor of interpretation in a world of "flawed words and stubborn sounds", is the profoundest test for the Augustinian reader. Indeed, as Fletcher remarks, "the mixture of pain and pleasure, an intellectual tension accompanying the hard work of exegetical labor, is nothing less than the cognitive aspect of the ambivalence which inheres in the contemplation of any sacred object. Whatever is *sacer* must cause the shiver of mingled delight and awe that constitutes our sense of 'difficulty'" (*Allegory*, 236). This cognitive ambivalence, however, generates in Augustine a continual concern about possible idolatry in the work of exegesis. Such a concern would no doubt arise in the reading of any text,

42. All of my quotations from *On Christian Doctrine* are taken from the translation by D. W. Robertson, Jr.

43. See *On Christian Doctrine* II.6.

but the most problematic field for the trial of true and false reading is found in the temporal and metaphysical space that separates the Old and the New Testaments. Most crucial here is the belief that the later text renders idolatrous any simple adherence to the historical narratives or to the formal, ceremonial prescriptions of the earlier text, while even the moral truths it embodies cannot be understood fully until regrounded in the gospel of the Incarnate God. Augustine and later patristic writers could fiercely debate the exact scope of the Old Testament's prefiguration of the New, but for the moment we need only note that Augustine's text considers allegorical interpretation to be more than an external method applied to Scripture. Rather, it is both an imperative and a tool of revelation itself. Christian "freedom" seems to depend upon the reader's capacity to allegorize. Hence an idolatrous reading, in which one yields to an absorbing nostalgia for the finality of earlier revelation, is a threat to the degree that it blocks the divine persuasions of the later Christian text and keeps the reader from recognizing how much the new readings of Hebrew Scripture must surpass that Scripture.[44]

Augustine's polemical reduction of the merely historical reader to an idolatrous literalist is balanced by his attack on those readers who do interpret, but only according to the "wandering error" of their own proud minds. *Cupiditas*, it turns out, is also able to coopt the allegorical strategy of opening up a textual surface and "using" it to refer to something beyond itself.[45] Only that something turns out to be "imaginations" unauthorized by God or his church. What is most striking about Augustine's attempts in Book II to define the danger of false allegory is that these follow from a long discussion of pagan idol-

44. We can illustrate the fear of such readerly idolatry if we recall John Freccero's argument that, for an Augustinian poet like Dante, the danger of merely literal reading and of a nostalgia for earlier, more secure centers of meaning could be represented by an encounter with Medusa, a mythic figure for the idolatrous power in words that turns the reader to stone, a monster whose gaze is really the reflection back from a text's unbroken surface of the stoniness that the reader had imposed on it. The spatial and hermeneutic turning away from the Medusa is thus what restores the erring pilgrim to a proper sense of ongoing revelation and to the promise of some future fulfillment beyond the realm of words. Hence Freccero, whose essay, "Medusa: The Letter and the Spirit," I have been summarizing here, identifies the threatening face of Medusa in *Inferno* (IX.52–63) with the veiled Moses of 2 Corinthians 3.

45. Indeed, false use seems to beget a pernicious uselessness that is worse than mere enjoyment: "Just as it is a servile infirmity to follow the letter and to take signs for the things that they signify, in the same way it is an evil of wandering error to interpret signs in a useless way. However, he who does not know what a sign means, but does know that it is a sign, is not in servitude. Thus it is better to be burdened by unknown but useful signs than to interpret signs in a useless way so that one is led from the yoke of servitude only to thrust his neck into the snares of error" (*On Christian Doctrine* III.9).

atry, where he attacks the worship of statues, the use of talismans, the indulgence in predictive prophecy—indeed, any attempt to replace the tropes of revelation by the "thousands of imagined fables and falsehoods by whose lies men are delighted, which are human institutions" (*On Christian Doctrine* II.25). For all of these, including allegory, may involve an attraction to "imaginary signs which lead to the cult of idols" (II.23), and so form the basis of man's unconscious alliance with demons. Allegory, that is, becomes more than a home of false significations; it is a haunted speech, a source of demonic infection, a tool of enchanting heretics. Most remarkable, however, is that for Augustine it seems to be the very conventionality and contingency of these signs and institutions which attract the demons and help to ensnare readers in their own curiosity and self-serving desires for spiritual authority.[46] Augustine's mythology of demons may thus allow us to define more precisely his anxiety about allegory. For although that mythology is perhaps underlain by more obscure superstitions and cultural traditions, in *On Christian Doctrine* it serves primarily as a way to both express and rationalize Augustine's feeling for the uncanny, contagious power of human words, images, and interpretations to possess the imagination. The demons of allegory promise freedom but return entrapment; if they break the fetishes of literalism, they may yet restore a more esoteric idolatry.

Such a crossing of empty sign with potent (even iconoclastic) demon is, again, a basic element in the ambivalent grammar of idolatry. Emerging as it does at the level of a concern with allegorical discourse, Augustine's account of demonic incursion may help us better understand Spenser's fear of those "gealous opinions and misconstructions" that seem to attend the necessarily duplicitous conceits of allegorical writing. What I have been saying about the double valence of idolatrous reading should also help define the urgency of Augustine's own guidelines about the proper means of interpretation—his stress on the historical authenticity of Old Testament narrative (however emptied of theological significance);[47] on the importance of look-

46. "All such omens are valid only in so far as through previously established imaginings, as if these were a common language, they are agreed upon with demons. Moreover, they all imply a pestiferous curiosity, an excruciating solicitude, and a mortal slavery. They were not noticed because of any innate validity, but they were made to have a validity through being noticed and pointed out. And thus they seem different to different people in accordance with their thoughts and presumptions. Those spirits who wish to deceive procure for each one those effects as they discern them by means of which he may be ensnared by his own suspicions and customary habits of thought" (*On Christian Doctrine* II.24).

47. Cf. James Samuel Preus, *From Shadow to Promise: Old Testament Interpretation from Augustine to the Young Luther,* 15–23.

ing at both the grammar and rhetorical context of the passage to be interpreted; on the relative perspicuousness of many passages in Scripture which can serve as an internal check on the reading of others, and so on. Such rules are, in a sense, propaedeutics against the invasion of the demonic reader; however philologically acute, they are aspects of a severely pragmatic but still magical rhetoric.

Augustine writes that "Scripture teaches nothing but charity, nor condemns anything except cupidity, and in this way shapes the minds of men" (*On Christian Doctrine* III.10). We should not take this to mean that Augustine uses allegory simply in the service of crass, psychological persuasion. No one, except perhaps Plato, is a finer witness than Augustine to the aesthesis or *eros* of figurative language; even in the more teacherly *On Christian Doctrine* this quality comes through in his account of the peculiar intellectual delight that attends the discovery of truths about the good work of ministers, the elimination of heresy, and the power of baptism hidden in the far-fetched similitudes of the Song of Songs (II.6). One is even tempted to say that Augustine's book turns interpretation into divination—negatively, to the degree that false readings can attract demons, but more benignly insofar as allegory lets one negotiate rhetorical and metaphysical difficulties so as to uncover Christ or God in the gaps of the text. Hermeneutic *caritas*, like the work of Plato's mediating daemons, is the agency that bridges human and divine. Still, what Augustine most often opposes to an idolatrous enjoyment of a text is not "love" but "use"—use in confirming not only the inner experience but also the doctrinal authority of *caritas*, use in driving a clear wedge between true and false readings. Indeed, for all his devoted attention to grammar, context, figurative texture, and literal history, Augustine seems willing to countenance quite violent misconstructions of the text so long as they serve his "edifying" purpose. This is because *caritas* is not just a trope or idea of love but also a synecdoche for the supernatural authority of Grace embodied in the sacramental and pedagogical institutions of the church as a whole; it is not simply the rarified, ever receding endpoint of a Platonizing hermeneutics, but an a priori hedge against interpretive freedom. The incarnation of *caritas* in the ecclesiastical Body of Christ makes of it a pragmatic tool as much as a sublime ideal. *Caritas* is a place where love and repression marry—as in Augustine's reading of the fertile sheep of Canticles 4.2, which figuratively give birth to the precepts of love, but which are also "pleasant" similitudes for the teeth of the church (militant saints) who cut off the errors of heretics and chew and incorporate their hard souls (*On Christian Doctrine* II.6). I have argued that allegory renders a text simultaneously empty and full, blind and transparent, and that, giving the powerful illusion that it is unveiling a text's secrets, allegory is able to exalt the reader's imposed interpretations to the level of revelation or *realia.* Augustine's appeal to the measure and myth of *caritas*, then, however divisive it may seem, can be read as the exegete's defense against the abyss of incommensurable, seductive, and catastrophic meanings opened up in a sacred text by the iconoclastic idolatry of allegory.

The Bishop of Hippo's commitment to doctrinal persuasion vitiates neither his fierce honesty about the limits and blandishments of human language in *On Christian Doctrine*, nor his clear awareness that the work of allegory must always locate itself within often insoluble conflicts of different texts and authorities. Augustine at least makes plain how difficult it is to distinguish allegory as a mode of unveiling from allegory as a mode of mystification, usurpation, and idolatry. To invoke a useful distinction of Ricoeur's, Augustine teaches us that we cannot always separate hermeneutics as an exercise in suspicion from hermeneutics as a recollection of meaning.[48] It is this pragmatic doubt that makes Augustine in turn so useful for my own de-idealizing approach to Spenser. As I will argue, the poet is disillusioned enough about the work of allegory to see how the revelatory and the idolatrous poles may infect one another, but equally aware that he is not quite in a position to offer any other myth or god-term (not even one so unstable as *caritas*) that might dissolve these dilemmas. Spenser plays the maddening game of revealing the liabilities and violences of allegory even while trying to reauthenticate it as a viable road to vision.

Augustine's somewhat embattled stance on allegory emerges out of his struggles with both pagan religion and heretical Christianity; it formalizes a number of responses to the problems of reading which will later fork into Catholic and Protestant alternatives. His work thus provides us with a background against which we can begin to measure the chaotic shape of those sixteenth-century controversies about allegory and representation which directly affected Spenser.

In speaking of the development of typology, we must remind ourselves that Christian tradition went far beyond Paul and the Gospels in turning the life of Christ into the fulfillment of Hebrew prophecy. Christ's first coming anticipated further revelation, especially an apocalyptic consummation that occupied a mythic and often highly

48. Ricoeur discusses this distinction at length in *Freud and Philosophy: An Essay on Interpretation*, 28–36.

elusive space and time. More important, what filled up the space between second and first comings was the continuing presence of God's Grace embodied in the universal church, the Body of Christ—like *caritas*, a trope that could ambiguously bracket elements of spiritual, magical, and political power. What I have called the legitimating function of typology became essential for a church fundamentally committed to the divination of its own history, doctrine, and ceremony, to what Ernst Cassirer rightly called a "theodicy of ecclesiastical order" (*Individual and Cosmos*, 10). Whatever its conceptual subtlety, a cosmology like that of Augustine—which saw history as an ongoing sentence, unfolding and continually recapitulating an eternally fixed, divine center of meaning—provided an authorizing, rationalizing myth for the church's systematic efforts to read itself over and above the New Testament as the real antitype of Scripture, both the mediator and end of all interpretation. Any alternative ideas of spiritual revelation, communion, or presence, any millennial or chiliastic claims that superseded the church's authority, thus tended to be read as heresy or idolatry. For the church was in a sense already incarnation and apocalypse, at least insofar as it claimed to provide the sole access to both. Hence the logic behind Spenser's imagery of parodic inspiration, incarnation, and catastrophic revelation in his depiction of the Catholic giant Orgoglio (*FQ* I.vii.9, 13, 18).

The poet's ironic, mythic simplification points to a central truth. No doubt church policy on the issue of exegesis was far from uniform; indeed, the relative adequacy of allegorical and typological reading was debated in the Middle Ages with more energy than is often realized.[49] Conservative thinkers often valorized typology as a check on the indulgences of speculative allegoresis, which (however much guided by reason) seemed liable to end in fantasy, fetishism, heresy, even the incursion of demons. But because it was the official word of the church rather than any internal difference between the two modes that really counted as the final test of interpretive correctness, allegory and typology might consort rather happily together. We should remember that despite contemporary insistence on the predominantly "historical" focus of typology, its materials—the schematized, theologically emptied narratives of the Hebrew Bible, the sacramental engines of the church, the doctrinal mysteries of final judgment, and so on—were as much inventions subject to human need as the most fantastic and abstracted conceptual allegory. It was the power and cost of

49. The complex medieval conflicts between different styles of typological and allegorical interpretation are surveyed in Preus, *From Shadow to Promise*, 9–149.

this "inventedness" which the Reformation and Renaissance most clearly discovered and which Spenser represents by his inflated fictive giant. The self-consciousness of authors in the period about the element of human distortion in the work of both kinds of allegory ended up disturbing formerly secure centers of interpretation and authority.

Allegory had, among other things, allowed the medieval church to accommodate a great variety of pre-Christian fables within its own synthetic system of signs. Such a task of accommodation was no doubt undertaken as a kind of sacred theft, an act of what Robert Graves termed "iconotropy"; the church translated and refigured the idols of the pagan gods instead of breaking them, imitating the Children of Israel who carried the gold and silver statues of the Egyptians into the wilderness with them (to use Augustine's apologetic emblem from *On Christian Doctrine*).[50] The result, however, as Reformers observed, was not only a Christianizing of the pagan but a paganizing of the Christian, or at least a secret muddling of differences between the two. Similarly, the combination of typology and allegory within a rationalized, fourfold hierarchy of polysemous meanings had the effect of ironically leveling or equating sacred narratives with the later abstractions and invented mythologies imposed on them. Hence a reformer like William Tyndale could complain that the readings of Catholics at once bled to death the literal history of revealed Scripture and ministered to an excessive faith in the church's own belated doctrines, saints' lives, and eschatological fables (such as the politically profitable myths of Purgatory and Hell): "And the lives, stories, and gests of men, which are contained in the bible, they read as things no more pertaining unto them than a tale of Robin Hood, and as things they wot not whereto they serve, *save to feign false descant and juggling allegories, to stablish their kingdom withal.* And one of the chiefest and fleshliest studies they have is to magnify the saints above measure and above the truth; *and with their poetry to make them greater than ever God made them*" (*The Work of Tyndale,* 139; emphasis mine). Tyndale even suggests that in so granting the power of salvation and damnation

50. Actually, Augustine uses the image of the Israelites stealing Egyptian ornaments to suggest how Christians should use pagan literary and philosophical works (*On Christian Doctrine* II.40), but it fits the general appropriation of pagan religious symbols and liturgical customs as well. Of course, it is too simple to say (as Hume or Gibbon might have) that the Roman church only perpetuated the paganism that it suppressed, or that its various saints simply substituted for the innumerable local and institutional gods which populated late Roman religion. For a study of the ways in which early Christianity transformed and revised the shapes of pagan worship, see Peter Brown, *The Cult of the Saints: Its Rise and Function in Latin Christianity,* 1–23, and passim.

to their fables the Papists go far beyond the ambitions of classical mythmakers. In line with such an argument, Protestant polemicists could identify the entire Catholic tradition, if not with pagan demonology and magic, then at least with their degraded survivals in the folklore of elves, fairies, and witches.[51] The Kingdom of God thus became the Kingdom of Darkness; the Age of Faith stood revealed as the Age of Illusion.

The overcoming of this illusion, the collapse of this faith, involves a welter of competing solutions, some of which I have touched on earlier in this chapter. We must be careful not to overestimate the proto-Enlightenment of the Reformation; it not only left intact many of the older medieval structures but fed certain renewed illusions that could be as catastrophic as what they replaced. It is often said, for instance, that sixteenth-century Protestants and Humanists helped restore a truer, more literal understanding of the biblical text, especially that of the Old Testament. But if we forget how much the philological revolution was prepared for by the work of medieval scholars, then we should at least recognize that the Protestant return to the literal text (and to the primitive church) was as much a historically conditioned act of imaginative reduction as a rediscovery of history. Luther's and Tyndale's interest in the Hebrew Bible remained conditioned by Paul's and Augustine's ideologically loaded distinction between Law and Grace. The important point is that such reformers' powerful, retrospective identification of the Christian faithful with the situation of the Israelites *sub lege*—still awaiting the promised help of God and bare of all efficacious means of gaining Grace for themselves—helped undermine the wonted sufficiency of the approved Catholic interpretations of Scripture. Similarly, Luther's more severely magical version of the Eucharist impugned the idolatrous, spellbinding quality of the Mass. His iconoclastic readings of Scripture depended on a historical mastery of text and tradition as well as a late medieval Nominalist skepticism; but he combined with these an antithetical violence toward Catholic tradition which no merely intellectual position can account for.[52] It may even be that his ascetic pursuit of the "letter," as opposed to the alleged "spirit" of doctrinal allegory, nourished itself on

51. The most comprehensive instance of this identification occurs in the last chapter of Part IV of Hobbes's *Leviathan*, "Of the Kingdom of Darkness," which draws the parallel between the Roman church (including its saints, sacraments, legal customs, interpretive traditions, and so on) and the Kingdom of Fairy in elaborate and comic detail.

52. On Luther's exegetical reforms, see Preus, *From Shadow to Promise*, 200–265, and Pelikan, *Luther the Expositor*, 48–137. I am also much indebted to Gerhard Ebeling's *Luther* for my general approach to the reformer. For the influence of Nominalist theology on Luther's thought, see Ozment, *The Age of Reform, 1250–1550*, 231–39.

the irony that this effort was exactly what some Scholastic interpreters would have considered the epitome of readerly idolatry. In any case, we must see Luther's reformation of attitudes toward Scripture within a dialectic of loss and gain. His wrenching of older historical and hermeneutic categories (bolstered by his vernacular translation) had the effect of making the sacred text at once more familiar, more of a stable ground of meaning, and at the same time more fully isolate or other—that is, less accessible to the shifting web of mediations which had accommodated the Bible to the wisdom, pathos, and "poetry" of the medieval church.[53]

This massive, self-imposed loss of mediation undoubtedly made possible a subtler appreciation of the literary texture of Scripture; it also fed the more urgent interest in applying scriptural texts and types to the personal situation of the interpreter rather than to doctrinal or ceremonial loci. If many exegetes continued to depend on Augustine or Aquinas, at least these writers ceased to be treated as quasi-divine authorities whose differing opinions always had to be laboriously reconciled. But the Reformation's extreme and often self-blinding myth of textual authority, and the very volatile notions of inner spiritual guidance and interpretive truth that were necessarily grafted onto it, raised as many problems as they solved. The Bible could be converted, as it was by some Puritans, into the singular grid through which every aspect of life had to be filtered, the measure by which all moral, legal, or ritual distinctions had to be raised or collapsed. The authority granted to the "spirit," when freed from its dogmatic moorings, could lead men to find in private thoughts revelations that could compete with or even supersede those of Scripture itself. Luther and Calvin might in turn reemphasize the unique presence and power of the Word revealed in Scripture, for both fiercely rejected any interpretation of 2 Corinthians 3 which converted Paul's Letter-Spirit dichotomy into a warrant for personal or institutional allegoresis, and they classed sectarian enthusiasts together with allegorizing Papists as opposite but equal manifestations of the same spiritual disease.[54] And on another level, Philipp Melancthon or Richard Hooker could emphasize the many "indifferent" matters of law, doctrine, and ceremony which Scripture had left open to the arbitration of human reason or historical necessity. Despite all such lim-

53. On the imaginative impact of the vernacular Bible in England, viewed especially through the writings of William Tyndale, see Stephen Greenblatt's chapter, "The Word of God in an Age of Mechanical Reproduction," in *Renaissance Self-Fashioning* 74–114.

54. Cf. Ebeling, *Luther*, 102–9.

iting and corrective measures, however, it is not surprising that the large dislocations of spiritual authority in the sixteenth century could issue in a fearful sense of almost universal idolatry such as haunts the following passage from Calvin:

> When . . . we are in a manner forced to the contemplation of God . . . we immediately fly off to carnal dreams and depraved fictions, and so by our vanity corrupt heavenly truth. This far, indeed, we differ from each other, in that every one appropriates to himself some peculiar error; but we are all alike in this, that we substitute monstrous fictions for the one living and true God. . . . Hence that immense flood of error with which the whole world is overflowed. Every individual mind being a kind of labyrinth, it is not wonderful, not only that each nation has adopted a variety of fictions, but that almost every man has had his own god. To the darkness of ignorance there have been added presumption and wantonness, and hence there is scarcely an individual to be found without some idol or phantom as a substitute for Deity. Like water gushing forth from a large and copious spring, immense crowds of gods have issued from the human mind, every man giving himself full license, and devising some peculiar form of divinity, to meet his own views. It is unnecessary here to attempt a catalogue of the superstitions with which the world was overspread. The thing were endless. (*Institutes* I.v.11–12)

Calvin's attack on man's "carnal dreams" and "depraved fictions" of deity is much indebted to an Augustinian sense of the infinite inflections of fallen love—evasive, perverse, blinding, usurping *cupiditas*. But the anxiety and claustrophobia of Calvin's rhetoric, the not un-Spenserian imagery of the flood and the labyrinth, emerge from an undercurrent of lost faith in the outward vehicles of revelation and a decided ambivalence about being forced back onto his own subjective authority. I assume that we may find Calvin's skepticism more persuasive, perhaps more irreducible, than the rationalistic theology he devised to counter it, but more important for the moment is the human breadth of his indictment. The Protestant is included as much as the Catholic, the religious man as much as the secular, the learned as well as the vulgar; the individual interpretation is no better than the institutional. Scarcely has the mind begun to form words or ideas about divinity, or find a vessel for its desires, than it falls into idolatry.

Yet the above passage, dark as it is, may provide a foil for certain aspects of Renaissance thought which could accommodate rather than evade Calvin's chaotic labyrinth and even justify the poetic labor of cataloguing the forms of idolatry. One might begin here by pointing to Nicholas of Cusa's arguments about the peculiar autonomy, the liberating incommensurability even of images that are said (by inadequate metaphor) to mirror God, his conviction that "no image will so faithfully or precisely reproduce the exemplar as to rule out the possibility of an infinity of more faithful and precise images" (*Of Learned Ignorance* I.11). Doubtless this statement may indicate something uncertain about the place of the absolute exemplar itself (even though it does not contradict Cusanus's assertion that earthly forms can be read as "finite infinitudes," "created gods" [II.2]). Given a cosmology that abandons hierarchy, homogeneity, and eternal self-identity, it at least suggests a less than objective measure for what is "faithful" and "precise." But Cusanus's words also make the endless flood of human images a basis for hope rather than fear. For this philosopher, as for many others of his time, the human ability to live within continuing uncertainty and otherness becomes a major testimony to our divine uniqueness in creation; indeed, even the fact that a person's gods must always reflect the individual limits of his or her imaginative eye could become a point of specific value in the quest for the proper forms of knowledge and worship.[55] Cassirer rightly took Cusanus's stance as the key to his reading of the Renaissance, for this sense of a great rift between human images and their divine exemplars—as well as a greater reticence about the inherited means of bridging that rift—helps to motivate the period's rich proliferation of icons and images in isolation from the pressures of religious orthodoxy. Such a situation does not mean that all religion is subjective or that the only true place for images is within the secular realm. But it does suggest a situation in which the boundaries between sacred and secular, or between true and false religion, become somewhat harder to trace. Images become important insofar as they are deployed within a fresher, if sometimes more anxious space of conscious imagination and illusion, one that may cut itself off from certain ties to established truth, tradition, and authority.

The contrast may be clearer if we turn from strictly religious and exegetical categories to literary ones. Dante was perhaps the last poet

55. Cassirer cites a passage from Chapter 6 of Cusanus's *De visione dei*, in which the inescapable and idolatrous self-reflexivity of human images of God becomes one key to understanding the true wonder of God's face: "The spiritual eye, in its limitedness, sees you, the goal and object of the mind's observation, according to the nature of its own limitation. Man is capable only of human judgment. . . . If the lion attributed a face to you, he would attribute that of a lion, the ox that of an ox, and the eagle that of an eagle [Cusanus is making a strange joke about the three apocalyptic creatures which surround the throne of God]. Ah, God, how wonderful is your face: the youth, if he would conceive of it, must imagine it as young, the man as male, the old man as old. In all faces the face of faces appears, veiled, as in an enigma" (*Individual and Cosmos*, 32–33).

who could appropriate all of human history and all known literature within a rigidly hierarchical eschatological poem—and even his work heralds the dilemmas of the later period by investing so much in the substance of his visionary world itself and in a final myth of order which seems to overgo both the authority of the church and the types of Christian history as they are formalized in the Book of Revelation. The work of the Renaissance leaves much of the Dantesque architectonics in ruin. The classical imitations and archeological researches of the Humanists; the huge imaginative investments of a Ficino, Pico, or Bruno in alternative sacred traditions like Kabbalah or Gnostic Hermeticism; Shakespeare's poetic and dramatic elaboration of folkloric "superstitions" about ghosts, witches, and fairies—all of these try to discover a history, a cosmos, and a magic over which medieval tradition had no hold, even at the cost of an endless esotericism, or an uneasy sense of loss, isolation, fragmentation.

The very eclectic chaos of Renaissance syncretism—in which emblems and images "begin to gravitate about their own madness," their own individual intensities of suggestion—tells us something about the breaking up of inherited systems of analogy.[56] If some writers attempt to valorize the independent power and decorum of non-Christian literature, whether as secular poetry or sacred wisdom, this does not mean that Christian revelation fails. Rather, it may only reflect a growing sense of the historical inviolability of the major vehicle of that revelation, the Bible, and an awareness of the dangers involved in the illusion that all other literatures and symbols find their ground in it. Spenser, for example, maintains a continual, dialectical play between alternative revelations, mythologies, fictions, and philosophies in his poem. Although he sometimes explores extreme types of imagistic relation or subversively interweaves what seem to be primitive and sophisticated modes of seeing, he never lapses into the blind identification of pagan and Christian such as Tyndale condemned in medieval discourse.

We might note at this point one last and finely ironic response to Calvin's words about human illusion, a response that appears variously in those Renaissance authors who make the inescapability of idolatry the very foundation of their writing (something that finds

56. Speaking of late medieval and early Renaissance forms of emblematic expression, Michel Foucault observes that "things themselves become so burdened with attributes, signs, allusions that they finally lose their own form. Meaning is no longer read in an immediate perception, the figure no longer speaks for itself; between the knowledge which animates it and the form into which it is transposed, a gap widens. It is free for the dream" (*Madness and Civilization,* 18–19).

echoes in Spenser himself). The chief theorist of such a stance is the sixteenth-century critic Jacopo Mazzoni who in his defense of the *Divine Comedy* argued that the poet, whether "fantastic" or "verisimilar," is involved primarily in the business of creating aesthetic "idols" rather than true *eikones* or icastic imitations.[57] Likewise, Petrarch, eschewing the theologically centered descriptions of his great precursor, composed highly wrought lyrics whose imagery evolved and dissolved itself in the pursuit of an "idol carved in living laurel"—the idol being both the erotic object, which constitutes and is constituted by the desiring fantasy, and the poem that seeks to embody the metamorphoses of object and fantasy.[58] With somewhat greater skepticism, if no less exuberance, Miguel de Cervantes constructed our founding revision of romance, in which the Knight of Faith appears as a madman whose heroic and erotic goals are the literalized and hyperbolical, if strangely impersonal, fictions of chivalric fable, a quester whose disillusionments serve only to feed further illusion. Despite what a critic like Sidney might tell us about a poet's never lying, writers such as Petrarch and Cervantes are still indebted to medieval categories that place their work in the realm of moral and epistemological error. Yet what must count as much for us in this investigation is the aesthetic and historical urgency of these authors' elaborated errors. Their fictions bear the burden of untruth; but standing as they do in the light of greater disillusionments with the absolute truth of the medieval synthesis, these writers may discover in such refined explorations of the idolatrous their only approach to something like transcendence, or at least a way of warding off the more dangerous illusions attendant upon Scholastic reason or theological allegory.

57. Mazzoni adapts his distinction between icastic and fantastic (or idolatrous) representations from Plato's *Sophist* 235–36. His position is strongly opposed by Tasso, who in his *Discourses on the Heroic Poem* argues that the writer of epics must create not idols but true, or icastic images, though such truth as these images had would be founded in a human, historical realm rather than in a supersensible world of ideas. I am of course simplifying a complex Renaissance debate on the nature and authority of artistic imitation surveyed most comprehensively by Baxter Hathaway in *The Age of Criticism: The Late Renaissance in Italy*, 118–25, 144–66, and passim. (Hathaway interestingly observes that "there was a strong strain of Pyrrhonism in Mazzoni which makes it difficult drawing a line between the finer ironic implications of his distinctions and the implications of their crass literalness" [125].)

58. On Petrarch's exploration of the trope of idolatry in his lyrics, see John Freccero, "The Fig Tree and the Laurel: Petrarch's Poetics," 37–40.

2

Mythmaking in Hibernia
(*A View of the Present State of Ireland*)

From this the poem springs: that we live in a place
That is not our own and, much more, not ourselves
And hard it is in spite of blazoned days.
Wallace Stevens

Mad Ireland hurt you into poetry.
W. H. Auden

I have described the situation of the allegorist, the iconoclast, and the idolater in terms of the metaphors, myths, ironies, and anxieties which complicate their work. A conceptual pattern and a terminological dialectic have, I hope, begun to emerge, as well as a kind of central narrative. The reader is no doubt impatient at this point to get on to Spenser's poetry and to see my system or story tested on the work of a writer who can be at once Dante and Cervantes, Calvin and Bruno. Just this movement, however, is what I must delay. It is not merely that we need more attention to the historical circumstances of the poet or to the cultural climate of his work. It is rather that I want to unsettle some ideas of poetry itself and interpose a few tentative observations about its powers between my earlier remarks and the commentary on *The Faerie Queen* that dominates Part Two. The following analysis of Spenser's prose dialogue *A View of the Present State of Ireland* is offered as a stumbling block, a heuristic delaying tactic that may indicate something about the relation of Spenser's poetic iconoclasm to the world at large, and about the ways in which poetry can become part of the unstable material of everyday life. The chapter is furthermore a *skandalon* insofar as it intrudes a more historically burdened text into the abstract spaces opened up in the previous chapter and yet makes over the message of an understandably obscure dialogue for my own allegorical purposes. Fundamentally, I want to suggest that between the lines of his fairly conservative treatise on Irish politics and antiquarian lore Spenser raises some rather radical questions about the nature of fable, imagination, ideology, and law which may change but also refresh our awareness of what is at stake in the poet's more strictly literary work.

That work belongs to a poet of exile. An English Protestant writing in war-ravaged Catholic Ireland, Spenser became the unofficial, unpatronized, and often disapproved of prophet of Elizabeth's *imperium* while helping to administer one of her government's most unstable and often ill-conceived colonial policies. The ironies of such a situation might help account for his apparent ambivalence toward the activity of poetic (as well as political) representation, his wariness of idealizations, the combination of alienation and devotion with which he renders his subjects, the willfulness and reticence of his tropes. The poet's own history of displacement might usefully gloss, if not quite explain, the fact that in writing of the Faerie Queen, his central figure of authority and value, he makes her the absent center of the epic that bears her name, a fragmented presence whose influence is yet diffused through many of the poem's uncertain, wandering heroines. Likewise, the strong but strangely mediated sense of place in his poetry might mirror the fact that despite a heroic effort to consecrate Ireland as his poetic "home," Spenser always remained a stranger there; he naturalized his epic in that alien landscape by calling it "the wilde fruit, which salvage soyl hath bred" (*Poetical Works*, 411). Even if it were only in Ireland that the middle-class Edmund Spenser could fashion himself into a landed English gentleman, his literary career remained tied to the imagined axis of the court of Elizabeth, so that the poet could only publish his account of his persona Colin Clout's saving return to an Irish home when Spenser in fact returned to London.

Perhaps we must say that Ireland was to Spenser both *heimlich* and *unheimlich*; in it he confronted something like his own unconscious, or at least a "salvage soyl" where nature, mind, and culture fought unresolvable battles. The stresses of that confrontation are the undersong of *A View*. They are also that without which *The Faerie Queene* as we know it could not have been written. One is tempted (for the sake of economy) to cut the epic free of the accidents of personal history, to say that Spenser like Shakespeare lived a life of allegory, on which his poems are the only adequate commentary. And indeed, I do not mean to use the *View* to support a genetic argument about the influence of Ireland on his poem. The psychology of representation is complex enough in Spenser's work, and to speculate about the nature of Spenser's personal reaction to Ireland might only provide reductive and redundant support for conclusions one can draw from the poetry alone. As Donald Cheney shows, for example, in his essay "Retrospective Pastoral: The Returns of Colin Clout," the humorous mask of an alienated, evasive singer, one who is both skeptical and self-indulgent, was already fitted onto the poet in *The Shepheardes Calendar* (1579), a work that predates his "exile." The generative place that is *not* the poet's own is after all as much within language, erotic consciousness, literary history, and time in general as within Ireland itself. The complex biographical fictions examined so well by Cheney may in the end be all we have available to help us measure questions of inwardness and intentionality in Spenser's poetry. Nevertheless, I want to offer a reading of some portions of the *View* as an introduction to the more abstruse modalities of Spenser's poem, particularly its treatment of landscape, myth, law, and religion. In part, this will help mediate the claims of historical and more circumscribed aesthetic approaches to the poem. More important, it will let us see the dialogue as a witness to the personal, existential urgency of Spenser's antimythological and demystifying turn of mind; such a reading is thus liable to complicate our understanding of the idealizing and visionary thrust of his mythopoeic writings. What follows will add support to the intuitions of older critics that Ireland was part of the ground of Spenser's "Faerie"—though only if we see that poetic realm as not just a world of philosophical ideals but the proving ground of the imagination's faith and fate, no utopia and yet a place of poetry.

Politics and Prophecy

Spenser's dialogue, when it is considered at all, is usually treated as a rather elegant piece of journalism, a firsthand account of the abuses in an English colony together with some comments on the possibility of reform. Nonetheless, the *View* is a quite shrewd piece of literary work. There is, admittedly, little real drama in the exchanges between the informant Irenius (whose name is from the Greek for "peaceable," somewhat darkly punning on Eire, Erin, Ireland) and his questioner Eudoxus ("well-taught"). But this formal fiction, set in England (at a reflective distance from its subject), becomes the frame for an intricate analysis of other fictions in both life and literature. For Spenser depicts Ireland not only as the home of rebellion, corruption, and chaos, which must be tamed by the forces of civilization, but also as a land in the grip of myth and illusion. W. B. Yeats complained that Spenser wrote of Ireland only as an official of the English state, and yet in a way he was just as prepared as the modern poet to recognize the subtle force of Irish imagination, mystery, and storytelling.[1] He was, however, more immediately struck by their dangers and costs. Spenser sees the Irish as a people enchanted by the false authority of custom, folklore, and superstition, by the false magic of ancestral names, tribal allegiances, even of their native language. And while Spenser never neglects a concrete analysis of particular actions and motives, he pays greatest attention to the larger structures of deception that sustain them, especially to the self-deluding and idolatrous attachments that can poison even the most sanctified forms of order. Indeed, this study of alienation and authority tends to present the English themselves as among the most effective agents of evil in Ireland, on account of the very rigidity with which they have instituted the machinery of colonial reform, making an idol of policy and refusing to accommodate their laws or statutes to the flux of time and human desire, or to the more chaotic laws of the Irish *genius loci*.

There runs through the dialogue a deep strain of skepticism about the place and power of such structures of order as myth, custom, and law, On the opening page, for instance, mythifying and demystifying approaches to the crisis in Irish affairs are brought into sharp conflict:

> IRENIUS: Marry, so there have been diverse and good plots devised and wise counsels cast already about reformation of that realm, but they say it is the fatal destiny of that land, that no purposes whatsoever are meant for her good will prosper or take good effect; which whether it proceed from the very genius of the soil, or influence of the stars, or that Almighty God hath not yet appointed the time of her reformation, or that He reserveth her in this unquiet state still, for some secret scourge which shall by her come unto England, it is hard to be known but yet much to be feared.

1. See Yeats, *Essays and Introductions,* 372: "Could he have gone there as a poet merely, he might have found among its poets more wonderful imaginations than even those islands of Phaedria and Acrasia . . . certainly all the kingdom of Faery, still unfaded, of which his own poetry was often but a troubled image." In fact, Spenser does praise the "sweet wit and good invention" of the local bards, deploring only the use of their talents to ornament the less praiseworthy deeds of renegade chiefs (*A View,* 72–75).

EUDOXUS: Surely I suppose this but a vain conceit of simple men, which judge things by their effects and not by their causes. For I would rather think the cause of this evil, which hangeth upon that country, to proceed rather of the unsoundness of the counsels and plots which you say have been oftimes laid for her reformation, or of faintness in following and effecting the same, than of any such fatal course or appointment of God as you misdeem, but it is the manner of men that when they are fallen into any absurdity, or their actions succeed not as they would, they are ready always to impute the blame thereof unto the heavens, so to excuse their own follies and imperfections. (*A View,* 1–2)

The language is prophetic, as Fletcher notes of the first speaker's words (*Prophetic Moment,* 213); perhaps more properly, owing to the emphasis on the secret design of Providence rather than on the open presence of the Word, it might be termed apocalyptic.[2] And yet even in so expansive and idealizing a rhetoric one may discern an implicit doubt, for it must be a quite uncertain prophet who strings together such a large number of explanatory keys to a historical situation, ascending from daemonic influences in the ground to astral intelligences and, finally, to the contradictory plans of God. It is telling that the verbal scheme that dominates the passage is what George Puttenham names "*aporia,* or the doubtfull" (*Arte of English Poesie,* 234); this is a figure that (following the lead of Alpers) I would even identify as one of Spenser's "master tropes."[3] As the poet uses it, here and elsewhere, the figure entails the multiplication within a discourse of such a variety of alternative perspectives as to call into question, or at least to delay, any divisive choice among those alternatives; in this particular passage, the figure creates a speech that continually suspends

2. See von Rad, *Old Testament Theology,* 2:301–15, and Martin Hengel, *Judaism and Hellenism,* 1:180–210, for basic discussions of apocalyptic and prophecy. While the two modes overlap and may completely merge in postbiblical writings, it is useful always to be aware of their strong differences. Classical prophecy stressed the radically disjunctive effect of God's Word and judgment in history, turning against all forms of predictive prophecy or divination based on any sort of deterministic scheme of temporal change. Apocalyptic writing arose from the grafting onto prophecy of a distinct tradition of wisdom literature and speculative cosmology. More crucially, the sophisticated literary resources of apocalyptic—its interest in secret revelations, its use of pseudepigraphic form to suggest "inspired authority," its retrospective misreadings of unfulfilled prophecy as literally predictive of present time, its elaborately dualistic visions of historical eons and cosmic catastrophe—bring it close to what earlier writers would have called "false prophecy," not to mention propaganda.

3. See Alpers, *The Poetry of "The Faerie Queene,"* 36–106, and passim. I do not think this critic ever uses the specific term *aporia* to characterize the steady piling up of independent images and verbal formulas which he sees as the poet's fundamental technique of description and narration, but this is what his study points to. Alpers's account of the poetic motives for such a technique, however, differs somewhat from my own.

itself between urgent concern about and admitted ignorance of the sources of the Irish crisis ("hard to be known but yet much to be feared," as Irenius says). The effect is that although the speaker moves toward ever higher forms of supernatural agency, the very number of proposed explanations guards him against privileging any one of them; thus he conveys the necessity of an appeal to providential control while avoiding too radical a determinism.

The second speaker provides a more explicit critique of the dehistoricizing impulse that lies behind the first speaker's words. In effect, Eudoxus declares Irenius's speech to be nothing less than a defensive and self-deluding instance of false prophecy. He does not, of course, deny the existence of a providential order, nor does he insist that man humbly give over his search for hidden wisdom. But to give history over to the workings of an inhuman fate, however warily, seems to him in effect only a way of excusing past follies and palliating human fears. Even more dangerously, such an appeal to the eschatological inhibits any future action that might successfully reform the situation that has raised those fears. To reason about events from effects instead of causes, as Irenius does, does not merely make for false explanations but obviates any explanation at all. Such a tactic closes off one's sense of the ever changing possibilities of the secular world and freezes events into isolated fatalities. It makes an end where one might find, or perhaps invent, a middle, a ground for choice of which Irenius's elaborately varied list is at best a travesty. Bound as he is within his defensive mystifications, Irenius alienates himself from both the stark choices of an authentically providential vision and the more pragmatic appeals that might be made to the awkward contingencies of history.

That Eudoxus's specific aim is to diffuse Irenius's evasive movement toward an eschatological perspective becomes even clearer in the passage just following the one quoted above. There he compares Irenius to the Englishmen whose fear of Ireland issues in the violent, visionary wish that the troublesome colony be destroyed by a deluge. This catastrophe suggests of course a regressive apocalypse, since the Bible makes it clear that no second flood will engulf the earth but, rather, that the Final Day will coincide with a total annihilation of the sea. More important, however, is Eudoxus's argument that such hopeless hopes can only be "the manner rather of desperate men far driven, to wish the utter ruin of that which they cannot redress, than of grave counsellors which ought to think nothing so hard but that through wisdom may be mastered and subdued, since the poet says that the wise man shall rule even over the stars, much more over the earth" (*A View*, 2). There is more than a faint echo here of the sublime claims made for human knowing in a work such as Pico's *Oration on the Dignity of Man*.[4] But insofar as Eudoxus's aim is largely to expose human illusions and undercut the desperate structures of wish and dream which skew revelation and block imaginative response, what might seem the hyperbole of a Humanist mage also takes on a biblical, iconoclastic coloring.

Such optimism as we hear in this passage will be qualified later on. For the moment I want mainly to suggest the ways in which Spenser's shifting rhetorical stances compose both a parallel to and a parable about the dynamics of political power and reform in the English colony. For throughout *A View*—even in places where the writing is less reflexive and the dialogic conflict less sharply drawn—Spenser tends to expose the stakes of moral or legal issues by framing them in terms of what might seem more strictly literary issues. That is to say, he relates political dilemmas to questions about what metaphor one chooses or what story one tells, as, for example, when he suggests that Irenius's way of telling too many possible stories in too diffident a manner may be as dangerous as telling one story that is wholly wrong. The literary and political concerns, then, continue to reflect upon each other throughout the work, especially in the context of Spenser's broader interest in the problems of representation, authority, and temporality. The above-quoted exchange may indeed stand as a representative anecdote for what seems to be the central anxiety of the dialogue: a sense of the risks inherent in man's pursuit of order and origins, and a fear of losing control of whatever work can be accomplished or knowledge won in the ever altering current of secular time by too ungoverned an appeal to the ideal, the atemporal, the providential.

Ireland, Ideology, and Law

Spenser's dialogue is full of digressions, interruptions, and secondary reflections—some of which have a strongly parabolic relevance to the argument—but it keeps hold of its various materials by means of several interlocking triads. For example, Irenius proposes to examine in sequence the sources of the Irish crisis, its present scope, and finally (in the closely argued conclusion), a project for its future reformation. Or, with a shrewd eye for the temporal dimension, he will

4. More precisely, Spenser alludes to the Latin adage *vir sapiens dominabitur astris*, attributed to Virgil (Spenser's "the poet") during much of the Middle Ages and Renaissance but apparently originating with the astrologer Ptolemy. See Burckhardt, *The Civilization of the Renaissance in Italy*, 2:486, for further references.

describe three distinct sorts of abuse: "Some . . . are of very great antiquity and long continuance; others more late and of less endurance; others daily growing and increasing continually as the evil occasions are every day offered" (*A View*, 2)—while within each category he examines successively the abuses in law, in custom, and in religion.

I want to begin with the critique of law, perhaps the most pungent, if not the most original, portion of the dialogue; one wonders, indeed, if its ominous suggestions were not the sole reason why the dialogue was never published in Spenser's lifetime, no matter how seriously the court advisors may have read it.[5] The greatest scandal it exposes is that English law in Ireland has been strangely transformed into an agent of corruption. For "the laws were at first intended for the reformation of abuses and peaceable continuance of the subjects, but have since been either disannuled or quite prevaricated through change and alteration of times; yet are they good still in themselves, but to that Commonwealth which is ruled by them they work not that good which they should, and sometimes also perhaps that evil which they would not" (3). Here again the problems of temporality coincide with those of representation, for what emerges from this meditation on the seemingly fatal paradoxes of mutability is the admonition that "laws ought to be fashioned unto the manners and condition of the people to whom they are meant, and not to be imposed upon them according to the simple rule of right, for then as I said instead of good they may work ill, and pervert justice to extreme injustice" (11). Spenser's point seems to be that the work of law must defend itself against the "prevarications" of time (the lies of things that stay the same as well as of things that change). For simple rule of right, even while it may serve as a powerful instrument of control and order, may become nothing but an empty fiction of right and justice, an idol that blinds the rulers to the actual stakes and costs of rule.[6]

5. As Renwick notes (*A View*, 171), Spenser's dialogue was entered in the Stationers' Register on 20 January 1596, but apparently further authority for its publication was not forthcoming. Despite its public suppression, the dozen or so surviving manuscripts can testify to the interest it may have held for Tudor officials.

6. Fletcher (*Prophetic Moment*, 282) discusses this same conflict between human order and changing time as the basis of his interpretation of Equity in Book v: "Conscience provides a psychological basis for equity through its balancing functions; the mind in its conscience is undivided, has no doubt about standards, judges equably. But it also achieves self-consciousness, and this leads the hero to take part in a historical destiny. Without an awareness of the continuing complications of judgments, that is, of their ever-changing conditions, the mind is incapable of seeing into the future or taking part in a significant movement through historical time. This historicity of conscience is enshrined in the legal formulation of equity as a corrective to the law. By insisting on this meaning of equity, Spenser gives to his Legend the direction of a legitimate prophecy."

Spenser, then, calls into question the adequacy of many English laws and statutes to deal with the Irish situation. But there is no question of accommodating colonial rule to the separate legal traditions that have grown up in Ireland. The poet's distinctions between the two legal systems are not grounded so much in abstract ideas of justice as in quite pragmatic notions of control and stability—the main problem with the Irish laws being that they seem to build endless potentials for rebellion, disorder, and discontinuity into the social structure, whereas whatever violence is occasioned by English law (setting aside that violence which serves the purposes of correction or threat) Spenser judges to have arisen from a human mishandling of what is fundamentally an equitable, or at least stable system of government. To frame the difference in terms of one of our most malleable cultural metaphors, I might say that what Spenser fears in the Irish is that, for all their "natural" (i.e., wild and uncivilized) qualities, their legal traditions recognize no form or illusion of natural continuity—whether in the shape of hereditary rights to power or place, fealty to a royal house, or tie of a family name and working population with a particular plot of ground—which might survive or rise above the inevitable disjunctions of historical time. As W. L. Renwick puts it in the commentary to his edition of *A View,*

> the English thought in terms of land and the family, the Irish in terms of the tribe and the individual. . . . The Irish chieftainship was elective, not hereditary. The election itself was a disturbance, and candidates often tried to drag in the government; and when a chief died, people in Dublin did not know who might succeed or what he might do. . . . So also with lesser men: they were tenants at will, entirely dependent on the chiefs, with no direct relation to the government because they had never known any comparable central authority. Finance was uncertain, for tenants paid no fixed rents but only variable customary dues and services as they were demanded. Even the land was unstable [!], for no dues were payable on uncultivated ground, and the restless population shifted from year to year within the clan territories. (*A View*, 177)

In such a chaos of egos set free, Spenser writes, the island's inhabitants "daily looketh after change and alteration, *and hovereth in expectation of new worlds*" (81; emphasis mine). Even where Spenser sees no hope of reforming the Irish according to the English model, he is at least insistent that no Irish manners, laws, or customs should seep into the English settlements in Ireland. (To this degree, Spenser's admonitions echo the primarily defensive statutes issued by many of the earlier Norman rulers of Ireland and collected in the famous Statutes of

Kilkenny [1490]. This document not only prohibited intermarriage between English and Irish, but made it illegal for colonists to speak the Irish language, use Irish names, wear Irish clothes, play Irish games, and even to ride bareback in the Irish fashion, as if in horror of any contact with an animal without the civilizing mediations of saddle, stirrups, and bridle.)[7]

Spenser's anxiety about the instability of rule in Ireland is quite evident, and yet even so it is perhaps dangerous to appropriate (as I have done above) such an easy metaphor as "chaos" to describe the situation. For the poet perceives the problem not as a simple need to impose an ideal order on an abstracted, Irish "disorder" but as the destructive conflict of two separate orders, each with its own severe logic, each taking a different account of violence, each codifying a different picture of morality, fidelity, scope of choice, and so on—even as Spenser also sees the failure to recognize such differences as the reason why the blind imposition of an order can so readily generate greater chaos than the one it was intended to reform. Throughout the dialogue he maintains a strict skepticism about the authority and permanence of particular laws or statutes, whether considered as agents for the imposition of control or as the embodiments of abstract moral norms. Given the loose style of argument in the dialogue, it is not at all easy to pin down what Spenser's exact description of "right" would be. What we can say, however, is that in such comments as that quoted above on the limits of "rule of right," Spenser is making use of a distinction (available in jurists as different as Jean Bodin and Hooker) between law as a philosophical and law as a political problem—that is, between law as justice (*jus*), whether based on natural or divine reason—and law as a matter of secular power and institutions (*lex*). The bare distinction can be found among classical and medieval thinkers as well, but the important point is that in the Renaissance the gap between *lex* and *jus* seems to widen dramatically, especially as the authority of the medieval *corpus juris* was challenged both by the new Humanist history and philology, and by a growing skepticism as to the commensurability of any human image with the divine reality that was its alleged metaphysical foundation.[8]

7. For a discussion of the statutes and their influence on later English colonial policy, see A. J. Otway-Ruthven, *A History of Medieval Ireland*, 291–95.

8. These remarks on Renaissance legal theory are especially indebted to Carl Joachim Friedrich's authoritative survey, *The Philosophy of Law in Historical Perspective*, 42–76, and to discussions in J. G. A. Pocock, *The Machiavellian Moment*, 3–30 and 156–218; Lawrence Manley, *Convention: 1500-1750*, 90–106 and 203–15; and Julian Franklin, *Jean Bodin and the Sixteenth-Century Revolution in the Methodology of Law and History*, 7–79.

In theorists such as Machiavelli, this position of radical disillusionment gives rise to a much more pragmatic notion of law as decentralized, relative, and largely unbound from "rule of right." Though all Renaissance theories of law do not go to the Machiavellian extreme of seeing legal institutions as largely coercive fictions—instruments of the will to power over the unstable text of time—they still tend to approach law as something that possesses both the liabilities and the blandishments of fiction. Law in the Renaissance begins to be understood as an inescapably human creation, a thing subject to the vagaries of tradition, national character, and political necessity. Law is thus as much a matter of desire and will as of reason; a law is not simply a rule that reflects eternal virtue but a virtuous trope, a remedial fiction. Insofar as a law may be the direct agent of reform, moving persons toward virtue in the very process of realizing virtue's dictates, and not simply a conservative force for maintaining the status quo, legal theory begins to come within the domain of a poetics of persuasion like that of Sidney. That is, laws resemble the concrete universals that make up poetry more than they do either the facts of history or the conceptualizations of philosophy; laws belong to the literature of power and love rather than the literature of knowledge. This also means that they can share poetry's implicit freedom from a priori moral constraints and metaphysical authority.

A View of the Present State of Ireland is a not un-Machiavellian document, both insofar as it refuses to grant any absolute moral rectitude to the workings of English law in Ireland, and as it looks clear-sightedly at the difficult interanimation of ideological fictions and military power in the progress of the Irish conflicts. It is Sidneyan to the degree that though Spenser does not gloss over the need for force in Ireland, he seems at moments to reconceive dilemmas of power as dilemmas of poetics. For instance, he insists that Ireland can be cured only by "the Sword of the Prince"—a metaphor that conveys the radical meaning and locus of the sovereign power which he wants to see exercised in Ireland. And yet he hastens both to soften and to rationalize such an extreme figure by referring it to the imposition of strong new statutes and civic or agricultural projects, as well as military might. Later he cites Machiavelli on Roman government in support of his argument that the queen's deputy in Ireland must have absolute power in the colony (*A View*, 169), as if to convey a sense that the one who *represents* imperial power must be that power's forceful, flexible trope rather than its empty cipher or allegory. (Otherwise, like Spenser's patron Lord Grey, the governor might become the symbolic victim of the very power he was supposedly embodying.) The risk

Spenser takes in choosing the author of *The Prince* to underline his point might seem to parallel the risk of granting the governor absolute power, however, and he characteristically appends to his strong initial assertion a long list of particular legal restraints on that absolute power he had so stressed at the outset—as if the need for such strong representation also bred the fear that it might turn into identification, usurpation, and tyranny. Such difficulties of balance in the "real" world receive no more stable or ideal solution in the explicitly poetic cosmos of *The Faerie Queene*. In Book v, for example, Spenser may choose to hold apart the image of effective violence against rebellion in the person of Talus from the idealistic justifications of violence personified by Arthegall. But in light of the questions about power and authority raised by *A View*, we may see just how willful and defensive such separations are. Indeed, as Stephen Greenblatt argues, Spenser's allegorical separation of idealistic rhetoric from the direct exercise of military violence ends up making Arthegall—the image of Lord Grey—peculiarly susceptible to the fundamentally rhetorical attacks of Envy, Detraction, and the slanderous Blatant Beast (Spenser's ironic if wisely evasive images of the state's official disapproval) after his final victory over the Catholic tyrant Grantorto (v.xii.28–43).[9] The allegorical dilemma is complex here, but the basic point I want to make is that, as we reflect on *A View*, it should be clear that Spenser's poem does not simply reclothe a blank, literal history in metaphor; rather, it exposes and explores the workings, limitations, and costs of a poetics that is in no way confined to the hieratic space of verses on a printed page.

The Genealogy of Idolatry

I will leave until the final section of this chapter an account of Spenser's most unsettling image of legal violence in Ireland and move now to his discussion of those specific Irish customs that seem most to perpetuate the civil disorder. The poet's pragmatic interest in the rhetorical nature and the historical contingency of law colors his account of these customs as well, and his delight in tracing their ancient origins—Eudoxus urges, "ye may at large stretch out your discourse into

9. See Greenblatt, "Murdering Peasants: Status, Genre, and the Representation of Rebellion," 22–23. For some related observations on the tension within *A View* between the traditional metaphors (especially agricultural and medical) by which Spenser justifies colonial rule and the less tractable facts of historical circumstance and political power, see Eamon Grennan's essay, "Language and Politics: A Note on Some Metaphors in Spenser's *A View of the Present State of Ireland*." Cf. also the skeptical assessments in Jonathan Goldberg, *James I and the Politics of Literature*, 8–10.

many sweet remembrances of antiquities (*A View*, 37)—is allied to a deliberate skepticism of both the available historical authorities and his own explanations. Supplementing the often "fabulous and forged" Irish chronicles with classical and modern histories, comparing "times, likeness of manners and customs, affinity of words and names . . . resemblances of rites and ceremonies, monuments of churches and tombs," Spenser (like Sidney's poet, "not . . . affirming anything") asserts that he will gather only a "likelihood of truth . . . a probability of things which I leave unto your judgement to believe or refuse" (39).[10] That he begins by implicating his own and others' historical writing in dilemmas of error and misjudgment is all the more interesting, because his account of Irish custom is distinguished by a peculiar attention to deceptive representations.

Spenser starts by considering the Irish husbandmen's way of letting their cattle wander almost wild during the summer months, to graze on the otherwise unusable ground of hills and "waste-places." Large camps are often set up in such areas, far from the civilities of village or town. What the poet objects to is that the camps, or "Bollies," tend to attract to such wild places great numbers of "outlaws or loose people," who would otherwise starve or be arrested, but who can there feed, clothe, and conceal themselves. More important, those who inhabit such camps tend to turn as bestial as the creatures they care for. What bothers Spenser is the work of a kind of corrupting poetry or literalizing metamorphosis, a metonymic infection of herders by the herded that Spenser brings out at the close of the following speech by Irenius in a sly countersimile: "The people that live thus in these Bollies grow thereby the more barbarous and live more licentiously than they could in towns, using what means they list, and practicing what mischiefs and villainies they will. . . . For there they think themselves half exempted from law and obedience, and having once tasted freedom do, like a steer that hath been long out of his yoke, grudge and repine ever after to come under rule again" (*A View*, 50).

A second custom about which Irenius complains, at even greater length and with a strange intensity, is the "wearing of mantles and long glibs, which is a thick curled bush of hair hanging down over

10. Renwick, in his commentary on *A View*, 188, notes the probable influence on Spenser of Humanist methods of comparative historiography, with its shrewd skepticism of literary authority and sense of cultural relativism. While admitting that Spenser may have been acquainted with Jean Bodin's massive *Methodus ad facilem historiarum cognitionem* (1583), Renwick shows that the comparative methodology would also have been available to him in such native English historians as Camden, Buchanan, and Smith.

their eyes, and monstrously disguising them, which are both very bad and hurtful" (50). The very commodity of the garment for the Irish way of life, something that might impress a modern anthropologist, quite appalls Spenser, for it is a human contrivance that helps to institutionalize what he sees as the most inhuman and uncivilized elements of the society. The costume allows thieves, outlaws, and all "wandering women" to live freely and safely outside of settled areas, since they can make of the mantle a home in all seasons—a tent, a bed (whether for sleep or sin), a shield, a hiding place, a mask. Under it the Irishman "covereth himself from the wrath of heaven, from the offence of the earth, and from the sight of men" (51). As for the glibs, "besides their savage brutishness and loathly filthiness . . . they are fit masks as a mantle is for a thief, for whensoever he hath run himself into that peril of law that he will not be known, he either cutteth off his glib quite, by which he becometh nothing like himself, or pulleth it so low down over his eyes that it is very hard to discern his thievish countenance" (53). The mantles and glibs are a shared covering for both sexual and political transgressions, tools of human deception which are nevertheless married to the innocent vicissitudes of the weather; they allow an inhuman power of change which is yet permanently embedded in Irish custom—grown, that is, into a second nature, an unnatural idol. They are in the end the very embodiment of a furtive, energetic evil that continues to resist the reforming work of the English governors; they are sartorial avatars of Proteus and Irish "mythologies" in their own right.

As M. M. Gray argued many years ago, the desperate, wild face of the Irish kern, covered with his brutish glib and living in a ravaged landscape, haunts Spenser's poetry in figures as different as Despair in Book I, the deathless Malegar of Book II, and the exiled Timias of Book IV.[11] The poet's account of the glibs and mantles indeed points to

11. "The Influences of Spenser's Irish Experiences on *The Faerie Queene*," 423–27. See, for example, the picture of the exiled Timias appearing before Belphebe "in wretched weedes disguiz'd, / With heary glib deform'd and meiger face, / like ghost late risen from his grave agryz'd, / She knew him not" (IV.viii.12)—lines echoed in the description of the starving Irish kerns quoted in footnote 32 to this chapter. Spenser's fascination with these bestial, deforming garments as *materia poetica* may itself be mediated by his interest in the folklore of the "horrid" wild man, studied most fully in Richard Bernheimer's *The Wild Man in the Middle Ages: A Study of Art, Sentiment, and Demonology*. A malleable myth of the primitive, this alien creature—sometimes comic and friendly, sometimes ghoulish and rapacious—undergoes various transformations in *The Faerie Queene*, from Orgoglio and Satyrane in Book I to Lust in Book IV and the gentle, wordless "salvage" in Book VI. As Hayden White notes in his essay on the ideological underpinnings of the myth, the inhuman wild man could also be seen (not unlike Spenser's uncanny kerns) as a sly natural magician and a master of disguise ("The Forms of Wildness: Archaeology of an Idea," 21).

a primitive but not quite natural power in Irish culture, a form of disorder which may yet seem uneasily allied to the kind of forces necessary to contain it. Such a dilemma is perhaps even more apparent in Spenser's account of a third disabling custom of the Irish. The problem seems transparent enough at the outset, a simple matter of Irish soldiers making too much noise in battle: "They came running with a terrible yell and hubbub, as if heaven and earth would have gone together" (*A View*, 54). Yet it is more than violent confusion, however apocalyptic its impression, which disturbs the poet, more even than the military efficacy of such cries. The problem is that such confusion is achieved by means, rather than in spite, of the commemorative and unifying powers of human speech, for Spenser makes a great point of the fact that the warriors are yelling out the numinous names of their first kings, or else "their captain's name or the word of his ancestors" (54). The case is similar to Sidney's account of the Arcadian rebellion that originates in the common people's prideful fascination with words and noble names, and with the illusory sense of power it grants them, at least insofar as in both poets we see apprehensible language overthrown through the very power of language over the mind.[12] In the case of the Irish cries, both force and confusion seem to arise out of a tremendous, collective appeal to origins, a necromantic, mythopoeic scream that for Spenser is nevertheless an empty superstition, a form of memory which distorts and kills rather than clarifies. If this yelling resembles the sacred battle cry of the ancient Hebrew tribes calling on Yahweh, which one theologian has identified as perhaps the oldest form of prophetic speech (von Rad, *Old Testament Theology*, 2:36n), it also recalls the false prophets so movingly described by Longfellow:

> For in the background figures vague and vast
> Of patriarchs and of prophets rose sublime.
>
> . . .
>
> And thus forever with reverted look
> The mystic volume of the world they read,
> Spelling it backward, like a Hebrew book,
> Till life became a Legend of the Dead.
> (*Poetical Works*, 192)

12. See Sidney, *Prose Works*, 1:323: "So general grewe this madnes among them, there needed no drumme, where each man cried, each spake to other that spake as fast to him, and the disagreeing sounde of so many voices, was the chiefe token of their unmeete agreement."

There is no question that for Spenser the knowledge of one's ancestry both sanctifies and educates, and that the backward glance of memory is an absolute necessity in making proper use of present and future time. "How can one avert pride and its subsequent fall?" asks Harry Berger, Jr., in *The Allegorical Temper*. "By a knowledge of who one is, from whom and from where one derives one's being, excellence, and power" (113). Yet we must remember that a titanic and seemingly autochthonous figure like Orgoglio, "puft up with emptie wind, and fild with sinfull crime" (I.vii.9), has grown great "through arrogant delight / Of th'high descent, whereof he was yborne" (I.vii.10); he is the narcissistic selfhood both pregnant and tumescent with the worship of his purported origins. Redcrosse learns his name and nation only after trial, failure, and grace, and finds for himself a genealogy that should humble as well as inspire him; and Arthur, though he is allowed to confront the tragic history of his homeland, is divided by a slight—but perhaps salvific—gap in the text from any absolute recovery of his paternity.[13] Blindly to assert the absolute authority of any one memory, name, or myth is to court idolatry; Spenser's strong desire to avoid any such false identifications may suggest that there is an ironic, demystifying intent behind the continual interweaving, skewing, and fragmentation of genealogies which occurs throughout *The Faerie Queene*. In our disenchanted present we are apt to be naively enthralled by the magical use of names in Hermetic philosophy or Kabbalah, but what Spenser shows us happening in Ireland is not any less a form of name magic. It is a deathly form of what one critic has called "the romance of the etymon," the mythopoeic enchantment of origins. One may recall, with a slight shudder, that the poem's first and most dangerous wizard (Archimago) is—etymologically speaking—a magus or idol of the *arche*.

Irenius's interlocutor Eudoxus manages to answer and extend this critique of magical speech by an even more sophisticated exercise in debunking. To the former's conclusion that the popular battle cry "Ferragh Ferragh" enshrines the name of "the first kings of Scotland, called Fergus or Feragus," Eudoxus responds:

> Believe me, this observation of yours, Irenius, is very good and delightful, far beyond the blind conceit of some who I remember have upon the same word *Farragh* made a very blunt conjecture, as namely master Stanyhurst, who though he be the same countryman born, that should

13. For further discussion, see Chapter 3, 119–24.

search more nearly into the secret of these things, yet have strayed from the truth all the heavens wide, (as they say) for he thereupon groundeth a very gross imagination that the Irish should descend from the Egyptians which came into that island, first under the leading of Scota the daughter of Pharao, whereupon they use (saith he) in all their battles to call upon the name of Pharao, crying *Ferragh Ferragh*. Surely he shot wide on the bow hand, and very far from the mark, for I would first know of him what ancient ground of authority he hath for such a senseless fable, and if he have any of the rude Irish books as it may be he hath, yet meseems a man of his learning should not so lightly have been carried away with old wives' tales from approvance to his own reason; for whether Scota be like an Egyptian word, or smack of any learning or judgement, let the learned judge, but his Scota rather comes upon the Greek *scotos*, that is darkness, which hath not let him see the light of truth. (55)

Except for the closing joke, of which more shortly, this passage sanctions a conjectural or scholarly pursuit of the origins of an enchanting name, though mainly in the service of disenchantment. Philology here works to dispel illusory etymologies rather than to authenticate true ones. The grotesqueness of Stanyhurst's faked regress to a sacred "Egyptian" origin indeed casts a skeptical light on the efforts of Elizabethan historians who sought to establish the *literal* continuity between the Tudor empire and its ancient precursors, whether religious or political.

Stanyhurst's mistake is a trivial one, of course, but there is something in it that disturbs the poet more than seems reasonable. Indeed, the real force of the passage lies in Spenser's having placed this account of the historian's "blind conceit" and "gross imagination" just after the description of the Irish battle screams. The latter phenomenon, a disease of an uncivilized nation, is thus recast by an implicit metonymy in the aberrant tactics of the most polite sort of historical writing. Both Stanyhurst and the Irish warriors, that is to say, fall into what Nietzsche might have called the idolatry of "believing backward."[14] In this passage of *A View*, as often in Spenser's poetry, we witness a situation in which the differences between primitive and sophisticated discourses start to collapse, the two levels infecting each other or resonating back and forth. The two instances of a "reverted look" might best be seen as the superimposed inscriptions of a palimpsest, save that in this case the "earlier" text also serves to rebuke

14. "By searching out origins, one becomes a crab. The historian looks backward; eventually he also *believes* backward" (*Twilight of the Idols*, aphorism 24, in *The Portable Nietzsche*, 470).

the later one, pointing as it does to the narrowing, regressive impulses that can underlie certain sorts of scholarly *Quellenforschungen*. Having exposed Stanyhurst's error, Spenser furthermore tries to move his own description (if only for a moment) beyond the awkward, necessary burden of constructing a historical narrative. For, coming as it does after two examples of clearly false speech, the poet's punning use of an obviously false etymology (Scota-*scotos*) shifts our attention to the disenchanting magic of words that have been liberated from the immediate service of historical explanation and naming and so are made available for the sanctified lies of fiction—the enlightening, ironic *scotos* of a "darke [but not blind] conceit." Spenser, then, neither wholly rejects nor embraces philology, but takes it as material for parable. His converting of the mythic source name into its own mockery repeats in a minor key the biblical rereading of Bab-el, "gate of god," as "confusion," and parallels the Golem's ironic change of a presumptuous "truth" into the word of "death."

Spenser's doubts about etiological functions of myth, his sense of how explanation collapses into mystification, are echoed somewhat later in the dialogue in a discussion of the origins of the numerous artificial mounds or "folkmotes" to be observed in Ireland. Spenser's avatar Irenius shows that these were once the sites of free meetings between neighboring clans or else served as fortified gathering places in time of war. "There were anciently diverse others, for some were raised, where there had been a great battle fought, as a memory or trophies thereof, others as monuments of burials of the carcasses of all those that were slain in any fight, upon whom they did throw up such round mounts as memorials for them, and sometimes did cast up great heaps of stones, as ye may read in many places of the Scripture; and other whiles they did throw up *many round heaps of earth in a circle like a garland, or pitch many long stones on end in compass*" (78; emphasis mine). Spenser recognizes the hills as sacred places of memory, and it is probable that he had similar sites in mind when he came to describe scenes of grace, order, and judgment, such as Arlo Hill, or Mount Acidale, where Calidore witnessed a ring of dancing nymphs which "like a girlond did in compasse stemme" (VI.x.12). And yet in Elizabethan Ireland these ancient hills have decayed; once places of free conference, they have become sites of close plotting, the resort of "all the scum of loose people" (77), who take advantage of the confusion of the gatherings to keep their devices secret. Here murders and battles start rather than end, and violent divisiveness has replaced peaceful communion, so that Irenius can see no other remedy than to suppress all such meetings.

As in the earlier discussion of the battle cries, Eudoxus answers Irenius's plans for reform with a mirroring comment on related questions of historical explanation:

> Ye have very well declared the original of these mounts and great stones, encompassed which some vainly term the old Giants trivets, and think that those huge stones would not else be brought into order or reared up without the strength of Giants and others, as vainly think that they were never placed there by man's hand or art, but only remained there so since the beginning, and were afterwards discovered by the deluge, and laid open by the washing of the waters or other like casualty. But let them dream their own imaginations to please themselves, but ye have satisfied me much better both by that I see some confirmation thereof in the holy writ, and also remember that I have read, in many histories and chronicles, the like mounts and stones oftentimes mentioned. (78–79)

The writer of these lines was no naive seeker after an Irish *genius loci* or any other inherited myths of autochthonous deities—beings, for example, like the native British fairies, of whose rich mythology *The Faerie Queene* takes so little real cognizance, just as it makes only oblique and fragmentary use of the indigenous materials of Arthurian legend. The speaker's disdain for such apparently innocent instances of Irish folklore may seem excessive, but Eudoxus needs to insist—against any myth of inhuman origins—on the place of "man's hand and art," on the pathos of human death and memory. Any narrative that erases our sense of these, whatever its aesthetic or social function, is suspect.[15] We might speculate on the relation of this passage to widespread Protestant attacks on the ecclesiastical manipulation of popular superstition.[16] More immediately relevant, however, is the way that Spenser implicitly refigures the fable of the antediluvian

15. Frye writes that, although such folktales as these are not quite like the major constitutive myths that explain or accommodate a culture to itself, that rationalize its "religion, laws, social structures, environment, history, or cosmology," yet they are "told to meet the imaginative needs of the community, so far as structures in words can meet these needs" (*Secular Scripture,* 6). One should observe here, however, that while Frye's characteristic emphasis on narrative patterning might help us see more starkly the parallel between Irish and biblical stories of giants, his approach commonly tends to evade the kind of messy questions about authority and belief which trouble Spenser, questions arising, for instance, out of the sense that a society's "imaginative needs" may be identical to its idolatries.

16. Spenser's own gloss (or rather, that of his unknown friend, E. K.) to the June eclogue of *The Shepheardes Calendar* provides a good example of the Protestant stance: "The opinion of Faeries and elfes is very old, and yet sticketh very religiously in the myndes of some. But to roote that rancke opinion of Elfes oute of mens hearts, the truth is, that there be no such thinges, nor yet the shadowes of the things, but onely by a sort of bald Friers and knavish shavelings so feigned" (*Poetical Works,* 443).

giants in order to comment on those who repeat it. We should first note that these creatures recall the giants and "men of renown" described in Genesis 6.1–4, born from the union of the daughters of men and the sons of God (often portrayed as fallen angels), whose wickedness moved God to drown the earth.[17] Spenser may or may not have recalled this text, with its analogues to classical tales of titanic rebellion. But what is more immediately intriguing is that his words suggest that the primitive giants can be read as the emblems of the minds that have conceived them. That is to say, the stories of the giants most directly reflect the inflated senses of men who "dream their own imaginations to please themselves"—a phrase that echoes both Old and New Testament descriptions of idolaters and false prophets,[18] and that also associates these Irish storytellers with those Englishmen whom Spenser thought abject mimics of God on account of their wish that Ireland be destroyed by a second flood.[19]

Spenser's way of seeing a conceptual or imaginative violence sedimented within ancient, fantastic stories of monstrosity finds a precise analogue in *The Faerie Queene*. The passage I have in mind is taken from Spenser's description of the book of "Briton moniments" which Arthur reads in the chamber of Alma's councilor Eumnestes (II.x.1–68). This volume too gives an account of a race of giants who first inhabited the British Isles, beastly, polluted, and violent beings who were banished by the mythic founder of Elizabeth's own royal line, the Trojan hero Brutus. And again, Spenser mocks the folktale that he repeats by making its monstrous subject an implicit trope for the imaginations of the men who originated the tale (as well as both identifying biblical and British history and making a mockery of that identification). What renders Spenser's genealogy of the giants doubly monstrous is that the delusive tale of their genesis records their genesis through illusion:

17. The interpretive history of this text is summarized by Speiser in his commentary (*Genesis*, 45–46). Speiser suggests that the Hebrew author (somewhat like Spenser) intended the reader to recognize the anomalous, folkloric character of the story and to view it as the product of man's morbid imagination, an evil myth of evil giants. He adds, with persecutory emphasis, that "the mere popularity of the story would have been sufficient to fill [the Yahwist] with horror at the depravity that it reflected. A world that could entertain such notions deserved to be wiped out."

18. Jeremiah especially makes use of similar phrasing: "Do the Prophetes delite to prophecie lies, even prophecying the deceit of their owne heart. Think thei to cause my people to forget my Name by their dreames, which they tel everie man to his neighbour. . . . The Prophet that hathe a dreame, let him tel a dreame, and he that hathe my worde, let him speake my worde faithfully" (23.26–28, Geneva Version).

19. It is a telling evasion that Spenser does not allude to Genesis 6, with its problematic, folkloric fable, even while he invokes the *historical* authority of Scripture to undermine the mythic etiologies of such mounds.

> But whence they sprong, or how they were begot,
> Uneath is to assure; uneath to wene
> *That monstrous error, which doth some assot,*
> That *Dioclesians* fiftie daughters shene
> Into this land by chaunce have driven bene,
> Where companing with feends and filthy Sprights,
> Through vaine illusion of their lust unclene,
> They brought forth Giants and such dreadfull wights,
> As farre exceeded men in their immeasurd mights.
> (II.x.8; emphasis mine)

Not all instances of genealogy in *The Faerie Queene* reflect this ironic treatment of myths of origin, or use mythic narrative to emblematize and criticize the very imaginations that create and shape those myths. Still, what should be clear by now is a strongly antimythological tenor in the poet's writing which the differing generic demands of historical narrative and poetic romance cannot obscure—even though in the latter mode Spenser's reticence about myth may take on a more complex, dialectical form. The lessons drawn from *A View* may help us understand why such sublime, magical *omphaloi* as Mount Acidale (VI.x) or Arlo Hill (VII.vi) are nonetheless so haunted by a spirit of demystification or exorcism. My final chapter will examine the description of such sacred centers in greater detail, especially the scenes of violation and loss, the strange modes of address and allusion which they occasion. For the moment, it may suffice to remind ourselves that in the case of Arlo Hill—that sacred site where the trial of the titaness Mutabilitie unfolds—the only thing that Spenser gives us in the way of an etiological myth is an account of how the hill's original divine inhabitants *abandoned* it. It is as if some contrived fall from original numinousness, some cure of the ground, were a necessary prelude to the later regathering of divinities in the last episode of his romance.

Mythopoesis and Its Discontents

I want at this point to juxtapose two passages from roughly the middle of the dialogue, passages that together offer an even more remarkable commentary than those previously cited on the burdens of the imagination and their effect on the poet in Ireland. The juxtaposition is not arbitrary, but my interpretation of the texts involved must be more frankly allegorical—especially since in neither case do these passages contain any antiquarian digressions, such as those on Scota or the giants, by which to link discussion back to more general questions about literary mythmaking. But the insight yielded into the situation of the poet and his attitudes toward language, law, and violence should more than justify any apparent dislocations of context.

The first passage is taken from an analysis of the immigrant Englishman's loyalty to his Irish home. Though Spenser is aware of the quite indifferent violence and repression with which many colonials treat the indigenous population, he is even more troubled by those long-settled colonists who have so adapted to life in Ireland as to become more "Irish"—that is, more rebellious, shifty, lawless, and deluded—than the Irish themselves. In their violent reversals of faith they disguise their origins, reject their native country, even renounce their English names; they attempt, that is, "to bite off her dug from which they sucked life" (65). As Greenblatt observes (*Renaissance Self-Fashioning*, 185), such cruel rejections of origin stem from the fact that another breast has, both literally and figuratively, taken the place of the first. For in giving an account of the sources of such faithlessness, Spenser stresses most the Anglo-Irish rebels' perverse attachment to the native but alien language of Ireland, something that is the unfortunate result of "fostering and marrying with the Irish . . . for the child that sucketh the milk of the nurse must of necessity learn his first speech of her," an observation that gives rise to some comments on the relation of language and education:

> The young children be like apes, which will affect and imitate what they see done before them, specially by their nurses whom they love so well. They moreover draw into themselves together with their suck, even the nature and disposition of their nurses, for the mind followeth much the temperature of the body; and also the words are the image of the mind, so as they proceeding from the mind, the mind must be needs effected with the words; so that the speech being Irish, the heart must needs be Irish, for out of the abundance of the heart the tongue speaketh. (68)

In this remarkable passage, the threatening face of Ireland embodied in the wild, alien kern is replaced by that of a seductive, absorptive mother who teaches a regressive mother tongue; Malegar is replaced by Acrasia. I do not propose to trace the argument of the passage—its joining together of nurture and speech, mind and body, love and imitation—to its classical and Renaissance sources.[20] But I quote at

20. The idea that we learn customs and virtue "as a child picks up his native language" goes back to Greek teachers of *arete* like Protagoras (Dodds, *The Greeks and the Irrational*, 183–84). Dante, in the *De vulgari eloquentia*, notes that children learn "vernacular speech" "without any rules in imitating our nurse" (*Literary Criticism of Dante Alighieri*, 3), and Du Bellay notes in his *Defense and Illustration of the French Language* that "the ancients used languages which they had sucked in with the milk of their nurses,

length because as significant as the general theory of linguistic influence is the subtly figurative, if somewhat confusing movement of the overall description. For example, the rather fine parallelisms and chiastic patterns ("words . . . minds / minds . . . words"; "speech . . . heart / heart . . . tongue") at once mime the secretive interanimation of body, affections, consciousness, and speech which so disturbs Spenser, and obliterate any clear perception of cause and effect. Indeed, the proverb that closes the passage in its original context actually insists that mind and heart condition speech, rather than the reverse: "O generation of vipers, how can ye, being evil, speak good things? For out of the abundance of the heart the tongue speaketh" (Matt. 12.34, Geneva Version). Spenser's closing biblical echo, though it links the corrupted Anglo-Irish to the recalcitrant gentiles of the Gospel and seems to authorize the idea of language's dangerous spiritual influence, if examined also manages to expose the arbitrary application of the fundamentally organic metaphor that underlies Spenser's explanation. For it reveals how uncertain is the causal relationship between "heart" and "tongue." This dilemma may, of course, be said to echo the chief element of anxiety in the passage, that is, the confusion of rational orders of action, explanation, and allegiance in Ireland which the learning of the Irish language perpetuates. But then it becomes even more intriguing that Spenser should display such a subtle series of rhetorical mystifications within a critique of exactly congruent mystifications in another sphere of language. For he indirectly exposes his own writing to an attack similar to the one he mounts against the learning of Irish.[21]

If the passage were less of a fragment, it might be more available to the analyses of recent critics devoted to uncovering the internally blocked or paradoxical nature of all theorizing about language.[22] One

---

and the unlearned spoke as well as the learned" (56). These works, which consider the dangers and advantages of copying a language not one's own, might have paradoxical relevance to Spenser's diatribe against the learning not of a classical language—a father tongue—but of a second vernacular or foster mother tongue. See William Kerrigan, "The Articulation of the Ego in the English Renaissance," 277–90, on the Renaissance association of Latin and vernacular speech with the imagery of paternity and maternity respectively.

21. Spenser's implicit distrust of *both* Irish and English may help explain why, as Ben Jonson complained, the poet "writ no language." Spenser's hybrid vocabulary, mock archaic diction, and complex deformations of syntax suggest an effort always to go beyond the limiting inheritance of spoken or written English. His poetry thus reinforces a sense of difficult, contradictory, contaminated speech, and does not try to chasten language—as Jonson thought necessary—by appeal to a putatively pure or classical source.

22. I have in mind here particularly the influential work of Paul de Man, though for a related application of deconstructionist methods to classical and Renaissance rhetorics, see Terence Cave, *The Cornucopian Text: Problems of Writing in the French Renaissance.*

could then say that Spenser's attempt to lay bare the origins of linguistic enchantment points to the difficulty of escaping that enchantment, and to the radically alogical or figurative nature of any discourse about sources. In this case, of course, such an approach to the text may appear a trifle labored. But it is at least a useful prelude to my own attempt to recover a more purely parabolic reading of the text's concerns with contamination and alienation, continuity and discontinuity, language and history, and of their reflections within the mythology of *The Faerie Queene*. Such a reading would do more than subvert the text's claims to matching its discourse to an autonomous reality or conceptual order outside it; it would live beyond the death of such claims, or perhaps, precisely in the moment of their death.

Proceeding partly within the terms of Spenser's romance, we might say that Irenius's resonant description of language as a natural rather than a purely intellectual force recalls the dynamic, generative mode of continuity unfolded in the Garden of Adonis (III.vi). Yet we may also find in his words the fear of language as a potentially corruptive power that will, far from furthering growth, actually close the mind up within its primitive origins, both cultural and physiological. This haunting fear of absorption and regression actually recalls not the dynamic processes of the Garden but the static continuities of the Bower of Bliss (II.xii), continuities that obliterate both memory and aspiration.[23] In the Bower, under the control of the demonic lover-nurse Acrasia ("false mixture"), human beings become unnaturally bestial, seduced not only by their untempered natural affections but also by the blandishments of a sophisticated mimetic art that is itself a human creation (just as the Irish are assimilated by their own "loose" herds and protean clothing). Such an intersection of the natural and cultural can only be cured by a severe, antithetical disjunction, which is what happens when the Bower is torn down at the end of Book II by the temperate, tempestuous Guyon.

This way of framing the passage from *A View*, however, may oversimplify the strange ironies of Spenser's imagery. As I noted, the English child brought up to speak Irish bites off the breast that has given him life because he has fed from the wrong source in the first place, a situation in which continuity strangely overlaps discontinuity.[24] In this

23. On this association, see the suggestive discussion in Greenblatt, *Renaissance Self-Fashioning*, 184–86. In addition to linking the Bower of Bliss to Spenser's experience of Ireland, this critic provides a shrewd account of the poet's interest in the violent ways that civilized discourse must "colonize" archaic or alien forces, even at the cost of self-reduction and repression.

24. Spenser employs a similarly complex imagery of conflicting sources and nourishments in his description of the work of Jesuit missionaries among the "blindly and brutishly informed" Irish papists: "I nothing doubt but through the powerful grace of that

context one might point to the ambiguous use throughout the dialogue of the imagery of "cutting off." This phrase can refer to a purifying, demystifying removal of a dangerous custom, a violence that is the very groundwork or ruinous foundation of reform; hence Spenser speaks of the "redressing and cutting off of those evils which I before blamed," adding, however, "and not of the people which are evil; for evil people by good ordinance and government may be made good, but the evil that is of itself evil will never become good" (*A View*, 95). The work of reform thus carries with it the possibility of too extreme a cutting off, not just a literal loss of life but also an invidious abandonment of the necessary continuities of labor, devotion, and historical identity, an abandonment that can seem the equivalent of moral death. (Spenser even perceives a possibility for self-abandonment, as in the image of the Irish thief who "*cutteth off* his glib quite, by which he becometh nothing like himself" [53; emphasis mine]; he also speaks of the ways in which the continual and often impolitic shifting of military leadership in Ireland does "great wrong . . . to the old soldier, from whom all means of advancement, (which is due unto him) is *cut off*, by shuffling in these new *cutting* captains into the places, for which he hath long served" [121; emphasis mine]). To generalize, we can say that the crisis of finding objects of love, or of turning toward the sources of life, identity, authority, and power, appears to be troubled by a fear of intersecting alternatives: fixation and disjunction, stasis and catastrophic change. Devotion to one origin may entail the defiling, wounding, or biting off of another; an idolatrous attachment to even the best of laws may convert that law to the worst, just as the seductions of iconoclasm may succeed only in alienating the iconoclast from the real power and object of reform. Indeed, fixation itself entails disjunction, since it is grounded in a choice (often delusive) that excludes or cuts off alternative modes of vision, the very exclusiveness of aim accounting for its effective, if divisive force. And this double bind is as evident in the Irish warriors who identify their collective, rebellious chaos with the power of an ancestral name as it is in the case of the massive, concentrated program of reform, conquest, and colonization that Spenser desires the English to undertake.

mighty Saviour [the efforts of missionaries] will work salvation in many of them. But nevertheless, since they drunk not of the pure spring of life, but only tasted of such troubled waters as were brought unto them, the dregs thereof have brought great contagion in their souls, the which daily increasing and being still more augmented with their own lewd lives and filthy conversation, hath now bred in them this general disease, that cannot but only with very strong purgations be cleansed and carried away" (85).

Returning to the passage from *A View*: there is something Wordsworthian in Spenser's description of the child's mind assimilating itself to the spirit of the place, his sucking in of words together with his milk. Yet the child seems to be sucked in by the words as well. One might recall here the theory held by psychoanalysts such as Melanie Klein that human language is always haunted by recollections of a preverbal, oral and bodily communion with the mother, an Edenic condition that becomes the unconscious measure of the mind's most extreme fantasies of love, power, and pleasure[25]—save that in Spenser the seductions of an original, yet foreign speech and those of the mother's breast are explicitly identified. To follow through the implications of this idea, I need to turn to a slightly earlier passage from *A View*, one in which the poet's account of a linguistic and bodily continuity grown into an idolatrous enchantment finds a more politically disturbing analogy, its *allegoria* or *ironia*. As part of his account of those Irish customs that Spenser supposes to descend from early Gallic invaders, Irenius observes that "the Gauls used to drink their enemies' blood and to paint themselves therewith, . . .

> . . . and so have I seen some of the Irish do but not their enemies' but friends' blood, as namely at the execution of a notable traitor at Limerick called Murrogh O'Brien, I saw an old woman which was his foster mother took up his head whilst he was quartered and sucked up all the blood running there out, saying that the earth was not worthy to drink it, and there with also steeped her face and breast, and tore her hair, crying and shrieking out most terribly. (62)

Read together, this and the earlier passage about learning Irish form an uncanny composite that would require the united insights of Blake and Freud to do it justice. Perhaps the most disturbing part of the later scene of disjunction and ingestion is that a supposedly rational, legal action—the "cutting off" of a traitor (one who had already presumably cut himself off from the proper ties of allegiance)—takes on for this old woman the lineaments of a ritual sacrifice, a demonic Eucharist and baptism. And although it is a state of virtual war which so alienates the woman from what should be the orderly work of legal

25. "A satisfactory early relation to the mother . . . implies a close contact between the unconscious of the mother and of the child. This is the foundation for the most complete experience of being understood and is essentially linked with the preverbal stage. However gratifying it is in later life to express thoughts and feelings to a congenial person, there remains an unsatisfied longing for understanding without words—ultimately for the earliest relation with the mother" (Klein, *Our Adult World and Other Essays*, 100).

reform, Spenser presses upon us the bizarre fact that this bloodbath is not a custom of war (as in the case of the Gauls) but a work of love. Instead of submitting before a legal spectacle of terror, this second foster mother is caught up in a compensatory act of mythmaking, one in which, to use Shelley's formula, love is tracked by ruin, by alienation, hunger, and envy. What the poet describes is at once a literalistic and a madly superstitious attempt to master the cutting off of death by rejoining endings to beginnings, the nurse consuming the blood of the child whom her own milk had nourished, now sucking "death instead of life," as if through her his divided body could become whole again. The scene is built upon a terrifying but implicitly tropological pattern of reversal and substitution—blood taking the place of milk, cannibalism the place of nourishment, age the place of youth, and incest the place of the normal order of generation.[26] Instead of the nurse's milk infecting the mind's words and images, the grown child's blood "steeps her face and breast." The image of a wounded or blood-stained breast is a nearly obsessive one in Spenser, but more crucial in the lines from the *View* is the author's description (perhaps projection) of an obsession in the nurse herself: she deems the blood spiritual and sacred as the result of the transforming agony that converts execution into ritual slaughter. Furthermore, to the degree that this ritual is itself somehow parodic or regressive, it constitutes a parody of the legal process that gave rise to it.[27] We may recall here (somewhat ironically) Montaigne's observation that cannibalism functions for primitive peoples as "an extreme and inexpiable" form of revenge, but also his use of the image of men eating men to mock the self-blinding myths of cultural difference erected by his cruel and "civilized" contemporaries (*Essays*, 1.30). Nations that can abide public torture or an Inquisition are themselves not far from cannibals. In this

26. Du Bellay provides an intriguing rhetorical analogue for this ironic parallelism of nurture and cannibalism, describing the Romans' way of internalizing the literature of their precursors: "Imitating the best Greek authors, transforming themselves into them, devouring them; and, after having well digested them, converting them into blood and nourishment, taking for themselves, each according to his nature . . . the best author of whom they observed diligently all the most rare and exquisite virtues, and these like shoots, as I have already said, they grafted and applied to their own tongue" (*Defense and Illustration*, 37). For the source of this imagery in Seneca, see Thomas Greene, *The Light in Troy: Imitation and Discovery in Renaissance Poetry*, 73–74.

27. Michael Seidel, *Satiric Inheritance: Rabelais to Sterne*, argues that the satiric act involves "a kind of perverse neutralization of historical progression," turning history into a pattern of universal victimization and creating "a frenzy around points of terminus," as well as "elaborate moments of regression where origins are ends and where, . . . as in Swift's *Modest Proposal*, all compensation is overcompensation and primal violations such as cannibalism are all too easily projected as sustaining the *lex per satyram*, the legal serving-up of bodies for the preservation of the system" (21).

light, we might see the mad nurse transfigured—along with the rest of the political disorder of which she is both a part and a victim—in Spenser's goddess of discord, Ate, who consumes a "living food":

> For life it is to her, when others sterve
> Through mischievous debate, and deadly feood,
> That she may sucke their life, and drinke their blood,
> With which she from her childhood had bene fed.
> (IV.i.26)

Such iconographic parallels suggest one way of drawing parts of *A View* within the mythic framework of *The Faerie Queene*. But I have tried as well to push toward a more speculative connection, for instance by juxtaposing the execution passage with the earlier account of a foster mother so that the two might (for a moment) seem the linked fragments of some lost canto of Book VI—variations of the Blatant Beast's wounding of language and imagination in canto vi, or a gloss on the confusion of cannibalistic, erotic, and religious appetites in the savages who bind the naked Serena to an altar in canto viii. As in the case of those texts, the execution scene asks for an analytic language that registers the insistent work of fantasy even in the physical violence of the historical scene. The mélange of literary, psychological, and theological terms in my own commentary is only partly adequate, for it tries to accommodate a text that, like many passages in *The Faerie Queene*, at once presses us to read it in the light of sacramental categories and yet calls those categories into question.[28] (It is especially problematic in this context to speak of a "demonic parody" of the Eucharist, since Spenser's is a period when the theological definitions of that ritual were in a radical state of flux and when reformers could even see the sacred *mysterion* of the Catholic communion as a version of the unholy chalice of the whore "Mystery.")[29] Indeed, in trying to give an account of such forms of mythmaking or idolatry, we cannot easily disentangle the fantastic from the real, the sacred from the profane, the civilized from the primitive, without being led into some reductive idealizations that would betray the poet's own complex act of attention.

28. The text forcefully illustrates René Girard's argument that "the difference between sacrificial and nonsacrificial violence is anything but exact; it is even arbitrary. At times the difference threatens to disappear entirely. There is no such thing as truly 'pure' violence" (*Violence and the Sacred*, 40).

29. As D. Douglas Waters notes, the cup held by the whore "was often used in Protestant discussions as a synecdoche for the Mass itself—even in cases in which Protestants attacked Roman Communion in 'one kind'" (*Duessa as Theological Satire*, 65).

The above analyses, in tracing the hidden ironies and errors of Spenser's discourse, and in circling around a problematic of language, are obviously indebted to a variety of post-Nietzschean critical perspectives. But it is more than an a priori philosophical conviction that prompts one to attend to the text's mystifications of origin, its confusion of endings and beginnings, the duplicity of its explanations and justifications, or else leads one to worry about the Romantic habit of imposing organic metaphors on the arbitrary processes of language. For these errors, ambivalences, and impositions are part of the machinery of mythological romance. And whether the poet encounters them in the historical disorder to which he is exiled or as a pathology latent in human expression itself they are dilemmas that he both embraces and attempts to cure.

As a preface to a consideration of Spenser's romance, I have been looking at how his prose dialogue confronts what one might call the mythopoesis of everyday life. I have tried to show how he describes both the structures and the destructive possibilities of the fictions that shape that life. As much as the poem proper (if one can use such a phrase these days), this life is the domain of the imagination. The Renaissance, indeed, never divided imagination from reality, nor saw that faculty at work solely in the sovereign activity of making literature. Imagination intersects with reality at every point; man shapes his life by an intricate texture of fantasies, sometimes conscious, sometimes unconscious. One aspect of this situation has been celebrated as the Renaissance's "rhetorical view of life"; I have tried to suggest the ways in which such a view shades into a darker awareness of man's self-entrapment by his own idols.

"Every individual mind being a kind of labyrinth, it is not wonderful . . . that almost every man has had his own god." If one wanted a map of Calvin's idol-filled labyrinth, the most obvious thinker to appeal to would be Bacon, with his acute sense of the interwoven mystifications embedded in custom, mind, language, and philosophy—the Idols of the Tribe, the Cave, the Marketplace, the Theater.[30] Though he would argue from Nature or Experience, rather than invoking the Word of God, Bacon is at one with Calvin in his uneasy awareness of the complexity of human illusion. However, to extract a fragmentary aphorism from the *Novum Organum* might tell us little more than we already know, unless one were fully prepared to analyze the peculiar taxonomic poetry that makes Bacon's account of his four, secular-

30. These peculiar taxonomic tropes (e.g., the reduction of Plato's cave of metaphysical illusion to the chaotic, private cave of the human mind, the arch identification of language and money in describing the idols of the marketplace, the description of the

ized idols so original. In place of such an analysis, then, I want to risk citing a passage from a later writer, William Hazlitt, who in avoiding either a religious or a philosophical critique of idols may bring us nearer to understanding the most problematic and liminal qualities of a Spenserian poetics of idolatry:

> Man is a poetic animal: and those of us who do not study the principles of poetry, act upon them all our lives, like Molière's *Bourgeois Gentilhomme*, who had always spoken prose without knowing it. The child is a poet in fact, when he first plays at hide-and-seek, or repeats the story of Jack the Giant-killer; the shepherd-boy is a poet, when he first crowns his mistress with a garland of flowers; the countryman, when he stops to look at the rainbow; the city-apprentice, when he gazes after the Lord-Mayor's show; the miser, when he hugs his gold; the courtier, who builds his hopes upon a smile; the savage, who paints his idol with blood; the slave, who worships a tyrant, or the tyrant, who fancies himself a god;—the vain, the ambitious, the proud, the choleric man, the hero and the coward, the beggar and the king, the rich and the poor, the young and the old, all live in a world of their own making; and the poet does no more than describe what all the others think and act. ("On Poetry in General," *Selected Essays*, 387)

From first to last, in his shift from imitative play to obsessive identification, in his ambivalent leveling of all points along this line, Hazlitt speaks from within the tradition of Spenser and is moreover writing a commentary on that tradition. With the possible exception of the countryman looking at the rainbow, every one of Hazlitt's examples has precise analogues in *The Faerie Queene*. The child, though admittedly a creature of Rousseau's, plays and recites according to the aggressive shapes of quest-romance. Looking back on him from the end of the passage, we may wonder whether he creates his play or it creates him, whether he hides or seeks, takes the part of giant or giant-killer, and whether this is innocent sport or potential idolatry (is he Don Quixote or John of Leyden?). The apprentice following the pageant may be Redcrosse at the court of Lucifera, Guyon in Mammon's cave, or Britomart in the House of Busyrane; the shepherd is Calidore or Coridon, the miser Mammon or Malbecco, the courtier Timias, the savage a member of the band of brigands in Book VI, the slaves and tyrants the inhabitants especially of Book V, among whom is Geryoneo, the oppressive ruler who turns his paternity into a blood-

---

world of philosophical theory as a theater) suggest that it is exactly at the critical point where Bacon must mark and attack his four classes of "idols" that he is ironically most what Shelley said he was (a poet), and no mere avatar of a disenchanted, rationalistic universe of atoms, causes, and facts.

stained idol, with a flesh-eating beast hidden beneath it. More important than these particular likenesses, however, is the diffuse, repetitive, and yet pressured movement of the whole passage, a movement that makes all of these forms of imaginative life disturbingly and triumphantly continuous. This continuity, or more precisely, this paratactic muddling of difference—one mode of a writer who would marry the imaginative impulses of criticism, poetry, and experience—is a powerfully jarring force; it conveys an iconoclastic intelligence that suspends or scatters any automatic attempts we might make to apply reductive distinctions to Hazlitt's examples. We may want to moralize and divide, separate true and false representation, split the deceptions of the self from deceptions of others, and expose the kinds of literalized or materialized figuration which poison the poetry of the miser, the slave, the tyrant, and the idolater. But this effort, the writer implicitly warns us, is something that is itself entangled with the possibility of idolatry; it is itself a labyrinthine quest for order which is tracked by anxiety and imagination and which proceeds always "with mazie error under pendant shades."

The moral shock that may arise from my juxtaposition of texts from *A View* is the result not only of recognizing in the picture of the old woman at the execution an ironic inversion of the account of language and education; the slightly less catastrophic communion of nurse and child in the latter passage is as much homologous with as antithetical to the first. Both are visions of the human mind entrapped in natural affections and contaminated by images of its own creation. Both scenes provide a disturbing view of the present state of Ireland and at the same time call into question the efficacy of what should be some sort of corrective discourse. It appears that we can depend neither on the analytic language of the dialogue itself, which seeks to expose the roots of corruption in Ireland, nor on the violent legal machinery of the English, which rather than opening up fresh gaps or establishing more alienating continuities should be setting things in order. Spenser conveys a sense, if not of the hopelessness, then of the sometimes extreme and debilitating moral cost of reform.

I do not mean to impose on these texts any such leveling of significance or value as might emerge from a purely structuralist analysis of their argument and imagery. The account of the execution, especially, may be for the writer as much an act of historical conscience as an attempt at symbolic reduction. As in the case of Spenser's much-quoted discussion of the military uses of contrived starvation—an all-too-real "modest proposal" that calls up sympathetic recollections of earlier famine and cannibalism—Spenser is both testing his human loyalties and straining the limits of his elevated moral perspective on the unreformed, barbarous Irish.[31] We should not, of course, sentimentalize his words. The description of the execution, with its floating spirit of revenge and its crazed witness, might even suggest something about the kind of ambivalent, sado-masochistic pleasure involved in our "sympathy" with a friend's or enemy's suffering. Still, such passages do at least involve Spenser in the labor of breaking down false and easy oppositions, putting partisanship and the hierarchies that generate partisanship on trial. The awareness that, for Spenser as for us, the negative structures of representation are profoundly congruent with the positive, and both are given to similar forms of mystery and usurpation, makes the study even of the pathological forms of mythmaking exemplified in *A View* fruitful rather than reductive. We must contend with the paradox that even the best of human and divine images may transform themselves into agents of death and life-in-death. Luther and Calvin recognized this dilemma when they watched the church that should have scattered the false gods become the very temple of their worship, the embodiment of idolatry. And for Spenser, the mythological poet, it is a situation that cannot be cured by either plugging new significations back into an older typological sign system or by purifying the ground of our belief by an absolute appeal to the bare text of Scripture. Rather, he develops modes of substitution and reduction which are at once more obscure, ambivalent, and liberating.

31. "Although there should none of them fall by the sword, nor be slain by the soldier, yet thus being kept from manurance, and their cattle from running abroad by this hard restraint, *they would quickly consume themselves and devour one another.* The proof whereof I saw sufficiently ensampled in those late wars in Munster, for notwithstanding that the same was a most rich and plentiful country . . . yet ere one year and a half they were brought to such wretchedness, as that any stony heart would have rued the same. Out of every corner of the woods and glens they came creeping forth upon their hands, for their legs could not bear them. *They looked anatomies of death, they spake like ghosts crying out of their graves, they did eat of the dead carrions, happy were they could find them, yea and one another soon after in so much as the very carcasses they spared not to scrape out of their graves.* . . . In short time there were none almost left. . . . Yet sure in all that war there perished not many by the sword, but all by extremity of famine, which they themselves had wrought" (*A View,* 104; emphasis mine). Note the ironic effect of the shift from figurative to literal cannibalism, the latter framed in turn by the extreme metaphors of "anatomies" and ghosts; note also the shifting of responsibility for the situation away from the English intruders and wholly onto the Irish themselves.

PART TWO

The Faerie Queene

3

Dialectics of Idolatry (Orgoglio and Arthur)

The rejection of idolatry meant not the destruction
but the liberation of the images.
Austin Farrer

The Giant

My first text is canto vii, and part of canto viii, from Book I of *The Faerie Queene*. Let me begin by quoting a summary of the narrative by John Ruskin, whose rather moralistic understanding of the plot makes it all the more useful for my own argument (especially because Ruskin, elsewhere a more flexible reader of the poem, knows exactly how reductive he is being and how strenuously he cuts against a critic like Hazlitt's refusal to "meddle with the allegory"):

> The [Redcrosse] knight leaves the house of Pride: Falsehood, [Duessa] pursues him and overtakes him, and finds him by a fountain side, of which the waters are "Dull and slow, / And all that drink thereof do faint and feeble grow." Of which the meaning is, that Godly Fear, after passing through the house of Pride, is exposed to drowsiness and feebleness of watch. . . . The Redcrosse Knight, being overcome with faintness by drinking of the fountain, is thereupon attacked by the giant Orgoglio, overcome, and thrown by him into a dungeon. This Orgoglio is *Orgueil*, or Carnal Pride; not the pride of life, spiritual and subtle, but the common and vulgar pride in the power of this world: and his throwing the Redcrosse Knight into a dungeon is a type of the captivity of true religion under the temporal power of corrupt churches, more especially of the Church of Rome. . . . In the meantime, the dwarf, attendant of the Redcrosse Knight, takes his arms, and finding Una, tells her of the cap-

> tivity of her lord. Una, in the midst of her mourning, meets Prince Arthur, in whom . . . is set forth generally Magnificence; but who . . . is more especially the magnificence, or literally, "great doing," of the kingdom of England. This power of England, going forth with Truth, attacks Orgoglio, or the Pride of Papacy, slays him; strips Duessa, or Falsehood, naked; and liberates the Redcrosse Knight. (*Works*, 11:253)

Here, then is the schematic opposition: Arthur versus Orgoglio, the knight in shining armor fighting the inflated giant, English chivalry and Protestant truth defeating the force of Roman idolatry. That appears to be the way that Spenser has imagined the conflict. Its shape seems as unalterable as that of a fairy tale, and yet the scene might have unfolded otherwise, the dialectics of the allegorical battle strangely changed. The idea of the giant was so reinvented by the Renaissance that Gargantua, a giant of debunking and deflation, an antithetical, anticlerical giant, might have taken Arthur's place in this fight against religious mystery. Indeed, in one pre-Rabelaisian narrative, the giant Gargantua (child of two colossi formed by Merlin from the bones of two whales and relics of Lancelot and Guinevere) actually traveled from France to Britain for the express purpose of helping Arthur, in his guise as King of the Last Days, battle the apocalyptic monsters Gog and Magog.[1] Such a far-fetched story might well have appalled Spenser—who seems to have disliked folktales about giants as much as he distrusted the ideologies of apocalypse—but it may suggest some of the complexity of the literary worlds in which his poem situates itself. Ruskin's summary is a noble, even a canny reduction, but it fixes terms that, as we work through the dense and shifting narrative, appear more fluid. Despite the violence of the conflict, Spenser seems at pains to complicate the straightforward, if apocalyptic dualism to a point of extremest ambivalence. If we try honestly to name it, the danger of Spenser's giant starts to appear hugely uncircumscribed, just as the scope of Arthur's power becomes a little hard to see. Measured by other Renaissance fables, the giant and the knight might even seem likely to change places—Arthur revealing an unsettling, ironic rhetorical energy that links him to the comic reformer Gargantua, while Orgoglio himself may drift closer to the chivalric Don Quixote, endlessly trapped in self-spawned illusion. Of

1. This tale is included in *Les Croniques admirables du puissant Roy Gargantua* (1534), attributed to François Girault; a French text can be found in *The Tale of Gargantua and King Arthur*, ed. Huntington Brown, 4f. The editor points to the popularity of the *Croniques* in Elizabethan England and even speculates that there existed an English translation that has since been lost.

course, there is little of Cervantes's or Rabelais's comedy in the next, and I do not doubt that the poet's impulses are both pious and prophetic: to unfold a "sage and serious" argument about the origins and overthrow of idolatrous pride. Yet Spenser both problematizes the nature of that idolatry, and seems unwilling to define any pure power of demystification to oppose it or to specify any gesture of iconoclasm free of the possibility of error. In canto vii, if anywhere, we see Spenser as an insistently moralizing poet, and yet his narrative proceeds not simply by conceptual, moral, or mythic simplifications but, rather, by strange refinements of contradiction and opacity.

Like Don Quixote and Gargantua, Spenser's knight and giant place in perspective many of the prior forms of literary history.[2] They not only recompose the elements of older stories, they require us to examine in changed ways the "motive for metaphor" and expose many of the arbitrary and idealizing aspects of literary strategies which one might have preferred to consider parts of a stable, rational cosmology of genres, images, ideas. Hence in what follows I treat the two not so much as allegorical representations of Pride and Magnificence, but as exemplars of antithetical, if mutually contaminating, modes of representation itself. Orgoglio interprets for us the poetics of Pride—delusive, idolatrous, catastrophic—while Arthur unfolds the poetics of Magnificence—disillusioning and iconoclastic, but redeeming certain otherwise dangerous literary enchantments. We are at a point where moral and poetic concerns cross: images of morality get involved with the morality of imagemaking, and the allegorical battle becomes a battle about allegory. Asked, "What does the Giant mean?" I could (and shall) generate a variety of answers that may do justice to what one critic has called Spenser's "play of double senses." But for the moment, what I am after is less a pleasant polysemy of hidden meanings than some sense of the dangers that attend the generation of any sense in the poem, and of the darker layerings of skepticism and self-reflexivity which produce the poem's fierce dialectic of surface and depth, image and idea, sense and nonsense.

Some points raised in Chapter 1 need restatement here. Medieval and Renaissance writers often sought a ground for allegory in an au-

2. On the revisionary strategies of Rabelais's and Cervantes's narratives, see Seidel, *Satiric Inheritance*, 60–94. Rosalie Colie, *The Resources of Kind: Genre-Theory in the Renaissance*, 117–18, is also enlightening on the power of a work like *Don Quixote* to assemble, analyze, undermine, and resurrect both the literary and social fictions of chivalry. Colie here and elsewhere makes the point that Renaissance literature often internalizes traditional "kinds" by making single characters into synecdochic figures of larger generic systems or modes of representation, and then setting them against other characters or environments similarly conceived.

thoritative metaphysics or cosmology of correspondences such as would guarantee the internal consistency and truth of allegorical images; they might also insist that allegorical interpretations simply unfolded the stable foundation of scriptural fable, sometimes in the light of such a cosmology. But such justifications are often little better than apologetic fictions and conceal allegory's more disconcerting powers. Certainly, a post-Reformation poet like Spenser is enough of a Nominalist to realize that allegory's aggressive, conceptual rhetoric can create as much as depend on such metaphysics or Scripture, and that such a rhetoric can give us the illusion of an idea's presence in a place where formerly that idea was not. Allegory, I have said, tends to work in the space of illusion and negation. To this degree, Walter Benjamin's observation that allegory signifies "precisely the non-existence of what it presents" (*Origin of German Tragic Drama*, 233) only restates for an apophatic modernism a much older identification of allegory with idolatry. Some such identification, in any case, underlies many sixteenth-century attacks on Scholastic allegory, which made a seeker after fourfold senses of Scripture as much of an idolater as a worshiper of saints' portraits or the transubstantiated host.

Recall the beautiful, enabling metaphor of Augustine and others, which figures reading as an effort to break the hard shell of fable enclosing the nut or spark of meaning. In such cases, Augustine suggests, the text itself may partially blind or confuse readers, humbling them but urging them on in their interpretive labor. Still, we must remember that locating the crucial mystery in the text is in part subject to the unstable will of the interpreter himself. Also, although Augustine may warn the reader against being seduced by the beauties of a text's fabulous surface or the merely historical sense of scriptural narrative, the reader is equally subject to the opposite delusion, namely, that he has access to a definite meaning hidden below the text. This may be in the end a subtler, more dangerous enchantment, for it opens up an abyss of infinite, empty, and possibly self-confuting interpretations, or, alternatively, provides a chance for the power of abstract names or images to fixate the mind (the false allegorist emerging in *On Christian Doctrine* as less a childish literalist than a heretical magus who consorts with seductive demons). It is in this context that one may begin to sense the limitations of Greenblatt's argument that allegory, by always pointing to a level of significance beyond the immediate surface of the text, is inherently nonidolatrous and "abjures all concealment" (*Renaissance Self-Fashioning*, 190). This is only about half the story—though it is that half which the allegorist, with his gesture of unveiling, would have us take for the whole. Allegorical writing, whether exegetical or literary, may break the idolatry of literal reading, but its demystifications tend to bear the burden of further mystery, rationalization, distortion, or lie. Spenser is acutely aware of this duplicity in allegory; if he generally gives up any such ideal safeguards against presumptuous misreading as Augustine's, it may be out of a suspicion that even *caritas* itself may be all too easily narrowed, infected, or institutionalized. At least I would argue that Spenser's willfully protean writing contains a violence against the powerful machinery of allegory which calls into question even such final measures of reading such as might be embodied in the grand but ambiguous figure of the Faerie Queen, Gloriana. In the attempt to combat illusions, the intricate, fantastic surface of Spenser's narrative may be all the more effective in restoring us to our senses—but largely because its eclectic opacity forces us to put off any absolute choices as to the ultimate sense of the allegorical fable. The poet finds a severe burden in the narrative's excess and endlessness, no doubt, one that emerges most clearly in the roving beast of slander whose spoiling of sacred images at the end of Book VI also heralds the end of Spenser's allegorical project and his poem's breaking down under the weight of its own courteous reticence and openness of meaning. The main point for now, however, is to see that Spenser's allegory does not simply unfold a prior scheme of ideas or a privileged system of fables but depends also on its sovereign power of surprise. It turns on its head and fragments the putative *sens morale*, suspending our questions about the relative priority of a myth or a moral.

The question remains, however: How are we to approach the text, assuming that we cannot evade the need to interpret and simplify? My pragmatic suggestion would be that we should not try to speak of a figure like Orgoglio as if he were an integrated philosophical counter or pursue the illusion that there is a coherent typological structure underlying the poet's description. Rather we should start by examining the moment of the giant's emergence itself, the emergency or crisis in the poem's allegorical machinery which gives the play of double senses its urgency.

For instance: going back to canto vii, in the account of Redcrosse Knight's dalliance with Duessa by the pool of Idleness, we can note that the giant does not simply break in on Redcrosse's lovemaking. He is rather a crisis that is oddly continuous with that lovemaking, even the "fulfillment" of it:

> Yet goodly court he made still to his Dame
> Pourd out in loosnesse on the grassy grownd,

Both carelesse of his health, and of his fame:
Till at the last he heard a dreadfull sownd,
Which through the wood loud bellowing, did rebownd,
That all the earth for terrour seemd to shake,
And trees did tremble. Th'Elfe therewith astownd,
Upstarted lightly from his looser make,
And his unready weapons gan in hand to take.

(I. vii.7)

The distinctly apocalyptic tone of the phrase "at the last he heard a dreadfull sownd" led S. K. Heninger, Jr., to see the giant as a figure for eschatological catastrophe, a divine judgment on the representative of lapsed spiritual truth ("The Orgoglio Episode," 128–32). Such a "spiritual" reading can be quite sensibly grafted onto a "physical" one; translated into the landscape, Orgoglio most clearly appears as what Stevens called "a giant of the weather," a mythic figure for an earthquake which shatters the deceptively blended sensations of the *pleasaunce* (out of which Duessa had previously emerged as a kind of insidious *genius loci*). In this way he closely recalls Virgil's Polyphemus, whose cry shakes Mt. Aetna (*Aeneid* III.672–74), just as his genealogy echoes classical and Renaissance theories about the generation of tremors. Still, it may help to recall that Ovid makes of the cyclops an erotic clown, a monstrous grotesque of a pastoral lover who slays his human rival (*Metamorphoses* XIII. 738–897). For at the "literal" level Spenser's narrative suggests that the crisis has a radically more erotic inflection. As a psychosexual or psychopoetic myth, the oppressive giant becomes a figure for the catastrophic and regressive aspects of a moment of sexual communion, its sudden fragmentation of time and consciousness. As a displaced, psychomachic projection of Redcrosse, the giant stands for the inflation of the knight's selfhood and the simultaneous overthrow of his true self; the giant is that force in the knight (ego and id at once) which obliterates the entire world in narcissistic phantasmagoria. Insofar as he is Redcrosse's creature, Orgoglio is also his orgasm (from the Greek, *orgasmos*, swelling or paroxysm) and his erection—that tumescence that is the synecdochic symbol of male sexual pride. And yet he is surely "an erection recollected in anxiety," a mythic figure measured against the consciousness of sin.[3] This arbitrary and fatal giant, the embodiment of idolatrous mystery, is also that involuntary genital motion that Augustine, in one of his most grotesque tropes, made the primary natural sign of man's fall from reason and Grace (*City of God* XIV.23–24).

3. I borrow the phrase in quotation marks from Donald Cheney (personal communication).

D. Douglas Waters and others have made us aware of how much sexual irony could fill Protestant attacks on the Catholic priesthood and its seductive, sacramental magic. Solemn accusations of demonism and witchcraft mingle with bawdy jokes in depictions of "Mistress Missa," the whole complex of images being underwritten by scriptural accounts of idolatry as a kind of spiritual whoredom (*Duessa as Theological Satire,* 1–20, and passim). Some sense of the biblical and satirical sources of Spenser's sexual imagery may then save us from trying to reduce it in an old-fashioned Freudian way. Still, I would think that Spenser is more than usually conscious of the kind of contagious, submerged feelings which such an accusatory religious rhetoric can liberate, and he makes it difficult for us to treat the sexual imagery as a strictly delimited metaphor for a theological or historical conflict. The sexual may be the repressed source of the religious. And yet the surprising violence with which Orgoglio bursts into the flow of the allegorical narrative makes it hard to measure his disruptive power exclusively in terms of either psychological, spiritual, or historical categories—indeed, Orgoglio's muddling of such distinctions may be an aspect of his dangerousness, rather than simply a reflection of the text's polysemy. John W. Shroeder ("Spenser's Erotic Drama") makes an interesting attempt to map out the sexual phases of the conflict through categories drawn from Aristotelian physiology, but there is really no way to reduce the temporal structure of the episode to any "natural" sequence (the imagery of sexual lassitude, for instance, both precedes and follows the phallic giant's advent).[4] Spenser does go on, after the above-quoted stanza, to offer an explicit genealogy for the giant, but his mythic explanation serves mainly to perpetuate the earlier complications—not only because it is unconnected with the immediate situation of Redcrosse but also because Orgoglio's genealogy (his "high descent") is itself subtly ironic:

> The greatest Earth his uncouth mother was,
> And blustring *Aeolus* his boasted sire,
> Who with his breath, which through the world doth pas,
> Her hollow womb did secretly inspire
> And fild her hidden caves with stormie yre,
> That she conceiv'd; and trebling the dew time,
> In which the wombes of women do expire,

4. Cf. Waters, *Duessa as Theological Satire*: "In harmony with the idea that most writers considered yielding to sin as an ironic double point in which one's outward felicity was accompanied by an inward weakness, many of the Protestants felt that spiritual fornication with the Mass culminated in a paradoxical encounter with the sin of pride" (68).

Brought forth this monstrous masse of earthly slime,
Puft up with empty wind, and fild with sinfull crime.

So growen great through arrogant delight,
Of th' high descent, whereof he was yborne. . . .
(I.vii. 9–10)

Here the sexualizing of landscape—such as takes on a more redemptive form in the Garden of Adonis—is the groundwork of chaos. The description indeed begins to recall the nearly parodic mixing of sexual and physiological imagery with theories about the catastrophic genesis of organic life such as we find in the mythicizing psychology of Sandor Ferenczi, especially with respect to the way Spenser thrusts together different phases of the generative process. Here sexual violence and pleasure mime the traumas of both impregnation and birth, sexual tumescence links back to the swellings of pregnancy, while the supernatural emergence of life fulfills itself only in a destructive "expiration." Furthermore, while the account of Pride's regressive or chthonic origins seems aimed at deflating the pretensions of the giant, it yet appears as if the giant's power grows out of his own attempt mythically to master that very genealogy. He is born and grows great through his own arrogant delight in his origins, as if by so identifying and even incorporating himself with them he could be self-generated. But the "Geaunt's" windy birth is at best a travesty of Adamic creation, in which the divine breath filled "red earth"; it is likewise a mocking recollection of the inspiration that comes upon the prophet "like the pangs of a woman in travail" (Isa. 21.3). Such false inspiration furthermore depends on a claim to divine parentage which the poet's words expose as deeply questionable: Earth is his "*uncouth* mother"—not only rough or inchoate but, etymologically speaking, "unknown" ("uncouth" coming from the Old English *uncuþ*, a word that retained its root meaning throughout the sixteenth century, during which time it also could mean "uncanny"); Aeolus is his "*boasted* sire," which is to say perhaps not his father at all but only the function of proud wish. The "blustring" Orgoglio with his "boasted" parent only fathers himself on his own wind, just as he mythologizes a mysterious mother out of his own ignorance of his origins.[5] In this he

5. One may think here of characters in Rabelais who habitually swear "by my paternity," meaning evidently not their ancestors but their own fathering phalluses. The allegorical figure of Pride in Prudentius's *Psychomachia* also makes a great point of displaying her heroic and royal genealogy. Compare, however, the (Protestant?) personification of Pride in Marlowe's *Doctor Faustus*, II.ii.112: "I am Pride. I disdain to have any parents."

resembles Blake's satanic poet or false messiah, building a heavenly home out of what he can steal from the abyss; or Sidney's "maker," who does not "build upon the depth of nature" but is "lifted up with the vigor of his own invention"; or last, Shakespeare's poet, who "gives to airy nothing, / A local habitation and a name . . . Such tricks hath strong imagination." What distinguishes the giant from such a poet, one hopes, is that he cannot be said to know in any degree either himself or his mystifications, since he only *is* his mystifications, nothing more.

In *A View of the Present State of Ireland*, Spenser characterizes native Irish fables about antediluvian giants in a vocabulary ordinarily reserved for idolatry, implicitly identifying the monsters of these fables with the "blind conceit" and "gross imagination" of the storytellers, those who "dream their own imaginations to please themselves" (79). Orgoglio, likewise, is really the catastrophic and illusory tale of his own genesis, or rather, an image of the power gained from the illusion of knowing one's own genesis. We can illuminate these observations, together with the earlier suggestion that Orgoglio is a travesty of "inspiration," by John Guillory's comments on the use of the words "imagination" and "fantasy" during the Renaissance. In that period, he notes, our typical post-Enlightenment opposition between imagination and reality was considerably less crucial than that between imagination and revelation, or human fantasy and divine truth.[6] It is characteristic of the Renaissance that the boundary between the opposed terms tends to wander considerably, as does the relative value placed on each term by different poets and critics. Guillory's most important point, however, is that imagination and inspiration are not simply contrasted as two opposite sources of poetic creation. Rather, the disturbing quality of the imagination, normally conceived of as a mediating faculty that connects sensation and reason by means of mental images, is its power to usurp or obscure the clear place of an inspired source, and so of divine authority. Hence its association in Christian tradition with the destructive "inventions" of heretical dreamers, idolaters, and false prophets. To apply the terms that Guillory borrows from Edward Said, imagination, a natural category that should be capable only of a secular *beginning*, mimics in its images, its claims on mind and desire, the characteristics of a truly atemporal *origin*, but for that very reason calls the place and nature of such an origin into question. For the moment, one can leave to one side Said's neglect of the possibility of a sacred origin within time (a

6. See Guillory, *Poetic Authority: Spenser, Milton, and Literary History*, 11–16, 27–28.

Hebraic or Romantic origin). The main thing is to see that for the Renaissance, imagination may not so much enhance as cut off the sort of poetic authority which can only derive from contact with an inspired origin, whether such contact entails a literal notion of afflatus or the possibility of an interpretive continuity with a sacred text.

What is at stake in this allegorical identification of Orgoglio with the false imagination of origins may become clearer if we contrast the above-quoted lines with the way that Arthur, Orgoglio's princely opponent, encounters his own genealogy. In Book II, canto x, of *The Faerie Queene*, Arthur and Sir Guyon, the Knight of Temperance, find themselves in the chamber of one of Alma's councilors, Eumnestes, a figure who (as opposed to the wilder Phantastes) seems to represent the orderly, retentive power of human memory. In that chamber Guyon reads a history of Fairyland, while Arthur reads at length in a history of Britain. The former text is continuously, even monotonously heroic and fantastic, though it is quite short, ending with an elegant, evasive allegory of the Tudor succession. The latter, however, is long and troubled, reporting acts of folly and betrayal which interrupt the tales of struggle and triumph.[7] Interestingly, whereas Guyon's idealized chronicle moves up to the present historical reign of Gloriana-Elizabeth, Arthur's book is a long fragment that breaks off with the death of Uther, that is, just before it should have reported the reign of the hero who reads it. Thus Arthur does not know or come to know either his own father or his own part in the history he scans:

> Thenceforth *Aurelius* peaceably did rayne,
> Till that through poyson stopped was his breath;
> So now entombed lyes at Stoneheng by the heath.
>
> After him *Uther*, which *Pendragon* hight,
> Succeding There abruptly it did end,
> Without full point, or other Cesure right,
> As if the rest some wicked hand did rend,
> Or th'Authour selfe could not at least attend
> To finish it: that so untimely breach
> The Prince him selfe halfe seemeth to offend,
> Yet secret pleasure did offence empeach,
> And wonder of antiquitie long stopt his speach.
>
> (II. x. 67–68)

7. The best analysis of the two histories is still that of Berger: see his *Allegorical Temper*, 89–114; also Fletcher, *The Prophetic Moment*, 106–21, on Spenser's use of British history as a "typological matrix" for his poem.

Though the poet strangely conceals, or rather tropes his strategy by the opposite possibilities of malice or writerly failure, Spenser himself is of course the one who has intruded this gap into the succession of kingship and narrative—perhaps in order to surprise us into recalling how much his text has doubled one over the other. And yet by breaking continuity and refusing closure, "full point, or other Cesure [Caesar?] right," Spenser prevents any claim that past legend or history might truly coalesce with the present tense of his narrative fiction. This complex gap is more than merely a device for achieving narrative suspense. The textual breach offends the prince's "selfe" by keeping him from the recovery of his paternity, and from the consciousness of his personal and historical fate. Arthur neither knows nor can he exploit his history; but neither can he be exploited by it. The politic breaking of the text prevents the kind of catastrophic overidentification of a self with its genealogical origins such as is apparent in Spenser's account of Orgoglio. Certainly Arthur avoids the sort of hysterical and often questionable search for exalted genealogies (personal, political, ecclesiastical) which ran rampant in Tudor England and in which, ironically, the Arthurian legends themselves played so strong a part. It may be true, as Isabel E. Rathborne has so beautifully argued, that the realm of "Faerie" (a word deriving from the Latin *fatum*) feeds on such idealized forms of dynastic power, and that it presents the coalescence within a single world of past and future images of England's greatness. Spenser's characters could thus be said to move (as she eerily phrases it) in "a mythical land of fame inhabited largely by dead heroes," like the classical Hades or Elysium (*The Meaning of Spenser's Fairyland*, 151). Without attempting to summarize the refinements of Rathborne's theory, we can at least see from the passage I have been considering that such coalescence is far from complete; it is even subject to ruptures created by the poet himself. A grounding in history and a knowledge of our origins may help us to live or to gain power in the world. But the "secret pleasure" (of knowledge? hope? nostalgia?) that Arthur's study provides is not unambiguous, and Spenser conveys a sense that one may read history or compose historical fictions in such a way that the specters of the great dead largely usurp the place of the living or empty out the present moment. Too strong a will toward genealogical continuity may create only a stronger discontinuity or failure in ongoing life, action, and narrative. Some such fate, at least, is hinted at in the last line of stanza 68. There, despite the hovering sense of heroic identification, Arthur's fascination with origins halts the flow of his words, a blockage that by analogy threatens to interrupt the process of the entire poem, of which he is the ideal center. This fear is supported by the disturbing echo of the line "Till that through poyson stopped was his breath" in the closing of stanza 68, "And wonder of antiquitie long stopt his speach"—as if that wonder were a version of sickness or betrayal. In such circumstances, an "untimely breach" may paradoxically rescue time and human life *in* time from the reductive identifications of reading.

The situation of the princely reader, however, is touched with a strange kind of humor. That it is "th'Authour selfe" who controls the uncanny gap between Uther and Arthur is oddly figured in the poet's subtle pun on the word "Authour," here almost a Carrollian "portmanteau" word containing the very names which that author sets apart. Spenser here authors the loss of a text as well as its presence. Indeed, he sets up a paradigm of *auctoritas* (in both literary and genealogical senses) which locates the book's authority in the parabolic undoing of authority—at least insofar as the history's claims upon the imagination are founded on an unbridgeable distance between the reader and the narrative of origins, as much as upon some direct continuity or interchange of power between the two.

I am tempted to read this passage as an ironic warning to critics not to get too caught up in the scholastics of source study. It may also be a reminder that we exist in a world where all real sources are somehow lost or contrived, and that the absence or denial of a source is bound to be as crucial as its presence. The very obliqueness of Spenser's pun may suggest that the poet can compass or control such contingencies only in parable; and yet Spenser's ironic assertion of his authority over the gaps and continuities of Arthurian history *is* justified to the extent that he founds his own account of Arthur on a void in the existing legends. As C. S. Lewis writes, "One feels like answering the letter [to Raleigh] in such terms as the following: 'You say *I chose the historye of king Arthure.* But you didn't. There is no Uther in your poem, nor Mordred, no Launcelot, no wars with the Saxons. It is not the history of Arthur you choose, but the bare name'" (*Spenser's Images of Life*, 137)[8] Lewis's observation is accurate enough, despite such broad exceptions as Spenser's choice of the idea of a chivalric quest cycle, the unstable identification of Britain and its imperial fate with that of Fairyland, and numerous other small details that echo the Arthurian material. Indeed, Spenser's most startling omission (more re-

8. Cf. John Upton, *Spenser's Faerie Queene*, 2:388: "Spenser departs from Jeffry of Monmouth, and the more romance history of Prince Arthur; and indeed from all the stories of our old English writers, in many of the circumstances relating to this British Prince, *that he might make a heroe for his poem, and not a poem for his heroe*" (emphasis mine).

markable than that careful pruning of the monastic and eucharistic symbolism found in the Arthurian Grail legends, a strategy he shares with other Tudor writers) Lewis does not mention at all. For Spenser has not given us *King* Arthur, or the history of a lord in full possession of his royal power; nor does he depict the slain hero whom folklore transmuted into the eschatological ruler of time past and time to come—*quondam rex, rexque futurus*.[9] Rather, we have a prince unmentioned in earlier legends, a lone knight-errant for whom political, genealogical, and erotic possession are always deferred. In this antiapocalyptic fiction, even his promised marriage to Gloriana is set at odds, as I shall argue later on. And yet it is just Spenser's invention of broken histories and deferred romances which accounts for the prince's fatal opposition to the giant Orgoglio, who represents both the delusive exaltation of natural or mythic origins and the usurpation of divine authority by the church of Rome.

Spenser opens up this broader historical dimension in his allegory when, after Orgoglio has dispatched Redcrosse to his dungeon, we get a sudden flood of allusions to the Book of Revelation which identify the giant as the master of idolatries, Antichrist. Orgoglio, the false genealogist, himself an empty fiction, concludes his own delusive romance with the figure of Falsehood by becoming the stage manager of *orgia*, mysterious rites. He sets up Duessa as an erotic and religious idol, the whore "Mystery," her power to fascinate and bind now reinforced by isolation, elevation, and terror:

> From that day forth *Duessa* was his deare,
> And highly honourd in his haughtie eye,
> He gave her gold and purple pall to weare,
> And triple crowne set on her head full hye,
> And her endowd with royall maiestye:
> Then for to make her dreaded more of men,

9. Frank Kermode notes that many Elizabethans wished to see in Arthurian legend not Malory's failing chivalric world but an image of "a unified Britain, and Arthur himself as King of the whole island, which, under the diadem of Constantine, was an empire according to *Leges Anglorum*" (*Shakespeare, Spenser, Donne*, 42), and that official propaganda associated the reign of Elizabeth with the restoration of this early imperial rule. But he also admits that "Spenser's poem throughout maintains a tension between the ideal and the actual, and he knows that the return of the Imperial Virgin, first prophesied for Constantine, has occurred only in a figurative and restricted sense" (49–50). Spenser, indeed, is as interested as Shakespeare in the failures or calcifications of the idea of a sovereign ruler and can present tyrannical empresses or "maiden Queens" like Lucifera (I.iv.8–12), mocking phantoms of Glory like Philotime (II.vii.44–49), as well as splendid incarnations of just rule such as we see in Mercilla (V.ix.27–50).

And peoples harts with awfull terrour tye,
A monstrous beast ybred in filthy fen
He chose, which he had kept long time in darksome den.

. . .

. . . seven great heads out of his body grew,
An yron brest, and backe of scaly bras,
And all embrewd in bloud, his eyes did shine as glas.

His tayle was stretched out in wondrous length,
That to the house of heavenly gods it raught,
And with extorted powre, and borrow'd strength,
The ever-burning lamps from thence it brought,
And prowdly threw to ground, as things of nought;
And underneath his filthy feet did tread
The sacred things, and holy heasts foretaught.
Upon this dreadfull Beast, with sevenfold head
He set the false *Duessa*, for more aw and dread.

(I.vii.16–18)

The Church is here, as Protestants claimed, a church robber, a *sacrilegus*.[10] For idolatry is sacrilege pretending to the status of the sacred; it has no proper power of its own but feeds on the death of other gods, steals from other revelations, and raises itself on the ruins of other ceremonies. Idolatry, paradoxically, is iconoclastic, but it does not therefore approach the demystifying work of iconoclasm. Orgoglio, like the leveling Anabaptist giant of Book v and the despoiling Blatant Beast, is a deceived and deceiving travesty of an inspired iconoclasm. His breaking of images is the breeding ground of oppressive mystery.[11]

Such an equivocation of sacred categories is partly a reflection of the poetic and historical crisis that Spenser explores in this canto; he is trying both to represent and dissect a situation in which matters of mystery and revelation become confusingly intertwined. Here I

10. Kermode notes that John Jewel "specifically calls the Roman hierarchy *sacrilegos*, which is in the contemporary translation 'church robbers', for refusing the laity the wine at communion" (*Shakespeare, Spenser, Donne*, 47), adding however that a variety of crimes like simony, absenteeism, idolatrous ornament, and so on—indeed the whole structure of usurped authority—made the church into a church robber.

11. Though different from Spenser's vision of the "iconoclastic idolater," the following lines from an anonymous Netherlandish reformer may suggest a similar irony in Protestant depictions of Roman idol worship: "They have against the express commandment of God, erected an infinity of beautiful images, paintings, and statues, gilded . . . like whores. . . . Finally, to sustain such an enormity by force, *they have burned the true and living images of God, living men, in order to make sacrifices to their images and dead idols*." The text is cited by Phyllis Mack Crew, *Calvinist Preaching and Iconoclasm in the Netherlands: 1544–1569*, 23 (emphasis mine).

must revise my too negative formulation that Spenser is an "antiapocalyptic" writer. Obviously, the poet has taken over the types of Whore, Beast, and Antichrist in order to give the allegorical conflict a dramatic shape. Yet though he appropriates the imagery, he does not naively claim the historical authority of apocalyptic. He raises millennial suspicions, as Joseph Anthony Wittreich, Jr., notes only to exorcise them (*Visionary Poetics*, 74); he undertakes the apocalyptic work of "unveiling" the visionary shapes of the present moment, yet he absorbs those shapes within a more complex poetic reflection. The kind of popular satirical or devotional emblems which sixteenth-century writers drew from the Book of Revelation—as exemplified by the woodcuts that illustrated Spenser's own early translations for *A Theatre for Worldlings*—do form the schematic armature of the episode analyzed above. Its immediate connection to the iconography of contemporary sectarian conflicts is indeed one of the things which helps give Spenser's scriptural archetypes "a context of Virgilian security," as Kermode argues (*Shakespeare, Spenser, Donne,* 22). The problem remains, however, that the apocalyptic images of the period are as much Spenser's subject as his source; he does not simply embellish them, he reimagines them from the inside.

Orgoglio, for instance, develops as we read about him from an earthly, psychosexual power into the biblical type of absolute idolatry. Despite the retrospective force of this type, one may plausibly wonder whether Spenser implicitly subjects the biblical image to origins that such a fixed, divinely revealed character should properly transcend. He at least makes it difficult (despite the obvious quantity of scriptural allusions) to locate clearly the point where, as Berger suggests, the text moves "from projection to apocalypse," from subjective to objective, from human psychomachia to divinely revealed types ("Book I: Prelude to Interpretation," 32). To inquire in this way about Orgoglio's human or natural "origin" may seem to confuse questions about the evolution of a poetic representation with questions about how the poet represents the evolution of evil. But the two problems are deeply intertwined here, especially since Spenser links the power of Orgoglio to the work of the imagination. Spenser is not Blake, of course, and he does not insist that we read all myths of divine or demonic being as the work of the poetic imagination (even in the case of those myths according to which we give demonic motives to the forms of human error). The poet actually attempts no final account of the giant in the context of either human or demonic origins. Instead, by entangling the scriptural imagery with so many alternative myths, as well as by presenting an ironic account of the giant's birth, the poet throws into question any singular pattern or sequence of forms by which we might contain the explosive array of allusions. What Berger might call the "evolutionary" shape of the narrative—its mingling of primitive and sophisticated types of idolatrous imagination, its generative linking of meteorological, sexual, political, and spiritual violence—thus actually possesses something like the critical force of a Nietzschean "genealogy," for its stark dialectical forms help undermine rather than confirm the authority of our cultural myths of origin.

Spenser's tactics do *not* simply grow out of a sense that any attempts to construct a true story of origins are epistemologically suspect. The more urgent problem is that, for all their probable falseness, such myths continue to possess an immense, catastrophic power of persuasion. To understand the force of Spenser's allegory here, we must see that Orgoglio is more than simply one actor in a larger apocalyptic drama. Rather, the giant is an apocalypse in his own right or, more precisely, a usurping reduction and grotesque synecdoche for the idea of apocalyptic revelation, Spenser's image of the part fancying itself to be the whole. Fittingly, Orgoglio interprets for us the institution that conceived of itself as both Incarnation and apocalypse, and that converted its own invented doctrines, laws, and rituals into the revealed antitypes or fulfillments of Scripture. But such fulfillments are in this case only instances of proud inflation, and Orgoglio's divinity only a delusive "enthusiasm" (literally, "having a god within").[12] The giant thus becomes an emblem of the tyrannical or idolatrous wisdom that presumes itself capable of comprehensively determining truth, of saying what is Letter and what Spirit, what veiled and what unveiled, what idolatry and what iconoclasm.

The Knight

Orgoglio is not bound, buried, or obliterated as Satan or Antichrist might be but simply and literally deflated. Our final vision of him is as a kind of punctured balloon. To fully understand this dramatic allegory for the undoing of idolatry, however, we must turn to the hero who accomplishes that work. Arthur enters canto viii in the guise of the Knight True and Faithful, sounding a horn that brings down the

12. Ebeling (*Luther*, 108–9) points out that reformers could describe as "enthusiasm" both the excesses of sectarian Protestants and the divinized fantasies of the Roman church, and cites a passage of Luther's which identifies enthusiasm with original sin, heresy, and idolatry: "To sum up, enthusiasm lurks in Adam and his children from the beginning up to the end of the world, as a poison placed in them by the ancient serpent, and it is the source, power and might of all heresy, including that of the papacy and of Mahomet" (109).

gate of the evil city, defeating Antichrist, the seven-headed Beast, and stripping the whore Babylon. Elizabethan readers, brought up on Bale's *Image of Both Churches* and Foxe's *Acts and Monuments,* would have been prepared to see in the text an allegory of English imperial power, charged with the burden of providential history, avenging the Protestant martyrs and rescuing the primitive purity of the English church from its captivity to Roman oppression. Still, the agency is somewhat hard to fix, and the conflict reaches its climax in a curiously negative moment: the giant himself is the one who uncovers the prince's disenchanting shield with a blow of his own club, as if Spenser thought it best to represent the overdetermined providence of God only by this extreme trick of ironic accidence and poetic justice. The apocalyptic patterning of the episode is stark, but Spenser's radical image of Arthur's power entails as much a reduction as it does a final clarification of the knight's character as described in the previous canto. *This* Arthur (on whom I will concentrate here) Spenser insistently interposes between the epiphany of Duessa and the rescue of Redcrosse. A strange pendant to the immense figure of Orgoglio, this Arthur first appears as an unnamed quester, blazoned with stars, jewels, and plumes, with an intricate, intellectual ornamentation whose sublime, Homeric panache would have made Wallace Stevens weep. The poet's extended formal description strives for a severe yet magnificent eloquence of the sort that Erasmus called *copia* or copiousness, as if by a kind of stylistic magic Spenser might cast out the tumidity and tyrannical *opsis* of Orgoglio (whose own plenty is ultimately a form of poverty and bathos).[13] Yet through all this gorgeousness, Spenser in his description raises urgent questions about

13. On this point, cf. Nohrnberg, *The Analogy of "The Faerie Queene,"* 50f. I cannot enter here into the debates about Arthur's fitness as the avatar of Magnificence. Hugh MacLachlan, "'In the Person of Prince Arthur': Spenserian *Magnificence* and the Ciceronian Tradition," summarizes the problem in some detail, like most critics emphasizing the moral and spiritual meanings of *magnificentia* ("great doing," a somewhat problematic translation of the original Aristotelian word *megaloprepeia*), and its close relation to the more typically heroic virtue of *magnanimitas* ("greatness of soul"). I would only suggest that Aristotle's own rather Mammonish or elitist definition of magnificence as "the proper display of riches in the pursuit of glory" also fits Spenser's purposes—though he presents us with a decorous, demystifying richesse, an allegorical artifice "made in lieu of many ornaments," rather than with the lesser magnificence available to mere wealth. (One might surmise in this context that Berger's splendid rubric for Spenser's style—"conspicuous irrelevance," a quality that is illustrated most fully by the description of Arthur—is an ironic appropriation of Thorstein Veblen's idea of "conspicuous consumption.") Ripa, by the way, though he considers Magnificence primarily a public, imperial virtue, associates it as much with poetic decorum as with simple grandeur; it stands for that power to fit outward gesture to deed and word without which the works of Magnificence would be "works of vanity, and mere madness" (*Iconologia*, 322; translation mine).

the power of human imagemaking. It is by admitting such questions, rather than by leaping directly into the more exclusive, absolute patterns of moral and figurative opposition which usually characterize the apocalyptic mode, that the poet works out his larger attack on the complex evil of Orgoglio.

Let me add that this odd uncertainty or reversal of expectation in the poet's treatment of final things is signaled throughout Book I. My remarks on Orgoglio as a usurping image of apocalypse may suggest one such signal, as perhaps may the fact that Spenser locates Arthur's fight with the giant conspicuously "in the middest" of things. A shrewd, archetypal critic such as Nohrnberg is correct to displace his account of this fight to the very end of his chapter on Book I, but this placement should itself remind us that the actual final battle of the book develops more clearly around a sacramental rather than an apocalyptic typology. There is a final tree and a final fountain of living waters in the New Jerusalem of Saint John's vision, but in that vision they are things won by redeemed souls after the battle rather than the agents that heal the hero during its progress. And when that battle is over in Spenser, the marriage of Una and Redcrosse, necessary to restore completely the captive Kingdom of Eden, is itself delayed. Book I's Eden of the end becomes, if not the original Eden of loss, then, strangely, an Eden of deferral, even while the interrupted marriage foreshadows all later deferrals in the poem.[14] The ending becomes a type of nonfulfillment (a paradox worked out more strangely in Book II, where it is an Edenic garden and not the dragon blocking it which needs to be destroyed). Spenser further reworks his biblical source by splitting apart the stark apocalyptic trope in which Jerusalem is *both* city and bride (Rev. 21.2, 9–10). He ultimately realigns the two goals, of course, and there is a sense in which, as Frye suggests, the defeat of the dragon is as much a means of gaining the heavenly city glimpsed from the Mount of Contemplation as it is a way of winning Una (*Anatomy*, 204). Still, this closing violence bridges no gaps between Redcrosse and Jerusalem—his agonistic, eroticized quest being fundamentally different from the nonsexual, ascetic, and passively visionary labors of the Hermit who shows him that Pisgah sight. Yet the "intervals and interstices" that Spenser opens up are not just located between clearly temporal or eternal perspectives, or between contemplative and active forms of devotion. Rather, we have a

14. For a discussion of delay and deferral as techniques in Spenser's narratives—one that strangely and elegantly grafts Derrida's theories of linguistic *différence* onto the archetypal poetics of Frye—see Patricia Parker, *Inescapable Romance: Studies in the Poetics of a Mode*, 54–77.

play of alternative *topoi* disposed so as to confuse any such traditional, rationalistic distinctions. Hence, for example, though on the mount it seems clear that Redcrosse's task is to "turne againe" from contemplative ideals to "earthly conquests," this opposition may yet turn back on itself; at the beginning of canto xi Spenser pointedly dismisses the military, Virgilian, imperial voices of his muse, so that it seems as if his story of the lone fight of one godly man in spiritual armor might after all be taking place in the head of the Hermit.

This reading suggests some support for Wittreich's contention that Spenser, while he denies any simple millennial claims, presents us with an apocalypse of mind; he displaces the struggles for revelation downward and inward within the reflective soul of individual humans caught in history (*Visionary Poetics*, 71–72). Still, just as the poet allows the "figures of the great apocalypse" to become a radical opening rather than a final measure for all later fictions in his poem,[15] he refuses to locate his fables clearly in either a mental, historical, or metaphysical space—as if the Protestant ideal of "internalization" were itself a potential illusion, an overestimation of the self's stability. Here as elsewhere, the poet seems to invest as much imaginative energy in his evasions of and substitutions for apocalypse as in any account of final revelation itself. It is in order to account for this investment that I need to hover at length over the peculiar figurative stresses of those stanzas preceding the mediate apocalypse of canto viii, stanzas which introduce the complex presence of the prince:

> At last she chaunced by good hap to meet
> A goodly knight, faire marching by the way
> Together with his Squire, arayed meet:
> His glitterand armour shined farre away,
> Like glauncing light of *Phoebus* brighest ray;
> From top to toe no place appeared bare,
> That deadly dint of steele endanger may:
> Athwart his brest a bauldrick brave he ware,
> That shynd, like twinkling stars, with stons most pretious rare.
>
> And in the midst thereof one pretious stone
> Of wondrous worth, and eke of wondrous mights,

15. A structural paradox lies concealed in Spenser's having placed the Legend of Holiness at the beginning of his epic cycle. Inevitable as it now seems to us, he thereby turns the machinery of typology on its head, or at least abandons one of its characteristic strengths. For he all but exhausts at the outset of his poem a symbolic language whose authority depends upon its being unfolded in the very last book of Scripture. This is not to suggest that there are no scriptural allusions in later episodes. But those that do exist are often hidden and strangely leveled with images drawn from other mythic "matrices" (to use Fletcher's term).

Shapt like a Ladies head, exceeding shone,
Like *Hesperus* emongst the lesser lights,
And strove for to amaze the weaker sights. . .

. . .

His haughtie helmet, horrid all with gold,
Both glorious brightnesse, and great terrour bred;
For all the crest a Dragon did enfold
With greedie pawes, and over all did spred
His golden wings: his dreadfull hideous hed
Close couched on the bever, seem'd to throw
From flaming mouth bright sparkles fierie red,
That suddeine horror to faint harts did show;
And scaly tayle was stretcht adowne his backe full low.

Upon the top of all his loftie crest,
A bunch of haires discolourd diversly,
With sprincled pearle, and gold full richly drest,
Did shake, and seem'd to daunce for iollity,
Like to an Almond tree ymounted hye
On top of greene *Selinis* all alone,
With blossomes brave bedecked daintily;
Whose tender locks do tremble every one
At every little breath, that under heaven is blowne.

(I. vii.29–32)

The "conspicuous irrelevance" of the description forces us to pause in our reading and holds the prince back for a moment from the rigid constraints of a narrative function or a precise name; we may thus feel even in these lines the sense of latent or deferred power that characterized the person of Arthur in relation to his genealogy. For example the "pretious stone," shaped like a lady's head in the center of the knight's baldric, though in some senses a magical amulet, a thing possessed for the sake of identity and defense, primarily focuses a further desire for possession within both an earthly and an astral realm (the jewel being "like *Hesperus* emongst the lesser lights" [I.vii.30]). As an image mediating past dream with future hope, the centered stone is part of what allows Arthur, as Cheney eloquently puts it, "to move with confidence in the memory of a vision pledged with the pressed grass of waking experience" (*Spenser's Image of Nature*, 70)[16] And yet, as

16. Like many heraldic emblems, Arthur's ornaments define desire as much as fixed character, something lost or quested for as well as a thing possessed or conquered. One may cite in this regard the successive definitions that John Florio gives to the word *impresa* in his *New World of Words* (1611): "An attempt, an enterprise, an undertaking. Also an impresse, a word, a mot or emblem. Also a jewell, worne in ones hat, with some devise in it." Quoted by D. J. Gordon, *The Renaissance Imagination*, 16.

critics have noted, in the description's moving pause the emblems of royalty, grace, election, and love which Arthur bears are mixed with disturbing memories of falsehood and pride. The armor glitters with a light like Lucifera and her palace; the gorgeous, red-gold dragon on Arthur's "haughtie" helmet—with its "greedie pawes" and knotted tail—both recalls Orgoglio's tyrannical beast and anticipates the final opponent of Redcrosse in canto xi. The "trembling leaves" of stanza 32 oddly recall those of Fradubio's woody prison, while the "bunch of haires discolourd diversly" on Arthur's helm exactly matches that which crowned the helmet worn by the evil enchanter Archimago when he disguised himself as Redcrosse. We might take this last instance of mirroring as being more a comment about allegorical imagery in general than about pride per se, a sly reminder of the diverse colorations and discolorations of which poetic discourse is capable apart from any set of fixed moral equivalents. But the general accumulation of prideful parallels is still unarguable. Christopher Marlowe, indeed, was enough impressed by the risky magnificence of the lines that he broke his usual habit of stealing from Spenser only descriptions of monsters like Lucifera, Orgoglio, and Mammon, and appropriated the almond tree stanza for his own heroic destroyer Tamburlaine:

> I'll ride in golden armour like the sun,
> And in my helm a triple plume shall spring,
> Spangled with diamonds, dancing in the air,
> To note me emperor of the three-fold world;
> Like to an almond-tree ymounted high
> Upon the lofty and celestial mount
> Of ever-green Selinus. . .
> *Tamburlaine*, Part Two, IV.iv.115–21)[17]

Marlowe piles up the details with a little more extravagance than Spenser, and adds his own touch of strange, synecdochic eroticism in a later line about the tree's having "blooms more white than Erycina's brow." But the large difference lies in his having given Spenser's words to Tamburlaine himself, for whom they are a prophetic vision of his own cosmic triumph (perhaps also the triumph of Marlowe's hyperboles over the threat of bathos and reductive moralization). What A. D. Hope calls Marlowe's "argument of arms"—the aggressive

17. See Roy W. Battenhouse, *Marlow's 'Tamburlaine': A Study in Renaissance Moral Philosophy*, 178–92, for a survey of the dramatist's borrowings from Spenser, especially his appropriation of allegorical images of destructive pride and greed.

identification of erotic, military, and poetic power which makes up the "magnanimity" of the hero (*The Cave and the Spring*, 117f.)—in Spenser takes the form of something more latent, more virtual if not more virtuous. In its original context the imagery composes a less catastrophic, less egoistic, and perhaps more subtly estranged vision of Arthur's power.[18] Now it might be argued that Arthur's triumph over the giant originates exactly in this sense of suspended fulfillment and in his ability to master the trappings of pride into a more articulate and balanced whole. But this reading may be little more than a moralistic idealization, a projection of the poet's aesthetic achievement onto the implied moral character of Arthur. Even if we accept it as a persuasive illusion of the allegorical discourse, it should not blind us to less easily rationalized ironies in the poet's imagery, especially those that engage the variegated problem of idolatry.

I want here to discuss two of Arthur's emblems, the dragon crest and the mirror shield. Aside from its internal parallels, the former recalls the violently beautiful chimera on the helmet of Turnus (*Aeneid* VII.785) from which also derives the crest of Tasso's Soldan (*Gerusalemme liberata* IX. 25). The figure also harks back to the heraldic dragon that Geoffrey of Monmouth said was inscribed on Arthur's helmet, memorializing his father Uther Pendragon (Hamilton, *Annotated "Faerie Queene,"* 103). Still, it is not the helmet's intricate allusive paternity that I want to focus on here but the dragon's power to fascinate. The creature is artificial and yet described as alive; the poet's words draw our attention both to the image proper and to the way viewers respond to it, how it "breeds" great terror and "shows" sudden horror. We thus witness a relation as much as see an image. In so concentrating on the dilemmas of vision, the deepest "source" that Spenser's text unfolds may be the etymological root of "dragon" itself, a word that comes from the Greek for "watcher": "*Drakon*, the snake, whose name is derived from *derkesthai*, owes his designation to the uncanny glint in his eye. He is called 'the seeing one', not because he can see particularly well . . . but because his stare commands attention. By the same token, Homer's *derkesthai* refers not so much to the function of the eye as to its gleam as noticed by someone else. The verb is used of the Gorgon whose glance incites terror, and of the raging boar whose eyes radiate fire" (Snell, *The Discovery of the Mind*, 2).

Of the Gorgon I will say more shortly. The point to make now about Arthur's dragon is that its power of visual fascination remains

18. For an oblique but powerful commentary on Spenser's image of the hero, and on the florid, visionary headgear that is at once expression, defense, and infection, see Wallace Stevens's "The Pastor Caballero" (*Collected Poems*, 379).

at once emphatic and oddly undirected. Its optical pull is not appropriated (as in the case of Duessa placed on the back of the Beast) to reinforce the mystery of pride, nor does the dragon's tail trap a struggling knight or drag down astral beings. The dragon's *enargeia*—his sensuous vividness—comes not from a naive pictorialism but from a mythicizing and a thematizing of the dynamics of looking, of seeing. Indeed, the description calls up the form of reflexive vision Benjamin called the "aura"—a quality that depends on our ability to invest an object with the ability to look at us in return. Spenser then would be attempting to shape our relation to his text and its images in a way that would produce the opposite of a static, blank, idolatrous seeing. Of course, from another angle it might be argued that for the poet to convert the unseeing image or artifact (even through trope) into a figure that somehow sees, fascinates, and desires us may be exactly to court that illusion of animation which would feed idolatry. But that the poet should have located this emblem of his chief hero at a threshold where magical vision cannot quite be distinguished from idolatry, or a proper image of the knight's self separated from the manifestations of a power beyond that self, is part of the dragon's peculiar, perversely clarifying force. In the long run, this allegorical watcher constitutes a talismanic defense against the reductions (the "evil eye") of allegorical reading—a paradox that is explored even more fully in the astonishing stanzas describing Arthur's chief weapon, his shield.

The shield is framed "all of Diamond perfect pure and cleene," unpierceable but closely covered with a veil:

> The same to wight he never wont disclose,
>   But when as monsters huge he would dismay,
>   Or daunt unequall armies of his foes,
>   Or when the flying heavens he would affray;
>   For so exceeding shone his glistring ray,
>   That *Phoebus* golden face it did attaint,
>   As when a cloud his beames doth over-lay;
>   And silver *Cynthia* wexed pale and faint,
> As when her face is stayned with magicke arts constraint.
>
> No magicke arts hereof had any might,
>   Nor bloudie wordes of bold Enchaunters call,
>   But all that was not such, as seemd in sight,
>   Before that shield did fade, and suddeine fall:
>   And when him list the raskall routes appall,
>   Men into stones therewith he could transmew,
>   And stones to dust, and dust to nought at all;

And when him list the prouder lookes subdew,
He would them gazing blind, or turne to other hew.

Ne let it seeme, that credence this exceedes,
For he that made the same, was knowne right well
To have done much more admirable deedes.
It Merlin was, which whylome did excell
All living wightes in might of magicke spell. . . .
(I.vii.34–36)

In canto viii, Orgoglio "reads his end" in that shield when he himself strikes off its covering veil. The irony and accidence of that moment may indicate both the peculiarly gratuitous quality of God's disenchanting revelation and the huge contingency and self-destroying negativity of the idolatrous power figured in Orgoglio. The moment is framed in such a way that one cannot quite distinguish the work of chance from the work of Providence, much less locate its agency properly in Arthur himself. In canto vii, however, even more maddening paradoxes present themselves, particularly if we seek a limiting or demystifying definition of the shield's fictive magic. For we can neither see in it the purely "marvellous" machinery of romance, nor take it as the agency of wholly superhuman power, nor rationalize its magic as metaphor and so convert it into a serviceable vehicle for religious or moral allegory.

Spenser willfully and systematically confuses our sense of the shield's magic in at least three ways. First, the poet's explicit references to "magic" by turns assert and undermine any clear pattern of opposition between the magic of the shield and all other magic, or between magic and countermagic. Thus, the simile ending stanza 34 associates its power with a magical influence over heavenly bodies, "As when [the moon's] face is stayned with magicke arts constraint." Yet the very first line of the next stanza calls into question the scope of that simile, and hence the scope of magic, for it asserts categorically that "No magicke arts hereof had any might, / Nor bloudie wordes of bold Enchaunters call"—suggesting that the shield is not only unaffected by magic but also, perhaps, not dependent on it at all. One momentary reaction to the second assertion might be for us to cast away our initial assumptions about the shield's magic power. But the fiction of magic quickly returns, and more strongly, when the shield's power is "explained" as being a creation of Merlin. This reference feeds the genealogy of the shield back into the larger Arthurian background of the poem. And yet its explicit purpose is to provide the shield with more historical credibility rather than with greater literary resonance: "Ne let it seeme, that credence this exceedes, / For he that made the same, was knowne right well / To have done much more admirable deedes." That is, the narrative offers to justify its fiction in an almost empirical manner and then "conducts its explanation by a series of statements which require fresh suspensions of disbelief" (Alpers, *Poetry of "The Faerie Queene,"* 178), supporting one palpable fiction by another. Against this interweaving of fictive coverings, how does one read the power of the unveiled shield to make fade and fall "all that was not such, as seemd in sight?"

Setting aside, for the moment, these Ariostan subtleties of self-reference, we can also note elements of uncanny, chthonic, or prideful magic contaminating the shield's purer, purifying powers. At issue is not simply the fact that Arthur bears the emblems of pride but that he imitates its actions. For in stanza 34 especially, the prince takes on the guise of a rebellious enchanter doing war with the gods of the sky. Most disturbingly, he turns against "silver *Cynthia,*" the moon goddess who is often associated with Elizabeth herself. Spenser here recalls the description of Turnus "frightening the heaven with his weapons" (*Aeneid* XI.351), but, more significantly, he echoes Medea's invocation of Hecate in Book VII of Ovid's *Metamorphoses*:

> By charmes I raise and lay the windes, and burst the Vipers jaw.
> And from the bowels of the Earth both stones and trees doe draw.
> Whole woods and Forestes I remove: I make the Mountaines shake,
> And even the Earth it selfe to grone and fearfully to quake.
> I call up dead men from their graves: and thee O lightsome Moone
> I darken oft, though beaten brasse abate thy perill soone.
> Our Sorcerie dimmes the Morning faire, and darkes the Sun at Noone.
> The flaming breath of firie Bulles ye quenched for my sake
> And caused their unwieldie neckes the bended yoke to take.
> Among the Earthbred brothers you a mortall war did set
> And brought asleepe the Dragon fell whose eyes were never shet. . . .
> Now have I neede of herbes that can by vertue of their juice
> To flowring prime of lustie youth old withred age reduce.
>
> (271–85, Golding trans.)

I quote at length from this passage—which also forms a major source for Prospero's address to his self-dissolving enchantment at the end of *The Tempest*—to remind the reader of the fundamental ambiguity and lack of clear moral distinctions in pagan magic. Medea's words interweave images of binding and unbinding, destruction and resurrection, titanic rebellion and Olympian control. They depend on a sovereign confusion as to the intentionality and scope of the daemonic order. It is this confusion rather than any definitive evil that makes pagan magic so powerful a threat to the ideally dualistic order of Christian tradition. Spenser has doubtless modulated the transgressive force of such magic here. The idea of rejuvenation (a grim, violent business in Ovid's story of Aeson) is displaced onto the almond tree simile, with its recollections of Joseph's flowering rod; the shield also has little to do with necromancy, except perhaps at the level of literary history. Finally, it might be said that Arthur's shield manages to sublimate, even if it cannot quite absorb, the sense of darkly sexual, feminine power—generative and destructive—suggested by Ovid's text. Nevertheless, enough of the original Medean enchantment remains in the shield to unsettle any attempts we might make to cure the weapon of its strange infections.

That sexual, spiritual, and political impulses should intersect in so symbolically charged a figure as Arthur should not surprise us. To the degree that he is Gloriana's knight, it might help to reflect on Yates's studies of the carefully wrought overlapping of sacred and secular images in Elizabethan royal iconography, a strategy that diffused and intensified the affective power of the throne while hiding from view many of the internal conflicts of Elizabeth's reign (*Astraea*, 86–87). The ambiguous weapon might also answer to something uncertain in Spenser's own situation. Thinking of the ambitious, alienated prophet-poet, a man cut off from the patronage of the throne that he so aggressively celebrates, a minor functionary in a troubled colony, an exile strangely in sympathy with Ireland and its disorderly natives—thinking of such a writer, one could argue that in the fantasy of such a shield as Arthur's, with its power to control, violate, and rebel, he found a figure to accommodate both his desires and his frustrations, even at the cost of considerable repression. If I hold back from privileging either concealed personal or political motives, it is primarily because such a move would tend to blur the poised and conscious paradoxes of Spenser's imagery. In particular, even given the sense of hidden energies, repressions, and conflicting desires which hovers around the shield, we need to ask: what can be made of a text that articulates its intricate mystifications of reference at the very moment when it seems most passionately to cling to an image of total demystification?

For the great difficulty of the shield is that it both illuminates and blinds, that it marks and simultaneously confuses the threshold between mystery and clarity, between mediated and unmediated revelation, and mocks any simpler myths of their difference. The shield is a power that the text seems to claim for itself and its hero, even in the process of making that power inaccessible, something both inside and outside the poem. Despite its apparent ability to undo false appearances, the shield evades formal or conceptual limitation. It not only destroys idolatry but also turns men to stones and statues or else annuls them entirely. Now some such power, Calvin or Isaiah might insist, is in the Word of God, but it is at some risk that we give the shield such a prior, external "source"—either in a doctrinal ideal or in the Bible's own tropes of ambivalent, superhuman power.[19] One could with as much justice suggest that Spenser invites us to turn his tropes back on the poem and so claim that it is really the *text* that is the shield (an identification implicit in many critical accounts of the weapon, though usually made with too untroubled a sense of what such a move entails). One might argue then that the poet's shifting account of the shield's power to metamorphose, obliterate, and blind works mainly to fragment the text's clarity of reference, to destabilize, blind, and humble the reader's "prouder lookes" by forcing him to confront the impenetrable ambiguities of the narrative surface. The text as mirror-shield defensively turns our narcissistic will to interpret back on itself, asking us to reflect on our own hermeneutic presumptions and presuppositions; it petrifies us in our quest for meaning and yet makes us all the more conscious of our susceptibility to the colors or shapes of rhetoric: "He would them gazing blind, and turn to other hew." In the end, to discover such ironic self-reference in the text is no less allegorical a strategy than any other, but it has this advantage for the moment: It suggests the way in which the figure of the shield lets Spenser make myths about the power—or desired power—of his own writing and yet gives him a tool to combat some of the illusions or diseases that such myths tend to foster, especially the illusion that there is some ultimate clarity which the allegorical text by itself could provide. Spenser thus teaches us to view skeptically even his own myths of demystification, his own stories of unveiling and iconoclasm, and, by extension, those of a whole religious tradition. To put it more simply, the shield defeats the Orgoglio in us which seeks a final meaning behind the text's bright, dark, reflective surface, or would reify its unsettled and unsettling tropes into a fixed iconic symbol or a fixed violence against the symbol.

Part of my aim in thus throwing the shield into perspective is to exhaust the will toward interpretation, to complicate all exclusive

19. Spenser's hyperbolical imagery of petrification, transformation, and annihilation recalls the sort of magical power Calvin finds in the utterances of Jehovah, who "is often said to blind and harden the reprobate, to turn, incline, and impel their hearts" (*Institutes*, II.iv.3), God's Word being able both to curse and cure, to break and reinforce the blindness of idolatry.

choices. Still, the project may seem to take too far the advice of Irving Massey that we must practice interpretation "not because we have not yet understood a work, but in spite of having 'understood' it, to reaffirm its opacity, to put it back into nonsense" (*The Gaping Pig*, 90). We may end up like Aeneas gazing at the shield of Vulcan, fascinated by the images but ignorant of their prophetic meaning. By way of closure then, let me offer a more scholarly speculation on the shield's origins, which may at least give a mythic center to some of the paradoxes mapped out above.

We know that the shield's most immediate source is the shield of the wizard Atalante in *Orlando Furioso*, a weapon used to defeat the hapless knights whom he traps in his enchanted castle (II.54–56). Similarly able to blind or stupefy those who look at it—though useless against those like Bradamante who wear Atalante's own magic ring (III.67–70)—the shield plays a part in a variety of comic and heroic encounters. Recovered and ultimately buried by Ruggiero, the shield is only one of an array of magical objects, such as the wizard's book of spells and his Hippogriff, all of which serve the poet as instruments of miraculous ironies, as tools for weaving, unweaving, and disjointing the complex plot structures of his romance. Haphazard and fantastic, sometimes defeating fraud and sometimes aiding it, the shield might be read as a figure for the uncertain motives of Ariostan poetry in general and of the romantic *eros* it satirizes.[20] Some early commentators may have been correct in taking it as an allegory of human trumpery and illusion; in any case, it is wholly characteristic of Spenser to take over such an Ariostan prop for his more severe, if no less ambiguous, purposes.[21] The broad points of connection with Spenser's romance may already be apparent, but I want to pursue further a more hidden bond. Spenser's description animates and reorients some questions that arise from Ariosto's having collapsed in Atalante's shield two other mythic shields—the evaded middle term in this case being the proper goddess of idolatry, Medusa. The first of these is the bronze mirror-shield that allows Perseus to glimpse and

20. Paul Alpers, *Poetry of "The Faerie Queene,"* 166–79, discusses in detail the ways in which the description of Arthur's shield weaves together both the diverse suggestions of Ariosto's romance and those of his moralizing commentators. A shrewd criticism of earlier source critics, these pages amount to something of a set piece for Alpers's ideas about the poem, especially in regard to its way of dissolving clear dramatic, descriptive, or allegorical form in order better to stir the exploratory responses of the reader.

21. William Nelson, *Poetry of Edmund Spenser*, 143, notes what a fine turn it is that in *The Faerie Queene* Ariosto's "trumpery shield becomes the divine power that destroys illusion." Satisfying as this sort of critical irony seems, it underestimates the element of trumpery which continues to attend both Arthur and his shield; it also assumes too clear a sense of the shield's "divine power."

decapitate the Gorgon. In the myth, Perseus subsequently uses the head of Medusa to petrify the sea monster attacking Andromeda, a scene that Ariosto strangely parodies in Ruggiero's imperfect use of Atalante's shield to save Angelica from the Orc (*Orlando Furioso* x. 109–10). It is by this ironic substitution of shield for head that Ariosto points us to the second mythic source: the shield of Athena. For it is to *this* shield, by a further process of transference, that Medusa's head was ultimately affixed.

The Medusa was read by some mythographers as a figure for both sexual fascination and spiritual idolatry, the source of a contaminating power that turns the worshiper into the image of the stone that binds him. Perseus's shield in this case becomes a defense of mortal vision, a medium that Burke compares to the defensive mirror of art (*Philosophy of Literary Form*, 63). The head, for Natalis Comes, figured the disruptive chaos of rebellion (*Mythologiae*, 223), but it could also represent its very opposite: violently displaced onto the gorgoneion of Athena, the snaky head becomes an austere emblem of authority, reason, and control, filled with all the numinousness of repression. Milton, in a very Spenserian passage of *Comus*, read it as a trope for that "noble grace that dash't brute violence / With sudden adoration, and blank aw" (451–52). The masque's concern with the threats to a virgin identity point to the sexual as well as political forces at stake here, and in this context we should also recall Freud's marvelous and grotesque reading of the image: the severed head is a figure not for *castitas* but for *castratio*, its multiple serpents and power to harden being ironic, retroactive defenses against the sense of wounded phallic potency which shadows the idea of decapitation (*Psychological Works*, 18:273–74). Such an interpretation, at least, would complicate my picture of Arthur's opposition to and involvement in the partly sexual power of Orgoglio. Still, it might be wiser to appeal to Fulgentius's suggestion that Medusa's head figures mainly the strongly amoral power of supernatural terror (if not the confusing terror of power), and to recall that the head or mask of Medusa could be used as an apotropaic emblem or talisman in the mystery religions, or affixed to the fronts of Greek and Roman temples.[22] As such, the goddess of idolatry would mark the difficult division between the sacred and the profane; she would represent the complex of mystery, anxiety, and desire located at the sacred threshold, itself the site of powers that may both curse and bless.

Spenser's complex treatment of the mythic images might be given

22. Cf. Leslie George Whitbread, trans., *Fulgentius the Mythographer*, 62, and Graves, *Greek Myths*, 1:129.

an interesting gloss by Tobin Siebers's work on the Medusa myth in its connection with the social mythology of magic (*The Mirror of Medusa* 1–27). Siebers wants to show that superstitious fears of invasive sorcery or the evil eye (associated with the threat of the Medusa) grow out of the need for societies to isolate internal tendencies to violence and to locate them within an identifiable enemy or victim. Against this figure they can then oppose a defensive, talismanic magic whose spiritual superiority is largely arbitrary. Within such a symbolic system of accusations, we begin to see the fascinating, troubling mask of Medusa as something that we impose on our enemies in order to oppose to their supposed power the putatively purer magic of Athena. Indeed, reading the story with an eye to its specularities, Siebers shows the ways in which the mythic plot of confrontation, decapitation, and transference points as much to the similarity as to the polar opposition of the two figures. In this myth of the female face, the goddess of wisdom merges with her enemy, her Gorgon shield becoming itself a narcissistic mirror that, rather than triumphantly bearing the head of a defeated opposite, exposes to Athena an image of her own origins.[23] It becomes a reminder of the blank conceptual and social violence that at first established and later must be concealed by such figures of sacred authority; it confounds "impiety and piety, savageness and civilization, monstrosity and divinity" (15). Siebers's larger argument (conducted in the mode of René Girard) may put off some readers, but his central gesture of critically collapsing mythic difference into uneasy identity helps us understand some of the force of Spenser's invention. Developing Ariosto's more purely witty, schematic conceit, Spenser draws the conflicting poles of the myth into a single, ambivalent figure and yet diffuses them in the shield's various powers to petrify, disenchant, blind, and metamorphose.

One last use of the Medusa figure may put Spenser's strategy in perspective. In the *Symposium* (1980a), Plato's Socrates punningly declares that an eloquent speech of Gorgias had struck him as dumb as the Gorgon's head that Odysseus had feared would keep him trapped in the underworld among the shadows of the dead As an avatar of Medusan enchantment, Spenser's shield also blocks any simple leap away from the infectious flux of language and memory into a higher world of ideal, timeless truths. But it does not therefore trap us in the nonreflexive verbal magic of the sophist. Similarly, if Spenser's allegory forgoes the sort of radical gestures by which Saint Paul would

23. Siebers, *Mirror of Medusa,* 10, actually cites a beautifully ironic retelling of the myth by Louis Marin, in which Perseus slays the Gorgon by using his mirror-shield to make her gaze at her own face.

unveil the blinding face of Mosaic revelation, he does not thereby restore the legalistic repressions of any "Synagogue." Rather, the myth of Medusa—the goddess of idolatry become the enemy of idolatry—allows the poet to make of the shield a place where rhetorical motives reach their formal limit, where rationalizations fail, where the dialectical will to possess and destroy cultural representations at once realizes and transcends itself. Elsewhere in Book 1, we can find less intricately abstract battles and more purely homiletic allegories, moments when Spenser more plainly founds his fable on the established, public icons of Elizabethan polity. In this central canto, however, the poet risks being at once more skeptical and more visionary, reaching after that illusory, nonexistent limit of representation that Burke called "pure persuasion" (*Rhetoric of Motives*, 267f.). The shield is the form of a persuasion, a presence, a mystery that at once undermines, chastens, and quickens the will to mystery, that restores a more urgent wonder to our disenchanted sight. It is an allegory that slays allegory. Only thus does the shield become the proper agency to defeat the idolatry of Orgoglio.

It is no doubt chilling to find that after all attempts to clear away illusion, one's type of transcendent revelation is an image of contagious fascination in which the opacities of imagination, divine vision, and idolatry are hardly separable. But such a discovery is liberating as well, almost a form of the sublime. In closing, I would appeal to the Romantic but oddly archaizing vocabulary of John Ruskin, whose later writings attempt similarly to frame the idea of an improved idolatry as one demystifying, if still ambivalent, solution to his most difficult questions about the nature of religious faith and mythological imagination. No man spoke more urgently than Ruskin about the regressive force of images, whether painted, sculpted, or written. But he still kept troubled faith in an ideal of imaginative representation as magical possession and identification. And, like Spenser, he was acutely aware of the hidden idolatries of minds supposedly free of idolatry: "Half of the poor and untaught Christians who are this day lying prostrate before crucifixes, Bambinos, and Volto Santos, are finding more acceptance with God than many Protestants who idolise nothing but their own opinions or their own interests" (*Works*, 10:451–52).[24] He adds that the worship of images is to be taken as an

24. This passage is taken from an appendix to volume 2 of *The Stones of Venice* entitled "Proper Sense of the Word Idolatry." Cf. also the chapters "Idolatry" and "Imagination" in *Aratra Pentelici* (*Works*, 20:220–71) and the whole of *The Queen of the Air* (*Works*, 19:291–423). In the latter book Ruskin notes how difficult it is "to disentangle

"imaginative enthusiasm . . . rather to be condemned as illusory and fictitious than as idolatrous, nor even as such condemned altogether, for strong love and faith are often the roots of them, and the errors of affection are better than the accuracies of apathy." In such a sentence as this the relations between fiction, idolatry, love, and faith are established only to be obscured and inverted. But, as in Spenser, the writer's will toward the embrace simultaneously of a disillusioning clarity of mind and the errors of affection carries the writing beyond any attempt simply to expose its self-contradictions. I will have more to say about "error" and "affection" in the pages that follow. For the moment, one might recompose the paradoxes of the above quotation and close this chapter by changing my epigraph from Austin Farrer's study of apocalyptic symbolism into a binding tautology: the rejection of idolatry means not the destruction but the liberation, the rebirth of idolatry.

---

in anywise the proud and practised disguises of religious creeds from the instinctive arts which, grotesquely and indecorously, yet with sincerity, strove to embody them, or to relate" (385). Indeed, Ruskin seems to have considered the very grotesqueness, fragmentation, and difficulty of much allegorical imagery the only things that saved it from idolatry.

4

Idols of the Quest (The Legend of Britomart)

Britomart through the Looking Glass

Arthur's shield is a mirror turning lamp. It bears a magic of illumination, of blinding reflectiveness, of metamorphosis. Its unveiling releases an ambivalent energy derived from an indeterminate, or rather, overdetermined otherness, an ultimately apocalyptic force that yet evades any attempt to fix its manifestations within the limits of traditional apocalyptic symbolism. The shield is the threshold between the poem's doubled impulses toward both mystification and demystification, a figure that at once focuses and chastens any attempt to work out a dialectical account of Spenserian idolatry and iconoclasm. Wielded by a knight of ambiguous ornamentation, the shield's power to defeat false imagery and magic also defeats the possibility of divining some sure power of disenchantment either within or without the poem. It is the emblematic agent of a mode of transformation whereby the poet moves not so much from magic to miracle as from magic to magic, even from idolatry to idolatry.

A later portion of the poem contains another allegorical object which in its similar ambiguities may help us gloss and set in perspective Arthur's shield—specifically the magical mirror that initiates Britomart's quest by giving her a vision of her destined beloved. As Nohrnberg notes, "the fantasizing of the erotic life in Book III," offers an unstable, secularized parallel to questions about the genesis of idolatry in Book I (*Analogy*, 444), and it is around Britomart's mirror that these problems are first elaborated. The magical artifact in this case is again the creation of Merlin, again it marries a power of enchantment to one of disenchantment. Nevertheless, the mirror in Book III is a glass that opens up vision more than it blocks vision, a mirror that in its ineluctable transparency seems precisely to reverse one's impressions of the shield's blank, opaque, and shining surface. It is a glass that reflects more than the viewer, for through it one gains access to a power that, if no less divisive than the shield's, seems less catastrophic. It shows a face or surface of fascination which becomes intimately bound up with the struggles for definition of the erotic selfhood.

"By strange occasion," the poet tells us, did Britomart first behold Arthegall,

> And much more strangely gan to love his sight,
> As it in bookes hath written bene of old.
> In *Deheubarth* that now South-wales is hight,
> What time King *Ryence* raign'd, and dealed right,
> The great Magitian *Merlin* had deviz'd
> By his deepe science, and hell-dreaded might,
> A looking glasse, right wondrously aguiz'd,
> Whose vertues through the wyde world soone were solemniz'd.
>
> It vertue had, to shew in perfect sight,
> What ever thing was in the world contaynd,
> Betwixt the lowest earth and heavens hight,
> So that it to the looker appertaynd;
> Whatever foe had wrought, or frend had faynd,
> Therein discovered was, ne ought mote pas,
> Ne ought in secret from the same remaynd;
> For thy it round and hollow shaped was,
> Like to the world it selfe, and seem'd a world of glas.
>
> (III. ii. 18–19)[1]

This Hermetic, microcosmic glass is a site where personal and political worlds cross. We are at first told that it serves as a tool of military divination, but the mirror's more subjective limitations are hinted at in the notion that it shows things clearly only so long as they "to the looker appertaynd." The glass's magic would thus seem very much

1. For a survey of the history of divination by mirrors (catoptromancy), as well as some suggestive comments on their use in Romantic and post-Romantic fiction, see Theodore Ziolkowski, *Disenchanted Images: A Literary Iconology*, 149–226. The round mirror (in common use in the sixteenth century) taken as a trope for mythological worlds also occurs in the "Fourth Day" of the "First Week" of Du Bartas' *Les Semaines*, a section of the poem which Gabriel Harvey claimed Spenser knew by memory. Du Bartas is describing the moon: "I think thy body round as any Ball / Whose superfice (high equall over all) / As a pure Glass, now up, and down anon, / Reflects the bright beams of thy spouse, the Sun" (Sylvester trans., lines 724–27), somewhat as Britomart's glass reflects Arthegall.

parallel to the power of Spenser's benign, demythologized figure of Genius, the god Agdistes, "that celestiall powre . . . "

> Who wondrous things concerning our welfare,
> And straunge phantomes doth let us oft foresee,
> And oft of secret ill bids us beware:
> That is our Selfe, whom though we do not see,
> Yet each doth in him selfe it well perceive to bee.
> (II.xii.47)

Still, this object, which Spenser speaks of as "*Venus* looking glas" (III.i.8), plays havoc even with so tentative a myth of the inward self as that in the lines just cited. Spenser's main use for the glass is to fix the romantic dilemma of the young heroine and precipitate a crisis in the narrative by introducing her "self" to the alienating, divisive shadow of an other: the hieratic vision of Arthegall clothed in the armor of Achilles (III.ii.24–25). As Anne Hollander writes, "mirrors have afflicted people for millennia with the fear of being trapped or attacked by something that lives inside the mirror itself and is only released by the viewer's gaze. That 'something' is simply the reflection, but this is freighted with the uncanny quality of separate life" (*Seeing through Clothes*, 392).[2] Arthegall does indeed acquire a "separate life" within the narrative of *The Faerie Queene*. But at this early stage in his career he may yet seem very much Britomart's creature. At least, insofar as the source of the apparition at this point is a mirror, we should take seriously the generative relation of Arthegall's image to Britomart's act of looking, if only to wonder whether the wound that the vision of him gives to her narcissism is not a further reflection of or on that narcissism. We might try to simplify the difficulties of the description by saying that Spenser is combining in Britomart the iconographic type of a *Vanitas*, whose mirror shows only the self and its illusions, with that of a *Prudentia*, whose glass reflects the truth of present or past[3]—but such schemata can only factor out and rationally moralize the critical ambivalences of Britomart's situation, telling us little about the uneasy magic at work there.

A psychoanalytic investigation of Britomart's love melancholy

2. Hollander goes on: "The danger of the mirror boils down to the risk of letting the infinite and wayward power of the human eye turn on itself and make an uncontrollable, destructive creature out of the self-image" (392)—which is to say, the danger of the mirror is congruent with the danger of idolatry.

3. The traditions behind these standard iconographic types are surveyed in G. F. Hartlaub, *Zauber des Spiegels*, 149–72

might only answer one allegory with another, but we need at least to sketch it out. If, for example, we sense a hidden incestuous motive in the fact that Britomart discovers the mirror within her royal father's closet, then her nurse Glauce's (admittedly negative) comparisons of the heroine to Myrrha, Biblis, and Pasiphae (III.ii.41), will complicate any single scheme of transgressive desire with more varied, polymorphous models (all taken from Ovid). That Britomart adopts not only armor but also a mask of enmity and that we first see her slandering her beloved before Redcrosse (III.ii.8) may suggest the presence of a vengeful or sadistic component in her love-quest (though of course her insults are a conscious rhetorical tool as well, a way of seeing her lover defended and "magnifide" in the eyes of someone other than herself). Even more interesting here, perhaps, would be to apply to Britomart recent psychoanalytic thought about the paradoxical structure of human identity, especially the notion that the outward, erotic drives of the ego originate in the displacement of an original narcissism onto an external or alienated image that continues to be "propped" on the primary narcissistic cathexes. Without being wholly ironic, we can frame the problematic of Spenser's narrative in terms of Jacques Lacan's revisionary psychological myth of the Mirror Stage. This theory ties the genesis of the desiring ego to its specular identification with its own fantasized bodily image, an identification that paradoxically depends upon and yet constitutes the hitherto nonexistent ego. Hence one's proper self is "always already" a figure, a nonplace, or "place devoyd," unfixed, but for that very reason liable to reductive fixation. Being grounded (if we can even use that word) in fantasy rather than in biology, such a mode of identification at once "symbolizes the mental permanence of the *I*" and "prefigures its alienating destination" (*Écrits*, 2). The idea of a Mirror Stage "is still pregnant with the correspondences that unite the *I* with the statue in which man projects himself, with the phantoms that dominate him, . . . with the automaton in which, in an ambiguous relation, the world of his own making tends to find completion . . . [with] the assumption of the armour of an alienating identity, which will mark with its rigid structure the subject's entire mental development" (3–4).

Lacan's account of the fate of the ego continues to be steeped in the pathos of quest-romance, his imagery infected with the anxious consciousness of idols, phantasms, and automata (golems, animate icons) which attends that quest. From Lacan, as well as from the Freud of the *Three Essays on Sexuality* or *Beyond the Pleasure Principle*, we take an awareness not only of the constitutive error of human *eros* but also of its essential relation to the error or wandering identifications and figurations of romance, especially in those situations where the object of desire and identification seems itself to turn into an enemy or blocking agent, or becomes merely the veil for some more hidden object. In the case of Spenser's heroine, one might suggest that the quest originates in a moment of both fantasizing an image of desire and being possessed by that image; this moment precipitates (as it may also be precipitated by) a certain anxiety as to that image's source or ontological status. Questions multiply: Is the image an illusion of one's own or imposed by another? Does it have a possessible form and location? Upon what labor is possession contingent? And so on. This anxiety, the dilemma of Narcissus staring at his reflection in the well, at once initiates and shadows the search for the image, a search that would end ideally in the impossible paradox of recovering that image fully as a property of both self and other—or else by achieving an illusion or dialectic of presence that might for a moment consume any distinction between them.

The generative mirror of Book III recalls not only Arthur's shield but also the dream that initiated his own quest, a dream in which he first glimpses his beloved Gloriana. The retrospective narrative of this vision is placed well after the complex description of the prince discussed in the previous chapter, after his defeat of Orgoglio, and may therefore seem something like a final account of his heroic election. Arthur reports that he woke from his sacred *somnium* of the Faerie Queen only to find "her place devoyd, / And nought but pressed gras, where she had lyen" (I.ix.15). Yet in that empty place he also finds room to hope. For despite the elegiac reference to "nought but pressed gras," with its recollection of the Bible's favored trope for transient flesh, the scene does not suggest a "cold hillside" of waking experience but contains rather a trace of the dream's ponderable reality, the delicate material evidence of present magic and future fulfillment. The dream disappears but touches the landscape with the numinousness of a felt loss that is of something other than mere illusion; it is this that Arthur pursues.

Such moments of empirical and epistemological questioning constitute the ideal point of the quest's origin, even if they are not literally the narrative's first episode or the passage with which the poet begins his composition. The vision in the mirror and the dream of Gloriana are examples of hierophanies (as Eliade would call them) which dislocate the consciousness of the quester who experiences them, and to some degree that of the reader who may identify with those questers. These visions fix a discontinuity not only between our ordinary sense of fantasy and reality but also between the diverse forms, *topoi*, or places of fantasy and consciousness themselves—hence between the images by which we measure past and future life. The burden of the quest-narrative then lies in the diverse attempts that can be made to close or at least relocate these crucial gaps, from which arises also the double potential of the quest for transfiguring or troubling the self, the movement, that is, between a sense of enabling desire and a continually renewed feeling of despair, distance, and loss. In this context we may recall Frye's useful and more or less Freudian definition of quest-romance as "the search of the libido or desiring self for a fulfillment that will deliver it from the anxieties of reality but will still contain that reality" (*Anatomy*, 193). Two qualifications to this are required, however, in the light of earlier arguments. First, the search for a "fulfilment" always risks binding or fixating desire, or else committing oneself to an illusion of ending that only leads the unassimilated portion of the original anxiety to be repressed; thus Arthur, for example, pursuing the materialized form of his dream image, is always in danger of falling into a preemptive idolatry of substitute forms of the goal.[4] These forms must then be evaded, broken down, or superseded, and yet this may be accomplished against a background of doubt as to the possibility of any finally sufficient iconoclasm. Second, such dilemmas mean that the quest *may* become endlessly extended, its goal continually deferred. The result of this, however, is that deferral itself becomes problematic, ambivalent—at times a real struggle to interpret and place the object of desire, at times a lapsing into completely contingent eventualities, merely random or entropic wandering (as much a potential form of idolatry as stasis). Given these circumstances, the fulfillment that the quester finds, if not inevitably idolatrous, may only be a peculiarly articulate form of the original anxiety, just as the reality that Frye says that fulfillment must contain may only be a more complex and potent from of illusion, even an illusion of disillusionment. Hence the quest for an end, which both animates and troubles desire, entails a continual questioning of endings, whether these endings take the form of triumph, recovery, or loss: it entails by extension a quest for the proper or sufficient lineaments of questing itself.

4. Such is the case in Arthur's pursuit of Florimell, when Spenser tells us that "oft did he wish, that Lady faire mote bee / His Faery Queene, for whom he did complaine: / Or that his Faery Queene were such, as shee" (III.iv.54). Lewis, *Spenser's Images of Life*, 133–34, remarks rather drily than Spenser's "one big blunder as a doctrinal poet" is that he does not emphasize the danger of Arthur's somewhat sentimental, even arbitrary wish that the present if fleeing lady substitute for the less accessible ideal of Gloriana; however, Spenser may be here revealing a more Ariostan sense of the way that all of the chaste or chased heroines of romance tend to merge with one another.

Returning to the opening of Book III, we can see an instability about the end image of Britomart's quest that parallels that of Arthur's, save that in the former case specific doubts about the reality or unreality of the image are complicated by questions about its origin within or outside the self:

> But wicked fortune mine, though mind be good,
> Can have no end, nor hope of my desire,
> But feed on shadowes, whiles I die for food,
> And like a shadow wexe, whiles with entire
> Affection, I doe languish and expire.
> I fonder, then *Cephisus* foolish child,
> Who having vewed in a fountaine shere
> His face, was with the love thereof beguild;
> I fonder love a shade, the bodie farre exild.
> (III.ii.44)

The rhetoric of Britomart's declaration and allusion is complex. On the surface she invokes the figure of Narcissus as a foil or counterexample, as a way of grounding her hyperbolic claim to an even grander illusion or fateful suffering. But we may sense some disequilibrium at work here, a turn that might be described by what Freud called "negation," in which a repressed content is allowed to manifest itself only at the cost of being denied. For hidden below Britomart's despair over the burden or shame of which she *can* speak is perhaps a more silent source of anxiety, the sense of some narcissistic component in her cathexis which she yet refuses to admit (since it is a victimizing love that turns the viewer into a mirror of the shadow or shade that she seeks, as lines 3 and 4 of the above stanza suggest). Britomart's nurse, indeed, seems quite aware of the narcissism that still contaminates the heroine's words, for she answers Britomart's complaint by further denying the similitude that Britomart herself must have thought she had already fully denied: "*Nought like* (quoth shee) for that same wretched boy / Was of himselfe the idle [idol] Paramoure; / Both love and lover, without hope of ioy, / For which he faded to a watry flowre" (III.ii.45; emphasis mine)—Glauce arguing in turn that Britomart herself loves "the shadow of a warlike knight," and that since "No shadow, but a bodie hath in powre," his person might be discovered by ciphers or divination.

We may feel that Glauce's rejection of narcissism is still haunted by some fascination with it (at least if we recall that the gentle description of the boy as "faded to a watry flowre" is echoed four cantos later in the elegaic image of "foolish *Narcisse*, that likes the watry shore"

[III.vi.45] at the sacred center of the Garden of Adonis). More immediately relevant, however, is that while what ostensibly overcomes Britomart's dilemma is indeed evidence of her lover's bodily reality, the things that allow her quest to proceed are rather a double illusion or pair of ironic tropes, both of which are apparent in Britomart's act of arming herself. For this act constitutes, first, a proleptic identification with her splendidly armed husband (one whose own armor is the vehicle of his agonistic identification with Achilles [III.ii.25]), and second, a defensive masking of the wound to her self-sufficiency caused by that very vision of him. Such tropes recall armor's function (historical as well as allegorical) as both emblem and defense; they point in addition to the relevance of Lacan's own chivalric metaphor, the "armour of an alienating identity," itself an elegant refiguring of the Freudian idea of *psychic* defense. Britomart thus bears with her, or pragmatically restructures, her original anxieties, rather than in any simple way escaping them.

With her "squire" Glauce, Britomart seeks out the wizard Merlin in the hope that he will be able to provide a fuller account of and cure for her illness. His prophecy of the virgin's imperial fate does seem to offer a firmer, teleological frame for the quest, but as usual the complexity and retrospective contradictions of Spenser's statements, images, and agents play havoc with any stable definition of the powers operating in the poem. We recall, for instance, that Britomart's glance in the mirror takes on its unsettling power not only because it raises questions about the status of self and other but also because the power of the glass and glance stands at a threshold between accident and necessity, "strange occasion" and binding fate. Merlin seems able to negotiate such a gap with enviable authority, not only distinguishing contingency from compulsion but also specifying the exact agency of control: "It was not, *Britomart*, thy wandring eye, / Glauncing unwares in charmed looking glas, / But the streight course of heavenly destiny, / Led with eternall providence, that has / Guided thy glaunce . . ." (III.iii.24). Britomart must then "submit her ways" unto divine will and thus fulfill her destiny. We need not pause over the vagueness of Merlin's words, or question too strictly how we should bridge the gap between those words and the less Christian and political, though still cosmic and providential, vision of *eros* which Spenser had framed at the opening of the canto.[5] Better perhaps to focus on the status of

5. Cf. III.iii.1–2, where Love is described as a "most sacred fire, that burnest mightily / In living brests, ykindled first above, / Emongst th'eternall spheres and lamping sky," a power that directs human actions rightly, even while "the fatall purpose of divine foresight, / Thou doest effect in destined descents, / Through deepe impression of thy secret might, / And stirredst up th'Heroes high intents."

Merlin's own authority as prophet-mage in this episode, and especially on the degree to which his power is bound up with a measure of dark or unholy science. This agent of truth, who was the first to mock Glauce's folkloristic cures and divinations, is himself given a rather peculiar, fairy-tale genealogy; he was "wondrously begotten, and begonne / By false illusion of a guilefull Spright / On a faire Ladie Nonne" (III.iii.13)—born, that is, out of demonic violation, or out of meeting of illusion with nothing or "none". That the enchanter is discovered, not unlike Busyrane ten cantos later, "writing strange characters in the ground, / With which the stubborn feends he to his service bound" (iii.14), is strange enough. But even more disquieting is the etiological fable (a marriage of Grimm and Kafka) that immediately precedes the account of Britomart's entry into Merlin's cave, a tale whose ironic picture of the magical work within that cave casts a shadow over all of Merlin's later attempts to propound a providential narrative. For it describes how Merlin's own noisy, spellbound fiends are laboring ceaselessly underground (even up to the present time frame of the narrative), trying to "bring to perfect end" a brazen wall around the Welsh kingdom, though Merlin himself had long before been captured by the traitorous "Ladie of the Lake." The magician, though effective, is thus also the victim of trickery and betrayal; his power is at once limited and inescapable, just as his project of controlling demons and erecting defensive enclosures can perpetuate itself even in the absence of conscious will or rational purpose.[6]

Spenser's curious tale is not, as one critic suggests, an image of a superstitious phase of culture which later episodes or images supersede. The tale haunts even subsequent philosophical debates about the nature of Providence, such as that arising from Glauce's questions about why Britomart needs to make any effort to pursue her quest if its end is predetermined. Like the earlier description of Arthur's shield, the poet's blurrings or confusions of magical causation defend against attempts to measure the progress of the quest by any usurping form of rationalization, whether it would entail reducing the narra-

6. Ernst Kris and Otto Kurz, *Legend, Myth, and Magic in the Image of the Artist*, 84–90, have an interesting discussion of the strong ambivalences that seem to surround such acts of building and the legends that they generate. The authors cite the argument of the German folklorist Friedrich von der Leyen among others to suggest that traditionally "great buildings are regarded as sacrileges, as in the Jewish story of the Tower of Babel; only demonic powers—or, in German legends, the Devil himself—can bring them to completion. Injustice, betrayal, and trickery are gruesomely associated with their construction" (*Das Märchen*, 77; translated in Kris and Kurz, *Legend, Myth*, 85). E. M. Butler, *Myth of the Magus*, 108, argues that the fable of Merlin's brazen wall was Spenser's own invention, although it recalls late antique and medieval legends that Solomon himself had bound his own demonic servants to complete the building of the first temple in Jerusalem even after his death.

tive to the arbitrary wanderings of erotic desire or linguistic reference, or placing that narrative under the control of necessarily fictional claims about divine compulsion. One might appeal here to Tzvetan Todorov's argument that the shifting and often ironic images of fulfillment in romance narrative have a way of unsettling the constitutive authority of whatever ideology has chosen that narrative as its literary vehicle (*Poetics of Prose*, 120–42), save that Todorov tends to speak as if the quasi-divine "narrativity" of romance were thereby taking its revenge on the structural presumptions of ideology or thematics. One could also say that Spenser is confessing something about the ineluctable fictiveness of his text and the figurative underpinnings of providential history (so that our confrontation with Merlin's ambiguous magic would resemble our encounter with the central *aporia* of the *Aeneid*, in which the pious hero leaves Hades through the ivory gate of false dreams after having seen the true future history of Rome). And yet such representational paradoxes seem no more to make sense of Spenser's difficult treatment of magic than do theological ones; they are for one thing contingent on particular frames of reference that neither we nor the poem can regard as absolute. Indeed, to take the poet's investment in magic seriously means seeing that the critical strategy (unavoidable in some ways) of showing how the fiction recognizes itself *as* a fiction is perhaps just one more form of reductive enchantment, since such a strategy tends to imply that we know what the scope and structure of such fictions really are.

The idea of enchantment is central to any theory of romance. For this reason I have tried to avoid rationalizing the literary manifestations of magic, whether this means taking magic as contrived metaphor or unconscious projection, though at different times it may be both. To further clarify my sense of the ambiguous place of magic in Spenser, I want to digress briefly in order to examine a few passages from Wittgenstein's *Remarks on Frazer's "Golden Bough."* Over and against what he feels to be the Victorian mythographer's reduction of magic to a kind of failed science, Wittgenstein in this text tries to restore a sense of both the psychological and existential urgency of magical gestures. His corrective move is to point out the unresolved residue of magical language in Frazer himself and to insist that primitive magic is really a self-enclosed, self-perpetuating language system that cannot adequately be judged by any more "advanced" discourse:

> A religious symbol does not rest on any *opinion*.
> And error [as a philosophical category] belongs only with opinion.

> Burning in effigy. Kissing the picture of a loved one. This is obviously *not* based on a belief that it will have a definite effect on the object which

the picture represents. It aims at some satisfaction and it achieves it. Or rather, it does not *aim* at anything; we act in this way and then feel satisfied.

And magic always rests on the idea of symbolism and of language.

The description [*Darstellung*] of a wish is, *eo ipso*, the description of its fulfillment.

And magic does give representation [*Darstellung*] to a wish; it expresses a wish.

What makes the character of ritual action is not any view or opinion, either right or wrong, although an opinion—a belief—itself can be ritualistic, or belong to a rite. (3e–7e)

The philosopher's words are illuminating; they help both to restore some sense of the radically nonempirical dynamics of magic and to remind us that any explanatory "opinion" attempting to contain those dynamics may itself be coopted by them. Yet this way of relating magic to questions of symbolism and language may be less than adequate for a Protestant poet such as Spenser, a writer for whom magic may often come under the category of *moral* error, illusion, or idolatry, and one who is so acutely aware that descriptions of a wish may not only describe its fulfillment but also point to its lack, as well as preempt or deform that fulfillment. In trying to retain a sense of both the burden of such error and the seriousness of magic, I am more drawn to a view of magic which would bring it close to what Vico calls "divination," a concept I have related to idolatry in Chapter 1. This association would entail a sense that magic's world of occult causation originates in the mind's warding off of its own ignorance and lack of control, its fear that all events in nature happen arbitrarily. To this suggestion one adds an awareness of the catastrophic effects of such divination, a sense that the mind tends to act under all too drastic, arbitrary, and antinatural modes of compulsion (what I would categorize as the demonic or the idolatrous). Here Wittgenstein's wise warnings to the empiricist are only partly serviceable. More to the point would be a development of Harold Bloom's Vichian observation regarding the blank contingencies of life lived within time: "All continuities possess the paradox of being absolutely arbitrary in their origins, and absolutely inescapable in their teleologies. We know this so vividly from what we all of us oxymoronically call our love lives that its literary counterparts need little demonstration" (*Map of Misreading*, 33).

It is against this sort of ultimate paradox and the anxiety it bears that Merlin aims his assertive negation: "It was *not, Britomart,* thy wandring eye, / Glauncing unwares in charmed looking glas, / But the streight course of heavenly destiny" (III.iii.24; emphasis mine). The strength of this declaration is in its factoring out and firm setting apart of the terms of Bloom's paradox. But the stated opposition of contingency and destiny finally remains with us only as a willful and largely defensive figuration of Britomart's situation; any merely literal or philosophical authority it might possess wanders away within the labyrinth of unanswerable questions about Merlin's magic which I tried to sketch out above.

As I have noted, Spenser fixes and then mars the firm distinctions between the poem's alternative concepts of chance and design, not only by multiplying his names and tropes for them but also by undoing any clear sense of the supernatural power of the magician who propounds them. This sovereign confusion, however, does not undo the will to secure a form of magical agency or explanation which can serve as the guiding purpose of the poem. Britomart's attempts to solve the paradoxes of her looking glass, her mystifying and demystifying adventures under ground, all end in further wandering. And yet these restore to us a form of wandering which recognizes the urgency of articulating a "streight course"—the true error of love—even if all easy questions about choice, compulsion, and control are continually set in suspension. The quester asks, "How do I see where to go? How do I know who or where I am, or when I have arrived?" Each question twists back onto the others; each generates answers that may block or liberate desire. For the freedom of the poet to choose, vary, and balance his figurations gains power only in the pursuit, evasion, or dislocation of a determinate antithetical or magical end, testing questions against answers and answers against questions. As Spenser tells us, this "play of double senses" is not only the work of the poet;[7] it is the ironic work of fate and the burden of life in time, where things intrude, break off, grow, and decay. *The poet writes both within and*

7. The phrase derives from Spenser's account of Britomart's wounding of Marinell, an event that unexpectedly fulfills the prophecy that the youthful warrior would be overthrown by a woman:

> This was that woman, this that deadly wound,
> That *Proteus* prophecide should him dismay,
> The which his mother vainely did expound,
> To be hart-wounding love, which should assay
> To bring her sonne unto his last decay.
> So tickle be the termes of mortall state,
> *And full of subtile sophismes, which do play*
> *With double senses, and with false debate,*
> *T'approve the unknowen purpose of eternall fate.*
> (III.iv.28; emphasis mine)

against this realm of error. Like Merlin, the poet binds his demonic tropes to "bring to perfect end" an enclosure, a brazen ring of narrative; but the poet himself is bound, and the troubled demons find their magical labor endless.

Idols of the Threshold

To recapture my argument up to this point: The quest-romance discovers its origins in a scene of conceptual trial or ambivalence, particularly one in which the quester must take a difficult stance toward some intruding image of desire. The quester—or the reader imagining him or herself in the quester's place—is caught within a net of contradictions, between suspicions of narcissism and feelings of otherness, between accident and necessity, between true prophecy and empty illusion. To appropriate the Freudian terms, the quester tends to be caught between introjection and projection, between the need to internalize the visionary object—even if this need entails the self-alienating process of feeding on shadows, as Britomart observes—and the dangerous desire to deny the object's origins within the self and to provide it with an external source or authority.[8] The fate of romance is continually to recognize and negotiate the threshold between such contradictory impulses; its response is continually to generate ideal heavens and hells, paradises and deserts, scenes of trial, entrapment, battle, and recognition, all of which always give way to others. Romance constructs clarifying designs and oppositions that it must both divinize and dissolve. For although it is only by the forward movement of the quest-narrative that the poet and quester are freed from the condition of deadening, static ambivalence, the onward movement of the quest and of its writing tends to set up further possibilities of blockage, further discursive paradoxes and retrospective contradictions that may draw out without necessarily resolving the initial ambivalence.

Merlin calls these originating troubles the "fatall lore" of love, the "hard begin, that meets thee in the dore" (III.iii.21). He is referring particularly to Britomart, but his homely metaphor suggests how indispensable to the situation of quest-romance is the idea of a thresh-

---

It is part of the paradox of the romance mode that Proteus should be both the god of infinite metamorphosis and duplicity as well as the propounder of binding, if ironic schemes of Providence.

8. Here, as in Freud's account of authority figures in *Totem and Taboo*, the motives of cannibalism and divination are complexly intertwined.

old. Fletcher, a crucial theorist of literary ambivalence, notes that at the threshold between what he calls the archetypal spaces of labyrinth and temple "there is a possible range of normal threshold-feelings: anxiety, readiness, blind hope." It is wrong, however, to suppose that we are dealing here merely with a sentimental intensification of natural feelings; rather, this continuum of response "measures the degrees of dread, and it refers specifically to a range of feelings aroused by the *sacer*, the taboo, the holy. For if within the temple the holy seems triumphant, in the labyrinth the holy is either lost or irrelevant, whereas at the threshold these differences are exactly what is put into question. The threshold tries the sense of the holy" ("'Positive Negation,'" 150). Fletcher's language is that of a religious phenomenology, but he is not unaware of how romance can retrope and psychologize the sacral situation. Happily for my own argument, he chooses to illustrate this shift by a moment late in Britomart's quest, when she meets Scudamour languishing outside the prison-palace of Busyrane, unable to pass its door of flames and so unable to rescue his trapped lover Amoret. Here, Fletcher says, Spenser's narrative accommodates both "a physical and mental crossover, so that the two merge in one single, unbroken psychosomatic drama." Scudamour's "mind" prevents his passage over the threshold, "but Britomart can pass over, and when she does, as with her other marvelous psychological breakthroughs, she achieves for Spenser an originating shift within English romantic sensibility. She enacts the exchange of psychic energies" (137).

But Spenser does more than psychologize the threshold between the sacred and the profane: he transforms a primary ambivalence about the sacred (the cursed or blessed) into a more self-conscious questioning of the nature and authenticity of sacred representation itself. The threshold to be negotiated is that between true and false divination, between a crossing that would be a sacrilegious transgression and one that would be iconoclastic. This movement, moreover, is contingent not just on prior or fixed states of mind but also on the unstable attitudes of the questers toward the crossing itself and on their diverse ways of representing the powers in conflict at that point in time and space.

Standing outside, it is Britomart who most fears transgression:

> What monstrous enmity provoke we heare,
> Foolhardy as th'Earthes children, the which made
> Battell against the Gods? so we a God invade.
>
> (III.xi.22)

And yet Britomart, who in the above lines seems to suggest a believing theodicy of the false Cupid, manages to negotiate the flames, as if her successful crossing of the false enchantment were partly contingent on her acceptance of it. At this point, at least, one traverses the threshold only by raising to an extreme the risk of transgression and death. She moves through the flaming gateway

> as a thunder bolt
> Perceth the yielding ayre, and doth displace
> The soring clouds into sad showres ymolt;
> So to her yold the flames, and did their force revolt.
> (III.xi.25)

There may be some irony in Spenser's use of the word "revolt," since in her passage through the flames Britomart resembles not so much "th'Earthes children" as the thunderbolt-hurling Zeus who defeated their rebellion. But it is significant that Spenser suppresses any direct mythological identification that would simply invert the opposed terms of Britomart's earlier comparison of herself to the titans. Success in negotiating the threshold brings with it continuing uncertainty as to the agencies involved in the crossing. While the absence of the likely divine name seems to demythologize the lightning figure, that name's phantom possibility still resonates within it and heightens the more than natural imagery of violent transgression.

Fletcher is right to speak of Britomart's crossing as "a single, unbroken psychosomatic drama," but nevertheless the psychological and mythological terms of the event are left relatively obscure. This obscurity may be a constitutive element of the crossing itself, for only in the case of Scudamour, who fails to cross, does the text provide an explicit symbolic characterization of an inward state shifting at the same time into a more precise sort of mythological naming (very different from Britomart's stark metonymy, "so we a God invade"):

> Whom whenas *Scudamour* saw past the fire,
> Safe and untoucht, he likewise gan assay,
> With greedy will, and envious desire,
> And bad the stubborne flames to yield him way:
> But cruell *Mulciber* would not obay
> His threatfull pride, but did the more augment
> His mighty rage, and with imperious sway
> Him forst (maulgre) his fiercenesse to relent,
> And backe retire, all scorcht and pitifully brent.
> (III.xi.26)

Scudamour addresses the unyielding barrier as a conscious enemy, but the ambiguous possessive pronouns—especially in the reference to "his mighty rage"—suggest the element of idolatrous identification that underlies this sudden divination of Vulcan. Anger leads us to personify inanimate objects that hurt or resist us, sometimes with rather comic results. In the case of Scudamour, however, the comedy of his narcissistic pride and "envious desire" gives rise only to the sort of catastrophic, delusive godmaking discussed above in my analysis of Orgoglio. For Scudamour, the threshold becomes not a door but a mirror, a threatening reflection. And unlike Britomart's looking glass, or those mirrors through which Alice enters Wonderland and Cocteau's Orpheus enters Hades, it does not give access to other worlds.

The House of Idolatry

Britomart, unlike Scudamour, in breaking through the fiery threshold of Busyrane's court only enters more complex forms of enchantment. Searching the palace's vast spaces, she surveys a grand series of tapestries depicting "Cupid's warres" against all of the Olympian gods, representations of his power to corrupt or metamorphose divinity and ultimately to displace the gods from their heavenly seats. At the "upper end" of this first great hall, the heroine comes upon an altar and, on it, an "Image all alone"—a darkly imagined statue of Cupid which sums up all that we have learned from the previous pictures:

> Blindfold he was, and in his cruell fist
> A mortall bow and arrowes keene did hold,
> With which he shot at random, when him list,
> Some headed with sad lead, some with pure gold;
> (Ah man beware, how thou those darts behold)
> A wounded Dragon under him did ly,
> Whose hideous tayle his left foot did enfold,
> And with a shaft was shot through either eye,
> That no man forth might draw, ne no man remedye.
> (III.xi.48)

As I have said before, idolatry is itself iconoclastic, a usurping identification, a sacrilegious form of the sacred. The idol stands in the place of authentic divinity or substitutes its concrete presence for the other's sovereign placelessness; and yet it makes for itself a nonplace, a space emptied of presence, a phantom place that is yet disturbingly similar to the obscure, shifting location that is the threshold. The idol is a false revelation, blinded and blinding. All of this Spenser brings out in his description of the statue. In line with much Reformation theology, Spenser suggests that the image is not so much deceptive in itself as it is made deceptive by its worshipers, who are themselves turned from true worshipers into fetishists as empty as their object. Hence the poet notes that "all the people in that ample hous / Did to that *image* bow their humble knee, / And oft committed fowle *Idolatree*" (III.xi.49; emphasis mine), while at the same time he asserts that the statue stands in a temple that is always *void* of worshipers, a house full only of "wastefull emptinesse, and solemne silence." The blindfold over Cupid's eyes is interpreted by iconographic tradition alternately as the cause of the god's random victimization of mortals and as a metonymic reflection of the blindness effected by his work.[9] The blind god blinds, a circumstance that Spenser further explicates by providing the unseeing god with a blinded victim, his eyes put out by the arrows of desire. The dragon itself may be a figure for the sort of reasonable, erotic wariness which is violated in Busyrane's House and so may derive from the creature who accompanies (and glosses) the chaste goddess Minerva in one of Alciati's emblems.[10] But the more archaic source for the dragon is the ever watchful guardian of the golden apple-bearing tree in the Garden of the Hesperides. This creature, whom Hesiod tells us is a younger sibling of the petrifying Gorgons (*Theogony* 270–74, 333–35), is a figure that points beyond any local moralizations of human love, standing more broadly for the apotropaic power with which we invest the idea of any sacred center, a figure for the manifest terror of the sacred which both sees and is seen by its worshiper. The doubly blind statue and the victimized watcher thus represent idolatry's sacrilegious triumph over and parody of such infolded, reflexive vision.

Beyond this hall Britomart enters another with even richer ornaments, in which gold bas-reliefs depict less mythological but more desperate forms of erotic conflict, particularly the catastrophic effect of love on human war and politics. She observes at the upper end of this

9. On the iconography of the blind Cupid, see Erwin Panofsky, *Studies in Iconology*, 95–128. Panofsky shows some interesting parallels between the rather grotesque pictures of the blind god in medieval art and those of other blindfolded figures such as Night, Death, Fortune, and the Synagogue. Although he notes that this last is often described by the phrase "*Vetus testamentum velatum*" (111), he never indicates its likely source in the Pauline figure of the blindingly veiled Moses, another type of idolatry.

10. See Alciati, *Emblematum liber* (1531), emblem 43; cited by Lewis, *Spenser's Images of Life*, 23.

chamber an iron gate. And it is through this gate, torn open by a sudden storm of wind, that Busyrane's masque will eventually spill.

If the statue of Cupid provides an anatomy of idolatry, the masque does no less. In it the statue becomes a living figure, guiding a triumphal chariot drawn by fierce lions, lifting his blindfold to gaze with sadistic pleasure at his captive, and in all suggesting a kind of erotic tyranny not limited to fixed images. The threatening theatricality of the procession—with "Ease" offering an uncanny, silent prologue to the sequence of "masquers" representing Fancy and Desyre, Doubt and Daunger, Fear and Hope, and so on—might itself have troubled some Puritan readers. But even more disturbing is the central depiction of the victim Amoret, wounded with Cupid's arrow and bearing her own bleeding heart in a silver bowl, a figure that converts theatrical display into an unholy rite of living sacrifice or necromancy, a parodic mass. What Thomas P. Roche has labeled its "dramatized personifications" (*Kindly Flame*, 76) in this context recall not only court pageants but the kind of reductive materializations of sacramental symbols which so horrified reformers.[11] The presence of the idol as well as the suggestions of a cultic ritual indeed mark Busyrane's House as a temple, like the Church of Isis into which Britomart also enters in Book v, canto vi. Britomart's own sleeping vision—its animation of a statue, its unreal and violent imagery—also suggests parallels with the nightly masque, which we might even refer to by contrast as "Amoret's Dream." But this latter would be at best a compulsive dream, no private phantasmagoria but an unwilling participation in the nightmares of Amoret's cultural tradition. It is as if Spenser were constructing a grotesque version of a Brunian "memory theater" filled only with those sophisticated, institutionalized structures of trope (idols of the tribe as well as idols of the cave) which feed upon and bind our most elemental fears, defenses, desires.

The analogues of mass, dream, and memory theater may suggest the radical character of Spenser's poetic machinery here, but they also evade any clear answers about the psychological sources of the masque. Indeed, we cannot devise any clear psychological plot or scheme of causes which would let us say, for example, that the masque derives from the virgin Amoret's own unwarranted sexual anxieties

11. Cf. in this regard John Jewel's complaint that "the rule and way to everlasting salvation" must come from God's word and "not from men's fantasies," and "that the sacraments may be ministered not like a masquery or a stage play but religiously and reverently" (*Apology for the Church of England*, 144). On the fundamental relation of Neo-Platonic magical practice to the ceremony of the mass—"with its music, words of consecration, incense, lights, wine, and supreme magical effect, transubstantiation"—see D. P. Walker, *Spiritual and Demonic Magic From Ficino to Campanella*, 36.

or that it is the unfortunate result of her male lover's oppressive, if conventional, strategies of erotic "Maistrye."[12] Much as he will do for Britomart, Spenser in this episode continually problematizes our search for sources—whether it derives from our need for ontological security or the comforts of moral accusation. What accounts for our analytic difficulties is not only the ambiguous status of allegorical personification in general but also that Spenser's vision of a human subject wounded in both mind and body by poetic conceits resolves itself not into an allegory of psychology but into a complex reflection on the project of allegorical art itself. As readers, we are placed at a threshold where the problems of erotic idolatry and those of poetic fiction are not at all easy to sort out.[13]

As an exercise in *theoria* or conceptual theater, Spenser's account of the pageant first of all attempts a critique of the masque form itself, banishing it from his poem with a full sense of its use as a vehicle of entertainment, metamorphosis, and indoctrination (though there is nothing reductively Puritanical about this attack on the theatrical form, which is being cast out more in trope than in reality). If a literary historian like D. J. Gordon finds it necessary to insist that a form of iconographic display such as the masque is emphatically "not an act of allegory or magic" but rather a "declaration, a substantiation, the creation of a self" (*Renaissance Imagination*, 23), then Spenser in his turn demystifies the masque even more fully by insisting on the paradox that it is *both* allegorical and magical. Indeed, he provides us with a kind of limiting case or preemptive apocalypse in which literary alle-

12. On these and related issues, see Roche's treatment of the masque as "an objectification of Amoret's fear of sexual love in marriage" in *The Kindly Flame*, 72–88; also A. Kent Hieatt, "Scudamour's Practice of *Maistrye* upon Amoret"; and Alistair Fowler, *Triumphal Forms: Structural Patterns in Renaissance Poetry*, 47–58.

13. Thomas Hyde's study of the iconography of Cupid ("Love's Pageants: The Figure of Cupid in the Poetry of Edmund Spenser") suggests the degree to which representations of the love god in Western tradition always led writers into a situation of crisis. Hyde shows that within a Christian literary milieu, any attempt at a poetic theodicy of the pagan *eros* tended either to break down into an instance of self-deceived idolatry or to produce an extremely self-conscious kind of fiction in which the fables of Cupid were either rejected as useless or used as allegorical veils to clothe more authoritative concepts and psychologies. The literary fascination of Cupid depends on his being more than just the cipher of a natural passion. Rather (as Hyde's work broadly implies) the god is a threshold figure for those cathexes mobilized by human imagery and mythmaking which exceed a merely aesthetic commitment to that imagery and which at the same time throw into question the desired clarity of any conceptual framework that might allegorically contain such excess. Cupid's career in poetic allegory is an effort to explore and sometimes rationalize dilemmas raised partly by the very attempt to represent the god. The climax of Hyde's argument is, fittingly enough, an intriguing account of the failed or parodic theodicy of Cupid in Busyrane's House ("Love's Pageants," 321–31).

gory is allowed to realize literally its strange semblance to or source in daemonic magic. Gordon's perspective, of course, aims at saving what is a pragmatic, politically burdened form of theater from being reduced by mystagogic scholars to a dehumanizing, infectious form of abstraction and mystery. Hence, like most recent critics, he emphasizes the degree to which the masque depends on the spectator's playful participation in its mythic fictions, on the composition and recomposition of the viewer's self and the assimilation of that self, within a courtly but fictive space, to a large complex of cultural paradigms. Nevertheless, so long as the masque depends on a self's participation in or identification with an image not its own, the form can hardly evade its strong structural similarities with both allegory and magic, and these similarities are what Spenser most urgently emphasizes.

My point is that Gordon's idealized account of a (Protestant or Humanist) "declaration," a (Catholic) "substantiation," or a (Romantic) "creation" of a self evades the more problematic Spenserian suspicion that the structures of the masque may tend to victimize or reduce the selves of its participants.[14] Spenser dramatizes this dilemma by the fact that, as Isabel MacCaffrey observes, the alien masque works a double magic, since it is for Amoret an entrapment but for Britomart a kind of exorcism (*Spenser's Allegory*, 112). From this dichotomy we might conclude that the only proper or safe stance toward the masque would be one of detachment, though we know that even in the more primitive Tudor entertainments such as Spenser knew the audience was asked to identify with or be absorbed, at least in part, by the fiction. As MacCaffrey sees, Spenser has cloven the typical spectator into two distinct selves that would ordinarily have been played off of one another. But the more radical corollary to her suggestion is that the masque of Cupid must somehow be read as *all antimasque*; that is, it constitutes a necessarily exorcized vision of chaotic enchantment to which the author provides no redemptive ceremonial antithesis.[15] (Such a reading is confirmed by Stephen Orgel's argument that the

14. I realize the element of anachronism here, since Gordon is interested mainly in Jacobean masques, but Enid Welsford in her study *The Court Masque*, 117–67, provides evidence that various forms of interpenetration or identification between audience and spectacle—including masking and unmasking, dancing and acting by courtiers, and so on—characterized earlier masques as well.

15. As opposed to general sorts of audience involvement, the antimasque proper is found only in late Elizabethan and Jacobean masques; Orgel (*Jonsonian Masque*, 8–9) suggests that the earliest appears in 1595, in Francis Davison's *The Mask of Proteus and the Adamantine Rock*. But Spenser could be said to show a dialectical extreme or potentiality in the earlier forms of allegorical entertainment which is usefully described by the later, polar terms "masque" and "antimasque," even though there is another sense in which he calls such a polarity into question.

figures in an antimasque are characterized by their total, literalistic absorption into the allegorical fiction that contains them and by their supposed inability to see their part in or break through the theatrical "illusion" [*Jonsonian Masque*, 13–14], a usually witty device that in the case of Amoret takes on more disturbing implications.) To put the problem in the extreme form it requires, I would say that Spenser shows us how the negative half of a dialectical pair (masque and antimasque) not only splits away from but usurps the place of the whole and, moreover, disguises itself as its opposite—much as Orgoglio had stood as a usurping synecdoche for and critique of the apocalyptic mode. In this form the masque-antimasque has wholly absorbed its one-time spectator, Amoret.

Even granting my earlier arguments against positing a source for the magical masque, we might find it fitting that Spenser has made the dangerously confusing and usurpative power of fantasy or "Fancy" the head masquer, being accompanied by its sometime synonym, "Desyre." Of course, the former's schematic position at the front of the allegorical procession does not require that we posit a genetic relation between it and the figures that follow, even though we *are* told that the apparently younger Fancy is the true "syre" of "De-syre" (like *phantasia*, an apparently unfathered or unfathering power), and that he gave the latter being "commune to them twaine" (III.xii.9). Such ambiguities of reference in the allegory may actually be Spenser's witty comment on the unstable distinctions and redundant agents of Renaissance faculty psychology. But the question of fantasy's part or lack thereof in the masque returns more seriously at the very end of the pageant, again in the context of speculation about the masque's origins:

> There were full many moe like maladies,
> Whose names and natures I note readen well;
> So many moe, as there be *phantasies*
> *In wavering wemens wit*, that none can tell,
> Or *paines in love*, or *punishments in hell*.
> (III.xii.26; emphasis mine)

The doubtful narrator suggests that we may read the masque as pathological projection, analytical psychomachia, or vision of damnation. Each of these alternatives (and my translation of Spenser's words is only tentative) has its own autonomous logic, and yet each seems to inhere strangely in or to stand as a possible metaphor for the others. The eschatological absoluteness of the last alternative may also suggest a kind of teleology in the list. But the categorical leaps between the three hypothetical sources have such an uncertain trajectory that any clear sense of hierarchy is obliterated. To this degree we need to measure the incommensurability of each alternative, the displacements between them, as well as their overlappings. Indeed, though we tend to use spatial metaphors like "source" or "place" (not to mention "displacement") in trying to sort out their relations, one result of Spenser's writing here is that both our literal and figurative notions of location are fragmented, as suggested, for instance, by the completely diverse functions of the preposition of place in the phrases "phantasies *in* . . . wemens wit," "paines *in* love," and "punishments *in* Hell."

Spenser is here taking an uncertainty endemic to all linguistic reference and putting it under a great deal of controlled, reflective pressure. The perception of some sort of insistent decentering in the poet's words seems to me so fundamental to a reading of the passage that when MacCaffrey observes exactly the opposite I cannot really begin to argue with her, for I am no longer sure we are reading the same poem: "[The sequence of analogues] deepens in seriousness and in degree of 'reality.' The blurring of ontological distinctions results in the superimposing of planes, *so that psychological, emotional and spiritual phenomena are seen to have a common center.* And so with imaginative and actual truth: fantasies—of Amoret, of Busirane, of the poet—are engendered by and rooted in a source that eventuates in the torments or joys of ultimate reality, Hell or Heaven . . . where in pure archetypal form live those essences in which human beings participate adjectivally" (*Spenser's Allegory*, 111–13; emphasis mine). It is a testimony to the difficulty of Spenser's mode that, whereas in commenting on Gordon I needed to insist on the primacy of a magical theory of language, in the case of MacCaffrey I must argue somewhat against it, at least insofar as this critic presumes that the text can be grounded in a firm structure of mystical or eschatological correspondences.[16] For this structure is as much the poem's victim as its inner principle of order. Spenser, after all, is hardly Dante or Pico, if even they fit MacCaffrey's scheme. MacCaffrey gives one a sense of the mythological and philosophical forms that are at stake in Spenser's

16. MacCaffrey insists that "behind Spenser's poem is a further implication: that in the timeless realm beyond history, in which all things shall one day be upfolded, the imagined and the real will become one, the crooked images be absorbed into their archetypes" (*Spenser's Allegory*, 75). This view at least needs to be qualified by the recognition that, as Colie puts it, "there is a great rift between human life and the life after death that runs through the whole *Faerie Queene*—we are nowhere assured of the relevance of what happens on earth to what will happen in heaven" (*Paradoxia Epidemica*, 349).

poem and of its continuing need to recover a nonnatural or visionary sense of place. Nevertheless, her use of what is in itself a more than blurry ontological vocabulary, her way of leveling the ambiguities in the use of "in" by making the poet move easily from "psychological" to "emotional" to "spiritual," idealizes out of existence the rhetorical difficulties of the text. In the end, this interpretation only obscures the radical nature of Spenser's verses.

My own bias understands the passage to work out a conflict within the writer, or, more accurately, it exposes a conflict between the writer and the tools of his allegorical project. The text reflects a struggle between the impulse to trace both psychological and eschatological origins for the apparitions represented in the masque (as MacCaffrey observes) and a defensive skepticism of all such finding. This struggle entails both a suspicion that any "finding" may only be the function of "invention" or fantasy, and a related fear of overestimating the absolute rightness of even a source authorized by tradition. Hence each successive item on the list discussed above suggests a greater degree of mythological abstraction at the same time that the expanding number of solutions suggests a greater uncertainty—not just in the slightly coy or innocent narrator but in Spenser himself. This hypothesis of a quest for a center tracked by a skepticism or fear of that center is arguably a mythological source of my own, and hence no more authoritative a solution than to suppose that the wavering referentiality of the poem is generic to all allegorical writing or else an emblem of the endless, impersonal dance of language itself (rather than a paradoxical defense against that somewhat deathly, lively dance). But my scheme at least has the advantage of showing a generative dynamic, a structure of motives for Spenser's writing which may account for the contrived rhetorical shape of the poetic text while taking seriously *The Faerie Queene*'s mythopoeic ambitions; it may also help us understand better the poem's marriage of an overdetermined mythic teleology with a profound, evasive freedom.

I have wandered a bit from my original discussion of the conceptual structure of the masque and the text's account of the masque's source and origin. Some of the questions raised in that discussion are answered but are also radically refocused at the critical point when Britomart crosses from the second chamber of Busyrane's House "into the inner roome, from whence [the masquers] first did rise" (III.xii.26). Within this room we glimpse a dark, infolded image of source and of relation whose centrality cannot be shuddered apart quite as easily as I have done with some of Spenser's other figurations of origin. But Britomart's quest for the disenchanting source of enchantment still unleashes no pure power of disenchantment nor concludes with any easy, unshaken recovery from magic.

I will not pause long over the nuances of the crossing itself. Instead of forcing her way through, Britomart must wait with "sleights and art" for the iron gate that shuts off the inner room to open of its own accord. She also attends a temporal as well as a spatial threshold: the passage from day to the second night of her vigil. She has seen the procession once, but to solve it she cannot allow it to emerge a second time, as if to witness its unfolding again were itself a danger, a temptation to repetition. When the gate does open she enters immediately. But in what she might have thought would be the tiring house of the masquers, she finds that they have all vanished—though of course we are never quite sure whether they were ever there to begin with. These are elusive details, but they may indicate how complex such moments of transgression are and how difficult it is to map the leap from the manifestations of magic in the outer chambers to their putative cause within:

> . . . they streight were vanisht all and some,
> Ne living wight she saw in all that roome,
> Save that same woefull Ladie, both whose hands
> Were bounden fast, that did her ill become,
> And her small wast girt round with yron bands,
> Unto a brasen pillour, by the which she stands.
>
> And her before the vile Enchaunter sate,
> Figuring straunge characters of his art,
> With living bloud he those characters wrate,
> Dreadfully dropping from her dying hart,
> Seeming transfixed with a cruell dart,
> And all perforce to make her him to love.
> Ah who can love the worker of her smart?
> A thousand charmes he formerly did prove;
> Yet thousand charmes could not her stedfast heart remove.
>
> (III.xii.30–31)

The second stanza reminds us that this is, perversely enough, both a textual and a rhetorical encounter, a scene of erotic persuasion—one in which, moreover, the persuasion and the pain of love are identified. We might here recall how, in *A View*, the picture of a child learning a language, though clothed in the relatively gentle imagery of maternal nourishment, could find an ironic mirror in images that intertwined the demonic and the bestial, the idolatrous and the cannibalistic. Canto xii's image of the wounded breast; the flow of blood which forms the medium of exchange between enchanter and victim; the deadly symbiosis that the reading and writing entails; the huge incommensurability of the magical ceremony and its psychological occasion—all of these suggest parallels to the kind of dilemmas which Spenser describes in his dialogue on Ireland. Along with other passages in his poem, such parallels suggest the forms of violence and victimization which may underlie even supposedly civilized modes of relation. And yet I list such analogues here not so much to solve our questions about the figures in the central chamber as to forestall one particular strategy for reading them. Spenser collapses the splendid shows of the masque to this vast, empty scene of reading and writing, thereby reminding us that the tortuous phantasms are the productions of language and poetry. For as even Ficino knew, the magician works less on objective demons and cosmological sympathies than on the creatures of memory and imagination. Yet the recollections of *A View* may also remind us that it would be only a subtler and more narrowing mystification to say that Busyrane the magician is a figure for the poet—unless the scene I have been describing also makes it considerably more difficult for us to say what a poet is or does.

The narrative that follows, if it does not resolve such disturbing ambiguities of reference, breaks apart and sets in motion the magically entangled figures of Amoret and Busyrane. Britomart's rude interruption of the scene serves the purposes of disenchantment, but again the progress of events makes it hard to sort out any pure power or intention of disenchantment. Indeed, Spenser indicates that merely to interrupt or break off even so damaging a spell is itself a danger, a delusive overestimation of one's powers. Frye suggests that "in romance all magicians, whatever the reality of their powers, have to renounce their magic at the end" (*Secular Scripture*, 144), the archetypal examples being Prospero's drowning his tomes and breaking his wand at the end of *The Tempest*, and Faustus's final cry of repentance and despair, "I'll burn my books." And indeed, Busyrane himself, when the Knight of Chastity enters

> Soone as that virgin knight he saw in place,
> His wicked bookes in hast he overthrew,
> Not caring his long labours to deface . . .
> (III.xii.32)

But this is disenchantment with a vengeance, for Busyrane at this point attempts to dispatch Amoret with another knife, a wound that, if inflicted, would literalize even more fully the "arrow in the heart" conceit. Britomart struggles with the villain, but in the process he turns his knife on *her*: "Unwares it strooke into her snowie chest, / That little drops empurpled her faire brest" (xi.33). The quester here begins to mirror the wounded object of her quest, and in her anger she almost slays the enchanter. Amoret prevents her doing so, however, since Busyrane's death would not bring to an end the spell he has woven around her. As Britomart earlier had to wait for the iron gate to open of its own accord, so she must now suspend any direct attempt to master her magical antagonist.

Up until this point in her passage through Busyrane's House, the heroine has been splendidly calm, if somewhat uncomprehending, as if caught in a dream of her own. To cross into the inner room should break the dreamlike texture of her experience and free her from impotent waiting, but it is exactly at this point that she is forced to wait under even greater constraints. Angry, hasty, wounded, Britomart must suffer Busyrane to undo his own illusions, rather than defacing or tearing down the poisoned imagery herself, as Guyon had done in the Bower. Indeed, the only time when she expresses anything like horror at the cruel magic in Busyrane's House is when she watches the enchanter *reverse* his spell:

> Full dreadfull things out of that balefull booke
> He red, and measur'd many a sad verse,
> That horror gan the virgins hart to perse,
> And her faire locks up stared stiffe on end,
> Hearing him those same bloudy lines reherse.
> (III.xii.36)

As neither the victim nor her rescuer escapes being wounded by the magician's knife, here Britomart must witness the disturbing fact that Chastity's spell-unbinding powers and long labors to free the imprisoned Amoret are in the end strangely dependent on the same magic that had previously bound her. The disease shares a space with its cure; the abolition of idolatry is not the death of magic.

Idols of the Close

Britomart in the end does manage to bind Busyrane with the very chain that had bound Amoret, a situation that ironically turns against itself Petrarch's image of the lover bound by Cupid in the first of the *Triomphi*. In Spenser's narrative it is the conjurer of Cupid, himself an incarnation of the poet of the first Triumph, who is so bound. Furthermore, just as Spenser provided no redemptive masque to follow the erotic antimasque, so there is in Book III no subsequent triumphal procession, no triumph of Chastity, nor any other of the extended, balanced series of subversions and usurpations which make up the larger architecture of Petrarch's sequence. The systematic poetics of triumph is itself undone here, as Britomart wanders back with renewed wonder through the House of Busyrane which has ruined itself, its glory "vanisht utterly, and cleane subverst" (III.xii.42). She is released into a world of quest rather than one of triumph.[17]

It may be that Britomart's trial in Busyrane's House is the extremest test of her thematic function as Knight of Chastity. Nevertheless, her successful overthrow of enchantment there serves partly to divert her from the original goal of her quest: marriage with the hero Arthegall. This fulfillment is delayed until Book V, and I want to end this chapter by looking at its central scene, Britomart's encounter with yet another idol and her dream of supernatural marriage in the Church of Isis. First, however, we need to pause over an earlier encounter, the lost or abandoned *telos* of Book III.

In the six-book *Faerie Queene* of 1596, an exasperated Scudamour leaves both Britomart and Amoret inside the House of Busyrane and is only reunited with his wife in canto x of Book IV. The 1590 version of the poem, however, which contained only the first three books, restores Amoret to her husband right after she leaves the ruined palace—Britomart being left as the one witness to a spousal embrace that closes the poem as it had proceeded up to that point:

> Lightly he clipt her twixt his armes twaine,
> And streightly did embrace her body bright,
> Her body, late the prison of sad paine,
> Now the sweet lodge of love and deare delight:
> But she faire Lady overcommen quight
> Of huge affection, did in pleasure melt,
> And in sweete ravishment pourd out her spright:
> No word they spake, nor earthly thing they felt,
> But like two senceles stocks in long embracement dwelt.
>
> Had ye them seene, ye would have surely thought,
> That they had beene that faire *Hermaphrodite*,

17. Roche, *Kindly Flame*, 88, makes a similar point: "As in Petrarch, The Triumph of Cupid is succeeded by the Triumph of Chastity, but Spenser saw that even this triumph might prove empty and thrusts his heroine into new situations in the legend of friendship."

> Which that rich *Romane* of white marble wrought,
> And in his costly Bath causd to bee site:
> So seemd those two, as growne together quite,
> That *Britomart* halfe envying their blesse,
> Was much empassiond in her gentle sprite,
> And to her selfe oft wisht like happinesse,
> In vaine she wisht, that fate n' ould let her yet possesse.
> (III.xii.45–46[1590])

Lewis, perhaps too simply, glosses this ravishing scene by means of the Mosaic figure of man and wife cleaving together and becoming one flesh; he also moves from this to a reading of the hermaphrodite as a kind of allegorical *imago dei (Images of Life*, 38). More circumspect critics, especially Cheney ("Spenser's Hermaphrodite"), have emphasized the degree to which Spenser frames this sublimated image of union with ironic or parodic elements. Without pushing a de-idealizing hermeneutic of suspicion too strongly, we may sense that this image of erotic ending evolves (or collapses) into a form of rigid, senseless death, a sexual death undoubtedly but one that is given a strange, concrete form in the allusion to the bisexual statue in the Roman bath. Within that pagan, slightly decadent field of images, the suggestion of metamorphosis and the fluid interchange of persons may seem uneasily coupled with a sense of fixation and calcification. Such an ambiguous wholeness is at once relieved and further compromised by the shadowy third figure on the scene, the alienated Britomart. For her the hermaphrodite means not possession but lack and desire, a happiness that fate denies her, a merging of sexual identities to which her own cross-dressing is at best an uneasy stepping stone. Some of the strangeness of the hermaphrodite image may indeed come from its being not only the poet's idea of what lovers looked like but also a visionary projection of the mournful heroine—as is suggested obliquely by the lines, "had ye them seene [as Britomart herself does], ye would have surely thought." Still, the image may then be a visionary revenge on the united lovers as much as a sign of Britomart's sympathy. For she is caught here between identification and alienation, between love and envy—those two opposite affections that Bacon thought most likely "to fascinate and bewitch," that "both have vehement wishes," "frame themselves readily into imaginations and suggestions," and "come easily into the eye" (*Works*, 3:392).[18] Hence it is through her eyes that Britomart pro-

18. "Envy" here seems especially likely to take on a visual or visionary form, as the etymology of *invidia* (to look askance or against) and the mythology of the "evil eye" suggest.

jects her inward fixation and confusion onto their immediate outward cause, elevating the lovers into an ideal of erotic union and yet secretly defiling that union by reducing the lovers to dead, idolatrous statues. Here we find returning in a minor key Britomart's earlier power to convert her own self-images into fateful, threatening objects of desire. No sooner has she retreated from the house of idolatry than idolatry and obsessive vision (the threat of the *eidolon*, the eye-doll) begin to reconstitute themselves.

Whether we want to locate the source of the image in the eye of Britomart or her poet, the hermaphrodite stanzas may stand as one of the best emblems of the emotive and representational ambivalence that characterizes Spenser's writing. Difficult as the stanzas are in themselves, however, we must also try to make sense of their cancellation from the six-book version of the poem in 1596. What is haunting about this circumstance is that it is the closest thing to a moment of literal iconoclasm in the compositional history of Spenser's poem, an occasion in which the idol is suppressed in reality, not just in fiction.[19] As one critic has suggested, Spenser needed to cast out even so beautifully ambiguous an image of ending in order to create a vivifying gap within his fable; the desire to please the reader with perfect closure falls before the poet's desire to continue his narrative, so that he willfully opens up a space of loss which requires the story of Scudamour and Amoret to go on being told (Goldberg, *Endlesse Worke*, 1–3). Such an appeal to the paradoxical motives of narrative (in the manner of Barthes) is useful here; its relevance to this particular situation is confirmed by the fact that, when the lovers seem finally about to meet again (IV.x), Spenser wholly occludes any account of their reunion, substituting Scudamour's own story of their very *first* meeting in the Temple of Venus (at the center of which is another hermaphroditic statue). Ending is not so much united with origins as made to occupy a curiously negative space, the extremely shadowy status of the original event itself being reinforced by Spenser's comparing Scudamour's successful theft of Amoret from the temple to Orpheus' failed recovery of Eurydice from Hades (IV.x.58).[20]

19. Maureen Quilligan, focusing on the ways in which the risky "publication" of the 1590 *Faerie Queene* is reflected in the more anxious sense of "publicness" and even censorship haunting the 1596 text, argues that "the cancellation of the hermaphrodite image would also suggest that the gynandromorphic flexibility that Spenser had asked of his readers in Book III would be canceled as well" (*Milton's Spenser: The Politics of Reading*, 203).

20. The fate of the early ending of Book III might lead us to speculate about the unwritten scene that should have been the visionary culmination of the poem, the "apocalyptic" marriage of Arthur and Gloriana. For despite critics' arguments that such a pro-

The kind of "iconoclasm" entailed by Spenser's cancellation of the hermaphrodite stanzas is as difficult to decipher as the image or idol itself. Indeed, the more seriously we take the difficulties of the passage, the more questions are raised about the motives underlying poetic composition, the authority or rationale for any poet's revisions, and the critical tact that should guide our investigation of rejected lines. The absent presence of the closing stanzas provides a greater than ordinary space in which to construct parables of literary cause and intentionality. I would only risk suggesting here that, whatever solutions critics find themselves proposing, ideas that are least indifferent to the element of crisis in the passage will carry most weight. That is to say, one needs an interpretative skepticism that will heighten rather than oppress the intensifications of image and meaning which give life to the poem. In determining why the poet changed his mind, one must try to do justice both to the inevitable arbitrariness of choice in poetic composition and to the complex patterns of compulsion that are at work in Spenser's mythmaking (assuming, of course, that arbitrariness and compulsion are even distinguishable).

The Isis Church episode falls in the central canto (vii) of Book v, "The Legend of Justice." It is a distortion, perhaps, to take this romantic, mediate dream text as the end of my own readings in this chapter (especially since it is the more epical, dramatic fight between Britomart and Radigund which successfully frees Britomart's lover from the bondage of false female power and makes possible their eventual marriage). And yet what I want to explore is exactly the intense, infolded tentativeness of the scene. What further determines my interest in Isis Church is the poet's complex picture of the way that his iconoclastic quester confronts a redemptive form of idolatry. More sublimely, if somewhat less problematically than the hermaphrodite

---

jected scene of union must somehow measure all our readings of earlier episodes, I suspect that the poet never could have composed it. Spenser's evident nervousness about any such eschatological moment (which I have commented on before) might help account for his suppression from the 1590 passage of any direct allusion to the Platonic-Aristophanic hermaphrodite of the *Symposium*—a somewhat grotesque, bisexual creature that Jove, in punishment for an attempted rebellion, divided in half, and that ever after attempts desperately to reunite its parts. Even if critics are justified in applying to Spenser Renaissance allegorizations of this text, still we must see how radically it ironizes this already ambiguous, humorous image of the cosmic origin and goal of human desire to convert it into an avowedly artificial, pagan statue (and placed in a bath, no less!). In the end, even given Spenser's reduced, demythologized, and depoliticized version of the hermaphrodite, the shadow of the Platonic image may have caused the poet sufficient worry to make him cancel the ending entirely.

stanzas, this episode implicates Britomart in a narrative of violent conflict and erotic communion which is the culmination of her explicitly visionary experiences in the poem.

Britomart comes across the temple seemingly by accident, after her defeat of the treacherous Dolon. She witnesses there a strange statue of the goddess, her priests and her cult, to all of which Britomart's own relation unfolds only slowly, through prophecy and dream. Critics have often noted the odd suggestion of self-worship in the lines that describe the heroine's first contemplation of the "Idoll" of Isis suppressing a crocodile: Britomart "Unto her selfe her silent prayers did impart" (v.vii.7). This is a familiar enough irony in *The Faerie Queene*, where questers often find themselves confronting externalized emblems of their own moral or psychic condition. But this ambiguous alignment of goddess and heroine is carried even further in Britomart's egocentric dream of identification and possession. Resting overnight within the central chamber of the temple, she has a vision in which she "dreams her own imagination to please herself," where she "becomes what she beholds" (as Blake would say of those who are trapped by their reductive image of the created world):

> Her seem'd, as she was doing sacrifize
> To *Isis*, deckt with Mitre on her hed,
> And linnen stole after those Priestes guize,
> All sodainely she saw transfigured
> Her linnen stole to robe of scarlet red,
> And Moone-like Mitre to a Crowne of gold,
> That even she her selfe much wondered
> At such a chaunge, and ioyed to behold
> Her selfe, adorn'd with gems and iewels manifold.
>
> And in the midst of her felicity,
> An hideous tempest seemed from below,
> To rise through all the Temple sodainely,
> That from the Altar all about did blow
> The holy fire, and all the embers strow
> Uppon the ground, which kindled privily,
> Into outragious flames unwares did grow,
> That all the Temple put in ieopardy
> Of flaming, and her selfe in great perplexity.
>
> With that the Crocodile, which sleeping lay
> Under the Idols feete in fearelesse bowre,
> Seem'd to awake in horrible dismay,
> As being troubled with that stormy stowre;

> And gaping greedy wide, did streight devoure
> Both flames and tempest: with which growen great,
> And swolne with pride of his owne peerelesse powre,
> He gan to threaten her likewise to eat;
> But that the Goddesse with her rod him backe did beat.
>
> Tho turning all his pride to humblesse meeke,
> Him selfe before her feete he lowly threw,
> And gan for grace and love of her to seeke:
> Which she accepting, he so neare her drew,
> That of his game she soone enwombed grew,
> And forth did bring a Lion of great might;
> That shortly did all other beasts subdew.
> With that she waked, full of fearefull fright,
> And doubtfully dismayd through that so uncouth sight.
>
> (v.vii.13–16)

Britomart's dream of her own transformation into the statue (reinforced not so much by physical description as by a studied ambiguity of reference in the use of the pronoun "she" throughout the above stanzas) no doubt suggests Paul's more benign idea of the faithful worshiper being changed by degrees into the image of God. Yet it is worth stressing the surprising hints of idolatrous worship and identification here (especially in what Spenser calls a "Church," and where the priests perform "Mas"), because there is so much in the conduct of this most esoteric of Spenser's visions which emerges as the result of a subtle evasion of potential forms of idolatry. The paradox of an iconoclastic (or iconotropic) idolatry is built into the decorum of the episode, and bringing it to the surface may help us better understand the difficulties of Spenser's description.

We can start by noting in the above lines and those leading up to them some strong recollections of what seems a thoroughly pagan brand of theurgic magic: the Pythagorean purities of Isis's priesthood, the dream that is sent to the celebrant during her sacred "incubation" near the altar of the deity, Britomart's image of herself "doing sacrifize," the Hermetic fancy of an animated idol (though this also recalls the moving statues of court masque). We might find diverse analogies to Spenser's complex plot of imitation, divination, and possession in Plutarch or Iamblichus, and yet these would mainly show us by contrast how much of the mere ritualism and doctrinal bathos Spenser has stripped away from the occult encounter. As in his treatment of the Eucharist and baptism, Spenser has cast the mysteries of Isis into a dream narrative that remains at the margins of systematic magic. Despite the sacred aura of the episode, there is no structured rite of initiation, no prescriptive ceremony, no collective repetition, no suggestion of catharsis, nor any interest in psychic salvation. Similarly there is little resembling the "Puritan" opposition of material body and occult soul or pneuma on which the eschatology of Greek and Roman mystery religion depended.[21] The dream confuses any such rationalized oppositions or mysteries, which could appear in the light of this obscure, sudden vision as at best a kind of failed poetry.

To define Spenser's strategy in terms of the absence of magical machinery, however, may be less than persuasive. That the poet strategically resists the rationalizing of the irrational comes through more directly in the complex ways he deploys some key mythological paradigms in his dream narrative, reinforcing a patterned density of analogy even as he confuses fixed polarities of value and authority. The vision of Britomart transformed into the gold and scarlet-clad goddess she had worshiped, for example, recalls both the figure of the Babylonian whore "Mystery" (also seated on a proud, sacrilegious beast) and the heroic "woman clothed with the sunne" of Revelation 12.1. Furthermore, whereas the latter figure appears in the biblical vision as great with child and threatened by a tyrannical, devouring serpent, only to be saved by an armed angel, in Spenser's text it is Britomart herself who manages to subdue the dragonlike crocodile, taming him even to the degree that *he* begets upon her his own supernatural child, a regal lion. (The whole sequence is given a truly oneiric rapidity, with the moment of conception strangely elided.) The crocodile itself had earlier in the canto been explicated as the symbol of both "forged guile and open force" (vii.7), and yet in the dream he first appears as the enemy of such threats: asleep to begin with, he awakes from his "feareless bowre" in order to suppress the destructive, seemingly causeless storm of fire that had spread outward from the disturbed altar, and that starts to consume its templar home. The crocodile, that is, starts to resemble the just, reforming monarch Osiris, if not Isis herself. And yet, having swallowed the rebellious fire, he just as quickly turns into a version of Typhon-Seth, the chthonic god of storm, betrayal, and barren tyranny who is Osiris's own brother and mortal enemy. His greedy, phallic violence is rapidly enough

21. See E. R. Dodds, *The Greeks and the Irrational*, 102–78, for a richly suggestive account of Greek shamanism, divination, and mystery religions, certain aspects of which both underlie and are excluded from the account of Isis Church. Much of the ritual material in the episode probably comes from later Roman authors such as Plutarch and Apuleius, although there also seem to be some details taken over from biblical descriptions of the Israelite priests (cf. A. C. Hamilton, *Annotated "Faerie Queene,"* 573).

turned into sexual play and generation, but it is no simple matter to see how this metamorphosis consorts with the phantasm's earlier postures of rebellion and threat.

Jane Aptekar, tracing out the ambivalent iconography of the crocodile in late classical and Christian writing, notes how strangely Dionysiac are the manifestations of the hieratic, Apollonian virtues of Justice and Equity in Isis Church. She points out that the goddess's chaste priests abstain from wine, at best a demonic communion drink in this episode, grapevines being said to have sprung from earth impregnated by the blood of rebel giants slain by Jove, so that their fruit stirs up "old rebellious thought"; and yet the passions of these early giants as well as the darkly generative power of the earth reemerge throughout the imagery of Britomart's dream (*Icons of Justice*, 104f.). Indeed, the volatile center of the dream—the holy fire that turns destructive, the sacred rage that turns into sacrilege, the restraint that is transformed alternately into tyranny and love—suggests that the church is the home of anarchic forces which yet cannot be clearly distinguished as natural or supernatural, sexual or political or cosmological. In this fantasy about power and its relation to the power of fantasy, Spenser gives us the picture of a fierce system of conflict, exchange, and compensation, a strangely shifting image of freedom and repression. From one angle, Aptekar is probably right to see in it subtle, almost Machiavellian lessons about the interanimated workings of law, force, and fraud; but while the pressure of political ideas in the episode serves to deepen the urgency of the sexual imagery, the insistent presence of the sexual complicates any presuppositions about the purity or detachability of the political argument (whether it unfolds according to conservative or more radical principles).[22] When Britomart retells the dream, one of Isis's priests tries to straighten things out by converting its iconoclastic phantasmagoria into parabolic prophecy, explaining the vision's symbolic reference to her eventual marriage with the just Arthegall, her tempering of his rough justice, and the birth of their child that "Lion-like shall shew his powre extreame"

22. Even if we followed Fletcher's lead in reading Isis as a figure for the singular idea of political Equity, Spenser's narrative would still work against our efforts to give it a rigidly ideological cast. For like the dreamers in Chapman's completion of Marlowe's "Hero and Leander," who meet no obvious gods of erotic order and disorder but "Ceremony" and "Dissimulation," Britomart dreams in Equity of a mythic principle of mediation. For Equity is a name for what we might otherwise call "the poetics of law" (*Prophetic Moment*, 282). Although in its prophetic aspect Equity is a divine principle that helps us measure the passing shows of time by the artifice of eternity, it is also the faculty that accommodates fixed rules to practice and balances principle against the contingencies of history, allowing neither chaotic occasion nor the agents of justice and law to inflate themselves to catastrophic dimensions.

(v.vii.22–23). Still, the priest's retrospective reading of the dreamed *hieros gamos* as a heroic prediction of the imperial future only comes to terms with a portion of the vision. It sublimates but in no way resolves or obviates the difficult structures of the poet's imagery in which the sacred, the sexual, and the political seem to merge.

One has reached this point before: an allegorical image full of reversals and allusive ironies, forms of transgression mingling with the ciphers of hierarchy, diverse levels of discourse that intersect within an almost obsessive construction of ambivalence. By way of ending here, however, some fairly plain questions (rather than epigrammatic paradox): What does it mean for the poet or the reader to labor to reach such points? Into what state do such intricate images throw us? From what are we released? And to whom, after all, should we attribute the desire for simplicity or stability of reference that the text undermines? To the poet? his audience? his tradition? Does each have its own ideal or illusion of simplicity? Would anyone even recognize simplicity or clarity as something he or she had really wanted from the poet in the first place, or really feared to have broken? From Britomart's point of view, it is perhaps the very metamorphic structure of the dream that makes it an instance of what I have called "redemptive idolatry." For the encounter in Isis Church, as opposed to her early mirror-vision, allows within the detachment of a dream a narcissistic identification that transfigures and enlarges the self, that does not block or sicken or victimize her sexual desires, and that seems to grant her a place within a mythic and political story which might provide more than "the armour of an alienating identity." But does it benefit us as readers that the text somehow steals from us any single figure or frame of value, any names that might bind or empower us? The priest, as I said, seems to have gotten only a part of the dream, but that part comes to him with the terror of a "heavenly fury" (v.vii.20). Would he or Britomart then have been better off if they had gotten the dream in all of its brave ambivalence? Or are we worried by the fact that the priest (who unlike Spenser seems not to have read Freud) so blithely glosses over the strange shapes of sexual violence and orality that twist themselves around the political symbolism? But might not this hidden violence be after all the very thing that so terrifies him, such that his reading of the dream would be as much a defense against as an explication of that terror? Perhaps the priest's reduction is a necessary one, since Britomart must live in the world and not in her dreams—though it is the world that will give her "ioyance of [her] dreame" (v.vii.23). But can it then really remain her dream, and not someone else's? Such questions are not simple to ask, nor can they quite be answered here, unless they have been answered already. If they are for the moment sufficient in themselves, it is because they throw more radically into doubt our own interpretive unfoldings of doubt, our own fetishizings of ambiguity and ambivalence. Yet having posed these questions, I find that what I really want to know is whether they could be Spenser's questions as well as my own.

5

Eden without Idols (The Garden of Adonis)

We were fashioned to live in Paradise, and Paradise was destined to serve us. Our destiny has been altered; that this has also happened with the destiny of Paradise is not stated.

Franz Kafka

Spenser's Garden of Adonis in Book III, canto vi, of *The Faerie Queene* has outwardly little to do with the dramatized scenes of idolatry and iconoclasm I have discussed so far. Nor does that episode contain anything like the scenes of visionary loss and disenchantment which are my subject in Chapter 6. Yet just for these reasons the Garden can offer a testing ground for the broader claims about Spenser's poetry which have emerged in my commentary. What I have said about Spenser's attitude toward myth and allegory should point up many of the strategies of inclusion, exclusion, and substitution which account for the extreme inventiveness of canto vi. To put it schematically, I have read the Garden as Spenser's attempt to find a myth of place, of presence, of incarnate power and love which yet seeks to evade the potential for idolatry which shadows such a search. This archaic yet revisionary garden responds to our impulses to fixate, literalize, and violate; it at once focuses and steals us from our nostalgias for other gardens. Spenser's mystic paradise is a retrospective and demystifying critique not only of the Bower of Bliss (II.xii) and the Garden of Proserpina (II.vii), but of all Edenic fables of origin, all apocalyptic longings for a final return, all inherited mythologies of birth, growth, and form.

Paradise, Paradox, and Place

Is it surprising to see a garden as the locus of idolatry and iconoclasm? One may recall how often the biblical attack on false worship called for the tearing down of groves and "high places," natural or cultivated sites that were thought to possess an inherent sacredness. Eden itself contained at its center the vehicle for the primal errors of pride and rebellious self-exaltation, while in the middle of the Garden of Love in Guillaume de Lorris's *Roman de la Rose* we find the displaced pool of Narcissus, the mirror of idolatrous *cupiditas.* In a lighter vein, one might cite Spenser's friend Raleigh, who in his *History of the World* gives an account of "those gross and blind idolaters" who "every age after other sink lower and lower and shrink and slide downwards from knowledge of the one true and very god," worshiping beasts, elements, the vegetable world—to satirize which he translates Juvenal:

> The Ægyptians thinke it sinne to root up, or to bite
> Their Leekes or Onyons, which they serve with holy rite:
> *O happie Nations, which of their owne sowing*
> *Have store of Gods in every garden growing.*
> (*History,* VI.iii; emphasis mine)

These are loose analogies, no doubt, but turning to *The Faerie Queene* we might note the paradox that it is a garden rather than a church that provides the most obvious site of iconoclasm. Despite the poet's fascination with the more radical gestures of reform, the poem contains no temple or church being broken down or stripped of its sacred ornaments, save by such defiling hands as those of Orgoglio's monster or the Blatant Beast. The physical violence of iconoclasm in a sacred context is indeed usually sublimated or defensively displaced into more complex sorts of mythic action—the poet giving us his most nearly literal rendering of the curative destruction of images in Guyon's tearing down of the profane Bower of Bliss:

> But all those pleasant bowres and Pallace brave,
> *Guyon* broke downe, with rigour pittilesse;
> Ne ought their goodly workmanship might save
> Them from the tempest of his wrathfulnesse,
> But that their blisse he turn'd to balefulnesse:
> Their groves he feld, their gardins did deface,
> Their arbers spoyle, their Cabinets suppresse,

> Their banket houses burne, their buildings race,
> And of the fairest late, now made the fowlest place.
> (II.xii.83)[1]

There are other places of illusion and false worship in the poem, many considerably more disturbing than the Bower. But Busyrane's palace dissolves by itself, as an extension of Britomart's transgression or forced counterspell. Mammon's cave remains untouched by Guyon's intrusion, being perhaps a vision of an elusive and permanent institution in the world, or at least not one reformable by iconoclastic violence. Orgoglio is deflated, but his popish palace, with its bloody sacrificial altar, simply recedes from view once its prisoner has been freed by Arthur. The contrastive emphasis on iconoclasm in the Bower may therefore make us see more clearly the threat of idolatry in a place where we might otherwise be inclined to ignore it.

There is nothing darkly unholy or mysterious about the Bower, though the figure at the gate does offer an enchanting chalice, an unselving drink. Nor is there really much of the trumpery of false pride or erotic cruelty, none of the evil, poisonous fruits that hang from the trees in the Garden of Proserpina. It is not the desire for worldly possession or total vision, the identification of the god and his image, that most characterizes the idolatry of the Bower but, rather, the lure of a perfect, prelapsarian relation of man and nature—whether this is found in an ideal mimesis in which art and nature coincide (a meeting that can be achieved only at the expense of confusing the necessarily distinct orders of the fallen world) or in a perfect, careless innocence in erotic relations. For there is sex as well as voyeurism in the Bower (*pace* C. S. Lewis), even though we see it only in its later phases of exhaustion.[2] Still, such sexuality as we witness is without generation, a pleasure whose slight touches of cruelty, greed, and sterility grow out of an ultimately desperate attempt to exclude a fallen world of struggle and change, but whose visual and sen-

1. For a more comprehensive reading of idolatry and iconoclasm in the Bower of Bliss, see Greenblatt, *Renaissance Self-Fashioning*, 157–92.

2. For Lewis's comments on sex in the Bower of Bliss, see *Allegory of Love*, 331–33. Though it is Lewis who rightly brought to the fore the problem of voyeurism in the Bower, he overemphasizes the degree to which that place represents "the whole sexual nature in disease." He insists that "there is not a kiss or an embrace in the island: only male prurience and female provocation," as opposed to the "frank" sexuality of the Garden of Adonis. This is accurate, perhaps, only in parable. We are as much as told that Acrasia and Verdant have been making love, but that may be less relevant than the fact that we are only shown their frozen, postcoital embraces—as if that were the ultimate end of love in the place.

sual fixations only yield to a strange kind of dissolution or entropy.[3] Hence the primary emblem of the Bower's seductions is the central tableau of Verdant sleeping in the arms of the witch Acrasia, the one "quite molten into lust," his weapons useless and shield defaced, the other (like his own nightmare) hovering over him, "greedily depasturing delight" through her "false eyes" (II.xii.73).

Though it simplifies the moral problematic of the Bower extremely, one might say that it is not so much the ideal of Eden as the attempt to make it present, to embody it in art and physical life, that can make the creation of a garden so dangerous. It is not at all easy, of course, to divide human nostalgia from the will to make present the objects of that nostalgia. But the garden itself may have been a particularly good locus for reflecting on the relation of desire to its realization, at least for Spenser and his contemporaries; as Terry Comito argues in his study, *The Idea of the Garden in the Renaissance,* what characterizes both literal and poetic gardens of the period is exactly the desire of artists to commit the presence of a sacred ideal of paradise to the physical world, to the creations of human labor and natural growth. Like the more explicitly symbolic monastic gardens of the Middle Ages, he argues, Renaissance gardens responded to a deep desire for a mythic potency in space, for possessing an original and timeless point of reality (an *omphalos,* Eliade would say). But as much out of its disillusionment with the symbolic modes of the Middle Ages as out of its compensatory worldliness, the Renaissance tried to construct its Edenic sites in the physical and political world, not, as Dante or Bonaventure, in a purely eschatological and visionary one.[4]

Comito's finely elaborated argument is crucial; he points to a problem in the history of the garden of which Spenser's Bower of Bliss and Garden of Adonis provide such a subtle analysis. Comito has a shrewd eye for the way in which formal and literary gardens "respond to their own aspirations" (178); he is sensitive especially to the shifting masks of nostalgia and to the ways in which the quest for paradise may be hindered by reduction or rationalization. Speaking of medieval gardens, he observes that "the theological imagination is of course as subject as any other to failure or evasion. The notion of Eden may be adulterated to a mere nostalgia for bucolic or sensual simplifications or it may be bureaucratized into a rigid allegory, made a mere name

3. On the dissolution of significant form in the Bower and its emblematic relevance to our view of the poem as a whole, see G. Wilson Knight's essay, "The Spenserian Fluidity."

4. On Renaissance attempts to find an actual geographical location for paradise, see Arnold Williams, *The Common Expositor: An Account of the Commentaries on Genesis, 1527–1633,* 95–102.

for abstractions" (35), not to mention the vehicle for antinomian or chiliastic apeals to the idea of final paradisal return.[5] He further recognizes how frequently a ruinous pride in display (whether mercantile or aristocratic), or the desire to flatter a mythologized monarch, formed the basis of Renaissance garden work. He sees, that is, how much these gardens could fall within the realm of Mammon and Philotime, as of Acrasia. (Interestingly, his most apt examples come from Elizabethan gardens like Cecil's.) But for all his sense of the complications of imaginative desire, Comito has a telling blind spot. As a critic he feels fairly confident that he can always see the true goal of the garden through all of the possible failures or perversions of intention, and that (somewhat in the manner of Frye) he can pluck the unambiguous imaginative heart out of these marred creations. And he opts at all times for a magical, incarnational notion of place as the aim of formal gardening. Hence he must dismiss as largely unpoetic or as merely doctrinal intrusion the insistence of a poet such as Milton that sanctity of place is the creation of those who dwell in that place, and no superhuman holiness[6]—a point that his deity underscores by setting Eden itself adrift during the deluge, "with all his verdure spoild," the garden later taking root at sea as "an Iland salt and bare, / The haunt of Seales and Orcs, and Sea-mews' clang" (*Paradise Lost*, XI.834–35). Comito thus underestimates the imaginative integrity of this impulse in both Spenser and Milton to spoil their own Edens. Though it has, like any stance, literalistic phases, without some awareness of this iconoclastic impulse we cannot understand the subtle dialectics of Spenser's mythmaking in *The Faerie Queene*.

One would like to say that the Garden of Adonis is Spenser's ultimate correction of the Bower, or that the Garden is the true form of which the Bower is merely a parody. The relation is of course much looser than this, but even without a point-by-point comparison we can see that the Garden of Book III continues to reflect the complex of nostalgias present in the Bower, at the same time that it evades its idolatries. The enticements of *opsis* and ornament, the temptations to a regressive voyeurism which seem to be built into the Bower, are replaced by a sense of mystery, refuge, and pleasure that goes beyond the merely visual and that requires of the poet an entirely different species of *enargeia*—if that rhetorical category is still even applicable.[7]

5. The idea of a "return to paradise" as a motif in Christian theology, as well as its relation to other myths of renewal and reform, are discussed in Ladner, *The Idea of Reform*, 63–82.

6. See Comito, *Idea of the Garden*, 36–37.

7. For a detailed analysis of Spenser's ironic treatment of sensuous pictorialism and visual illusion in the Bower of Bliss, see John Bender, *Spenser and Literary Pictorialism*, 175–97.

There is no verbal rendering of visible appearance per se, nor any questers like Guyon and his Palmer whose presence in and movement through the Garden might provide the illusion of spatial and visual experience, or serve as a point of identification to give continuity to our impressions. Having encountered the Garden in an extended, etiological excursus (as part of Spenser's attempt to explain the birth and education of Belphebe and her twin sister Amoret, preceded by the charming, Alexandrian idyll of Venus's search for the lost Cupid), we can only link the significance of the place back to the larger narrative of Book III by the most oblique allegorical means. And within the description of the Garden itself, surfaces, persons, and structures continually recede and give way to others, each explaining and failing to explain the one preceding. The Garden, Spenser first tells us, is firmly encircled by two walls with opposing gates, yet not only is it a space of continual departure and invasion but it continually reveals new thresholds and new centers. The reader must follow the description through a twisting series of perspectives such as lead Rosalie Colie to term the landscape "anamorphic"—though in the poem there is no single, even if unnatural point of view from which all of the artist's deformations might realign themselves into a more recognizable image.[8] The proliferation and compounding of poetic *topoi* both animate and confuse one's sense of *topos*; this sacred place paradoxically gives to place no inherent sacredness, at least to the degree that "place" is turned into an experience subject to the poet's continual undermining of our *sense* of place. Place, that is, becomes a wholly paradoxical category, a phenomenon that depends more on the text's mysteriously mobile will to find a place than on any clear idea of a place inside or outside the text's maze of tropes.

There is one thread, however, that may help solve a portion of this maze and align it more closely with Comito's idea of the Renaissance Garden. Spenser does not quite plan a paradise in a world of human agents. Yet he does commit his cathexes in the idea of paradise to a place of worldly change and stress, and to a myth of earth's "venereal soil" (if not to the earth itself or to its shifting geography and political history). In canto vi, the breaking of images that dissolved the Bower of Bliss has become preempted or obviated by an awareness of "so faire things mard, and spoyled quight" (III.vi.40), which is itself an integral *part* of the Garden, the ruinous work of time as much as the la-

8. See Colie, *Paradoxia Epidemica*, 337, fn. 8. Colie is specifically referring to Spenser's having designed his paradisiacal landscape as a map of human sexual anatomy, but the general term "anamorphic" may serve to characterize other visionary and mythic distortions as well.

bor of material reform. This commitment of paradise to time thus defends against both idolatry *and* iconoclasm; and yet it emerges most fully only through a series of conceptual and metaphoric paradoxes, some of which I will try to sketch out briefly before proceeding with further analysis.

The Garden is at once a hidden, supernatural breeding place set apart from the world and at the same time something accessible, planted deep inland "in fruitfull soyle of old" (whereas the Bower, like Milton's barren Eden, is isolated and at sea).[9] As scholars seem to agree, this "first seminarie" of all living things is Spenser's intricate reworking of the old myth of seminal reasons or *logoi spermatakoi*—these being the hidden seeds or causes of earthly species, deeds, and ideas which are born in the mind of the Creator but only unfold in (while giving shape to) the chaos of historical and physical life.[10] But the clues as to the mythic location of this home of order confuse us, for it at once intersects and stands outside of the world of mortality. The "naked babes," for instance, that fill its walled spaces, and that the porter "Genius" clothes with "fleshly weedes," leave the Garden so they can enter life and return again after what seems to be organic death, only to be restored and planted again in this strange afterlife. The other, more abstract sorts of "forms" which grow in the Garden "borrow matter" from the womblike Chaos that lies beneath it, and they too seem ripening in the Garden in preparation for "invading" the state of life; yet in this case there is no way of telling whether they invade a space that lies inside or outside the Garden. And though such forms "are variable and decay, / By course of kind, and by occasion,"

9. Fowler asserts that "when Spenser says 'well I wote by tryall, that this same / All other pleasant places doth excell' (III.vi.29), he means that he has made love, and enjoyed it" (*Numbers of Time*, 137). This is so touchingly (and imaginatively) literalistic that one hesitates to remind oneself how uncannily Spenser has rendered the questions of both sexual experience and physical location in the Garden.

10. See Robert Ellrodt, *Neoplatonism in the Poetry of Edmund Spenser*, 70–90, as well as the extensive discussions of this background in John E. Hankins, *Source and Meaning in Spenser's Allegory*, 241–72, and Nohrnberg, *Analogy*, 519–68. The myth of "seminal reasons" is widely diffused in Christian and Neo-Platonic writing, since it seems to have provided a way of reconciling Platonic and Aristotelian notions about the relation of eternity and time, form and matter. Most crucial, perhaps, as Nohrnberg notes (539), the myth could help rationalize the paradoxically double power of God over both original and ongoing creation. The "seeds" were neither natural nor strictly eternal; rather, they were "kinds," "species," and "potentialities" that possessed a kind of sempiternal reality. The idea of seminal reasons provided a guarantee that something survived the death of creatures and institutions within time, and that even unborn events and beings found their causes within the established orders of Providence. The *logoi spermatakoi* were thus the means by which the eternal *logos* assured its control over the temporal world; they placed the power of the first cause within a realm of secondary causes.

they are in no way caught up in the sort of eschatological cycle suggested by the fate of the "babes," who seem to *descend* into a world of "sinful mire" rather than (like the "forms") emerge out of it. These different cycles of decay and renewal may seem to overlap, or represent two phases of a single, larger process,[11] leaving us with a Garden that appears at one time to be part of the world of life and death, at other times outside it, at still others a second realm that contains life and death in a fashion wholly unlike that of historical, human existence. Out of such confusion, however, emerge a revision of heaven and a revision of earth that seek to do justice to our needs for both.

There have been innumerable attempts to define the deeper logic of the allegory more fully. Very persuasive, for instance, is Nohrnberg's suggestion that the Garden of Adonis develops the complex Renaissance idea that mortal, sexual generation can be an essential, if paradoxical means for humans to achieve an immortality; it is a sphere in which the otherwise isolated, defensive virtue of virginity both sacrifices and perfects itself (*Analogy*, 524–33). Canto vi could thus be seen as a mythic commentary on Shakespeare's sonnets to his unmarried friend; this garden realm of unborn and reborn life would be a visionary image of the meeting of male and female potency in the pregnant womb, and more broadly of what Gerard Manley Hopkins called "time's vast, womb-of-all, home-of-all, hearse-of-all night." Even allowing for such possibilities, however, what I want to stress here is the degree to which Spenser pushes us to consider the poetic motives as well as the philosophical meanings of his allegory; his way of representing time in the Garden reflects implicitly on the ambivalent strategies of the imagination itself in generating myths about time.

The life of the Garden is in time, but Time himself appears in the Garden as the "great enimy" to the processes of transformation and growth. We glimpse him first as a Saturnian mower who cuts off life with his scythe, but also as one who, by a more troubling elaboration of the inherited icon, "flyes about, and with his flaggy wings / Beates downe both leaves and buds without regard, / Ne ever pittie may relent his malice hard" (III.vi.39).[12] This dark personification of Time

11. Nohrnberg, with the aid of some rather suggestive diagrams, works out this complicated overlapping of cyclical phases in much greater detail (*Analogy*, 530–32). Cf. also Colie, *Paradoxia Epidemica*, 340–41, for comments on the doubled paradoxes of Substance and Form, Being and Becoming in the Garden.

12. On the iconographic history of Time the Mower, especially in his relation to the sickle-wielding, castrating Cronus (= Chronos), see Panofsky, *Studies in Iconology*, 69–93.

is not present at the opening of Spenser's description of the Garden; rather, we watch it emerge suddenly, though not unnaturally, out of the milder account of change in the earlier stanzas, especially the lines that note that "formes are variable and decay, / By course of kind, and by occasion; / And that faire flowre of beautie fades away, / As doth the lilly fresh before the sunny ray" (vi.38). Insofar as a somewhat impersonal theory about the mutability of forms modulates into a more elegiac, human fear, the text seems to respond by bringing forth a more human and personal monster. It is at this point in canto vi that the threat of the scythe-bearing demon seems most pronounced, the burden of earthly time the heaviest. Yet, surprisingly it is also exactly at this point (in particular following the image of Venus lamenting her dying children [vi.40]) that Spenser is enabled to leap into his most willful account of the Garden as a place of supernatural refuge—as if that image could only be projected from a ground of deep anxiety and mourning. Spenser does not attempt to leap out of time. Still, this movement is introduced by the nearly tautologous assertion that if Time *were not* in the Garden, nothing in the Garden would be bothered by time: "But were it not that *Time* their troubler is, / All that in this delightful Gardin growes, / Should happie be, and have immortall blis" (III.vi.41). The "pleasaunce" begins to be seen, in spite of Time, both as the locus of an original, envy-less innocence where "franckly each paramour his leman knowes" (vi.41) and as a late home for those who have suffered pain and exile, like the young gods Cupid and Psyche, or the god-man Adonis who is enwombed and embalmed there, set in a grove "of every sort of flowre, / To which sad lovers were transformd of yore" (vi.45). Such a grove is still part of time, a world of memory and metamorphosis. And yet it may seem as if the momentary surmise that time might be excluded ("But were it not . . . "), had somehow magically dissolved or obviated the earlier, anxious personification of time. Indeed, Spenser has shifted his position so far that, in the very next stanza, the emphatic and even redundant *presence* of temporal change in the Garden is exactly what defines the strong wonder of the place: "There is continuall spring, and harvest there / Continuall, both meeting at one time" (III.vi.42).[13]

In this passage the poet's transformation of or defense against the threat of winged Time becomes especially complex. The paradise still

13. Spenser is most obviously adapting his image of continuous growth from the Gardens of Alcinous (*Odyssey*, Bk.VII), whose trees bear fruit in both winter and summer. He may also be reflecting on speculations about the season proper to the first Creation or the Garden of Eden such as are found in Renaissance commentaries on Genesis; for discussion see Williams, *The Common Expositor*, 63, 107–8.

allows no fixed, immortal happiness; it excludes the high, fulfilled realm of summer (dominant in the deceptive Bower) as well as the zero state of winter. It does contain the other two natural and culturally defined seasons, but these cycle about one another in a totally unearthly dialectic. The above-quoted lines are so familiar that we may forget how precarious Spenser has made his myth of unity and temporal continuity, even at the formal or metrical level. The verses' poised combination of parallelism and chiasmus delicately reinforces the sense of balanced order, and yet this impression is unsettled by a serious and ironic *dis*continuity. For the uncharacteristically strong enjambment isolates the second "continuall" at the head of a line; reached by a syntactic leap, completing a chiasmus where one had not expected it, the repeated word becomes a surprising, discontinuous, initiating continuity—as if it were more a strident, paradoxical figure of desire than a simple statement about a mode of time experienced without doubt. The enjambment is a minor cut of Time's scythe, internalized by the verse; I point to the irony of its precariousness not out of cynicism but to suggest something about the internal tensions on which the writing of this Garden seems to feed. For it is immediately after the above-quoted stanza that Spenser is enabled further to project an image of the extremest and perhaps most paradoxical of human wishes, that of a wholly natural, magical artifice, a magic such as would precisely invert the deceptive, ornamental mimesis of the Bower. Thus "in the middest" of the Garden he places a "gloomy grove" and "pleasant arbour," a place

> . . . not by art,
> But of the trees owne inclination made,
> Which knitting their rancke braunches part to part,
> With wanton yvie twyne entrayld athwart,
> And Eglantine, and Caprifole emong,
> Fashiond above within their inmost part,
> That nether *Phoebus* beams could through them throng,
> Nor *Aeolus* sharp blast could worke them any wrong.
> (III.vi.44)

The *topos* is an ancient one, but what is crucial about it here is the way in which Spenser has positioned this liberated, defensive shrine in the overall sequence of imagery. Following as it does from so severe, if somewhat shifting an awareness of temporal loss, the description of the grove offers consolations whose scope and stability we may find are far from easily determined (especially after examining the figures enshrined within, as I shall do shortly). The important point is that a sense of time and its anxieties is allowed to come through even in so ideal a refuge, particularly in the recollection of discontinuity and the suspicion of destructive invasion. Even at its center, then, the moving eternity of the Garden becomes a site of continual emergence and emergency. Though in no way an explicit space of trial (except for the interpreter) the Garden reveals itself as a place that enlarges, challenges, and chastens our desires for paradise, rather than simply flattering or mocking them as the Bower does. Gods then do grow in the Garden, but of what sort they are we cannot be sure.

So far in this chapter I have played rather freely around the question of allegory in the Garden. To the degree that the Garden itself seems to complicate the impulse toward divination—toward the locating of gods or the sacralizing of space and time—it also complicates the impulse toward allegory, which can be an agent of divination. The need to seek for "other meanings" obviously hovers in all of the stanzas I have cited, but these forgo any clear sense of conceptual place as much as of natural or perceptual location. This strategy may make more sense if we see that the will to, or desire for, allegory is as much the subject of canto vi as its literary method, and not simply because allegory can be seen metaphorically as a process of transforming and generating sense, or as the death and rebirth of meaning. Spenser's strategies in this episode also reflect the fact that the influence of such gardens as we find in Genesis or the Song of Songs was partly determined by their accessibility to mechanisms of ecclesiastical allegory which could read such places as figures for the supersensible facts of divine creation, human beatitude, or institutional, sacramental power. Such allegorical sublimations of the garden led, paradoxically enough, to some of the most sensuous and ornate medieval literary works, especially in those cases where the richer classical garden *topoi* such as the *locus amoenus* were grafted onto the spare descriptions of the Bible.[14] Given, in fact, a Protestant sense of the intellectual and imaginative dangers of medieval institutions, the threat of the garden as a place of allegory might seem strangely congruent with that of the garden as a place of sensuous delight; the nostalgia for a place of spiritual or sexual wholeness might intertwine itself with a nostalgia for

14. Curtius's discussion of the classical and medieval *topos* of the *locus amoenus*, and its importance as a set piece for rhetorical display (*European Literature and the Latin Middle Ages*, 183–200) has, unfortunately, little to say about the Hexameral garden or its relation to allegorical tradition. For a brief but more critically useful account of the ways in which medieval writers tried to balance an interest in sensory vividness with the need for supersensible significance in their depictions of paradise, see Hans Robert Jauss, *Aesthetic Experience and Literary Hermeneutics*, 68–73.

an allegorical center of power and authority. Hence both of these nostalgias emerge and submerge continually in canto vi. My point is that for Spenser the traditional methods of reading and rationalizing the mythic garden have become a crucial part of the Garden. Stories of gardens are not just the occasion for allegory: allegory dwells and grows in the garden. Such a situation defines in part the motives for Spenser's treatment, for it is only as a struggle with the inherited allegories of Eden and the other myths linked to it that we can begin to comprehend the poet's rewriting of paradise.

Allegory in Eden

Or *Eden* selfe, if ought with *Eden* mote compaire.

The Faerie Queene (II.xii.52)

I have spoken a number of times about the complex, dialectical effects that the poet achieves by his canny multiplication of echoes from his own and others' poetry. The lesson may be reiterated in respect to the problem of gardens by citing some lines from Patricia Parker's *Inescapable Romance*: "The landscape of *The Faerie Queene* is broad enough to contain Eden as only one of its many prospects. The very immensity of Spenser's poem seems to subvert the monopoly of such loci, just as the characteristic syncretism of its imagery undermines the priority of a privileged 'source'" (76). This view may seem too radical, too modern a reading of Spenser's intentions, but in some sense it is not radical enough. For instance, one might observe that in *The Faerie Queene* Eden is reduced to little more than a prospect, one that is glimpsed briefly and emblematically in the closing cantos of Book I, yet with its traditional centrality not only displaced but also usurped by the vaster, more intricate landscape of the Garden of Adonis. The lineaments of Eden, of course, underlie this and other embowered places as well—"what can *Adonis horti* among the poets mean other than *Moses* his *Eden*, or terrestriall Paradise?" asks Henry Reynolds in his *Mythomystes* (76).[15] But the relation of the Garden of Adonis (as a major myth of "source") to the biblical paradigm of paradise (as literary source) must be measured within a dialectic of differences and by how Spenser not only mirrors but also transposes, realigns, inverts,

15. Again, the reader should consult Nohrnberg (*Analogy*, 515–18, and 539–49) for the most comprehensive survey of those medieval and Renaissance ideas about Eden and the terrestrial paradise which form the backdrop to Spenser's account of the Garden of Adonis.

conceals, or suppresses certain elements of the Edenic myth, and of the whole network of scriptural types of which that myth is a part.

Syncretistic allegory usually served as a way of harmonizing earlier and later mythologies; it accommodated but also covered over shifts in ideology or poetic sensibility, forging new wholes rather than splitting them apart. Yet the wholes remained under internal tension nonetheless. Parker observes that the syncretism of a romance like Spenser's reveals an underlying irony, a fragmentation of mythic sources which is closer to the mode of Gnostic allegory, at least as it is characterized by Hans Jonas: "Unlike the allegory of the Stoics or of syncretistic literature in general, gnostic allegory is itself the source of a new mythology: it is the revolutionary vehicle of its emergence in the face of an entrenched tradition, and since it aims at subverting the latter, the principle of this allegory must be paradox and not congruency" (*The Gnostic Religion*, 94). As I have argued in my first chapter, even more modest forms of allegory and allegorical allusion contain similar traces of irony and paradox, notwithstanding that they tend to suppress any explicit recognition of them in order to reinforce the crucial illusion of continuity with past texts and authorities. Spenser, by contrast, seems to revel in the most extreme sorts of paradox—though the kind of "subversiveness" brought out by Parker and especially Jonas should not be taken to mean that Spenser is somehow mounting an attack on the inherited authority of Scripture or that he is trying to replace Scripture with his own myth. The sublime, usurpative literalism of the antithetical mythmaker—the Gnostic or the sectarian millennialist—is hardly Spenser's mode (as it is often Milton's). But neither does the poet make any easy appeal to some center or authority outside the poem, whether a structure of doctrinal power or a master paradox (such as the Incarnation), that might circumscribe the exfoliating meanings of his own paradoxes. Rather, Spenser employs aspects of earlier garden myths in ways that transform both the continuities and discontinuities of allegory; he refreshes, complicates, and sets in perspective both the myths themselves and the interpretive will that works on them.

To show with any economy how this works in the Garden of Adonis I need to trace out some webs of major and minor allusion whose persuasiveness must be largely cumulative. Starting with the most general observations, we might say that in canto vi Spenser gives us neither a garden of the beginning nor a paradise of the end but, rather, a garden of the middle—not a place we have been thrust out of nor something we can only hope for but something that, he splendidly insists, is at all times present, if hidden. As if conscious that we compose myths of lost gardens so as to rationalize our uneasy sense of life in time through blaming of a primal transgression or Fall, Spenser gives us a garden that is neither quite free from nor wholly burdened by such a catastrophe. This Eden does contain relics or recollections of a fall: in the wounded father-figure Adonis concealed at its center; in the dark person of Time that moves through the Garden; even in the description of Venus "walking through the Gardin" and lamenting "the losse of her deare brood, her deare delight" (III.vi.40), a god who strangely recalls the Yahweh of Genesis 3.8, "walking in the garden in the coole of the day" in search of the sinful couple who hide themselves among the trees, unaware that they are now subject to the laws of labor and time. But memories of a prelapsarian creation are also strongly present. Among the most interesting is the fact that this garden of delights retains its own version of a divine *logos,* for the creatures there recall that "mightie word, / Which first was spoken by th'Almightie Lord, / That bad them to increase and multiply" (vi.34). The echo of Genesis 1.22, 28, is obvious, but equally remarkable is the curious fact that Spenser makes this later command into God's *first* Word, as if it had taken the place of that original *logos,* the *fiat lux,* by which God drew the world out of nothingness. We might explain the dilemma away by saying that, of course, there were no creatures alive yet to hear the actual first words, but if we choose not to trivialize the difficulties of the text, another idea may emerge. Spenser, in appropriating for his own Garden the biblical command to the creatures of Eden, not only endows that Garden, like the original earth, with continual generation but also suggests the paradox that in his Garden the word of continuity *is* the word of origin, that the Garden is a place of both eternal firstness and of eternal mutability.[16]

Possibly Spenser is here reflecting on his reading of Hexameral writers and offering a fictive solution to their attempts to reconcile the first words of Genesis, "In the beginning . . . ," with the idea of a creation *ex nihilo* or with the doctrine of an eternal godhead existing prior to time and substance (prior, that is, to temporal beginnings). Still, the poet's way of raising these issues in his complex fable is not conditioned by the need allegorically to accommodate scriptural fable to theological truth. The writer does not seek to rationalize, since poetry in canto vi has become at least as much the measure of theology as theology the measure of poetry. That Spenser is seeking to appro-

16. Hence, in the Garden, the "Father of all formes" is "eterne in mutabilitie," both originating and preserved by the mythicized dynamics of change.

priate the radical mythic perspectives of Genesis without burdening himself too much with genetic or ontological claims comes through in the fact that his own tale of origins contains no cosmogony per se, no fable of any sort about the birth of the world. The strange freedom of the Garden indeed lies in its being an eternal paradise thrown uncannily into the labyrinth of time, as I have suggested. In struggling to compose such an image, Spenser manages to achieve a more powerful restatement of and reflection on cosmogonic myth than we find even in his "Hymn in Honour of Love," where the poet combines the plot of Genesis 1 with an Empedoclean or Orphic image of Love wrenching into order the combative, self-destructive elements of primal chaos.

No doubt the Garden draws on complex traditions of speculative cosmology and Hexameral myth, but there is something more playful and paradoxical in Spenser's disposition of his images that makes their relation to those traditions difficult to define. One would like, for example, to find the key to Spenser's description of the Garden in the kind of subtle, dialectical models of temporal being invoked by Frank Kermode. This critic takes the Garden of Adonis as an allegory of the *aevum*, the medieval idea of a mediate realm of time existing between the chaos of secular history and the eternal timelessness of divine being. The *aevum* is a liminal space, suspended between potency and act, a garden realm that was taken to be the home of the seminal reasons, or that helped fix a place for such ontologically ambiguous creatures as angels and translated saints; as a "time fiction" it served to define a dimension in which medieval thinkers could give a kind of sempiternal existence to otherwise fragile, historical institutions such as the ideas of empire or kingship (*Sense of an Ending*, 74). To the degree that Kermode suggests how the *aevum* could be a conceptual tool facilitating human movement within history and politics, a fiction that could authenticate or ground other cultural fictions, his reading might serve to enrich my later argument about the Garden as a place of poetry. But the limitations of such mythic rationalizations for a commentary on Spenser are severe. For ideas like the *aevum* are, in a sense, exactly the sort of calcified poetry which the canto attempts to unsettle; they are as much a part of the problem explored in the Garden as its solution. Furthermore, we cannot invoke such philosophical sources without trying to account for the poet's way of having yoked them together so complexly with other discrete mythic loci. For the overriding difficulty of Spenser's Garden is that in it the ideas of an Eden, a created and creating world, and a fatal fall, all seem to intersect and contain one another. The intricate analogical machinery of the poem elides or runs together mythic *topoi* that one would otherwise think it necessary to distinguish, and that are commonly disposed into an orderly, unfolding plot with a sacred beginning, middle, and end. The interpreter of the Garden of Adonis must indeed make sense of the awkward fact that in the context of Spenser's fiction even authoritative names like "Creation," "Fall," or "Paradise," lose simplicity and stability, or threaten to become slightly brittle ciphers.

As elsewhere in the poem, some of these names or events exist only by implication, and we must not only search them out but evaluate the consequences of their being so occulted. One of the best examples of this sort of concealment occurs toward the end of *The Faerie Queene*, in the opening of the Mutabilitie Cantos. There the poet, introducing his metaphysical fable about the troubles of temporal life, glosses over traditional ideas about the origin of these troubles in a paternal, Adamic transgression, and speaks of them as the "pittious worke of *Mutabilitie!* / By which, we all are subject to that curse, / And death in stead of life have sucked from our Nurse" (VII.vi.6). The passage is of course a kind of allegorical riddle, a way of identifying temporality with the consequences of the fall. And yet though the poet can hardly expect the reader to forget the terms of the biblical myth, his allegorical veil also subtly elides (or begs the questions raised by) mythic theories regarding the causal relation between the first transgression and the curse of temporality, mainly by allowing the effect to substitute for the cause. If this strategy is an anxious, abstract defense against a theology of human guilt, it is also an implicit parable about the nature of personification, that process by which we elevate abstract names into potential gods, sources of power or punishment. In these lines, as in his later exploration of the ambiguous status of the titaness Mutabilitie herself, Spenser continues the work of his writing in the Garden of Adonis, namely to meditate on the structure, the dangers, and the consolations of our fables of origin.

Spenser's tenuous recombination of myths in Book III, canto vi, produces something like a Gnostic or Manichean vision of creation as inextricably bound up with the consequences of a supernatural or cosmic fall; the Garden, that is, seems to be a place in which time and death spring up at one moment, not unlike what happens in the just quoted verses about the "worke of *Mutabilitie.*" But more in line with the orthodox theology of Augustine—which despite any anxious feeling for the losses of temporal existence insists on both the goodness of creation and the redemptive presence within it of the incarnate Christ—Spenser embeds within these fallen/unfallen gardens his own vision of a dead and reborn god. The wounded source, Adonis, appears as both the victim of time and the divine vessel of a form of temporality that might preserve as well as destroy. Indeed, as his identity is shaped by other associations in the canto, Adonis appears to be both the fallen Adam *and* the redemptive Christ. These identifications come through most poignantly in the description of the inner bower of the Garden, the untouched *mons veneris* that is even so the place of ongoing generation. There, among the metamorphic emblems of "sad lovers" we glimpse a central tableau that Frye refers to as "an erotic pietà" (*Fables of Identity*, 82), in which Adonis as Adam/Christ is watched over by Venus as Eve/Mary, both mother and bride:

> There wont faire *Venus* often to enioy
> Her deare *Adonis* ioyous company,
> And reape sweet pleasure of the wanton boy;
> There yet, some say, in secret he does ly,
> Lapped in flowres and pretious spycery,
> By her hid from the world, and from the skill
> Of *Stygian* Gods, which doe her love envy;
> But she her selfe, when ever that she will,
> Possesseth him, and of his sweetnesse takes her fill.
> (III.vi.46)

This picture has little of the wanton spying, histrionic suffering, and sentimentality that we find in the tapestries illustrating the history of Adonis in Malecasta's house (III.i.34–38); indeed, as a scene of restoration it pushes beyond the usual, tragic conclusion of the myth.[17] The

17. The image of Venus mourning Adonis as a substitute pietà is also apparent in the last tapestry in Malecasta's house. Spenser may have derived this iconographic conceit from Francesco Colonna's *Hypnerotomachia Polyphili* (Venice, 1490), where the two figures are similarly depicted on a monument to the dead Adonis at the center of the Garden of Venus on the isle of Cythera, a monument crowned with a statue of Venus and Cupid which further mirrors the arrangement of the Madonna and Child. I should add that, insofar as in the Garden of Adonis Spenser has interwoven a scene of mourning with a *hieros gamos*, he approximates the symbolic ironies studied by Leo Steinberg in his essay, "The Metaphors of Love and Birth in Michelangelo's *Pietàs*." The scene at the center might also be placed in the light of Marcel Detienne's structuralist reading of Adonis and his cult in *The Gardens of Adonis*—particularly Detienne's interpretation of the god as a myth of spices and perfumes. This critic sees the story of Adonis's troubling birth, loves, and violent death as unfolding the ambivalent functions of these marginal substances in both sacrifice and seduction, that is, their influence as uncertain mediators between gods and humans, men and women respectively. Detienne's study may at least remind us of the doubling of erotic and elegiac motives in Adonis's being "lapped in flowres and pretious spycery" (strewn "like a corse" with emblematic blossoms, as Florizel says to Perdita, but also "like a bank for love to lie and play on. / Not like a corse; or if, not to be buried, / But quick and in mine arms" [*The Winter's Tale* IV.iv.129–32]).

combination of mournful contemplation, pleasurable repose, and active desire also contrasts strongly with the sense of static entrapment, exhaustion, and devouring voyeurism at the center of Acrasia's garden (though the embalmed and strangely inert body of Adonis is not quite an unambivalent emblem). Likewise, however much Adonis seems to combine the fates and powers of the first and second Adam, he sustains a crucial measure of difference from both. This pagan god in all of his redundant identities thus eludes both the easy analogies of a rationalizing syncretism and the more strenuous deformations of typology, which ask that a later myth be taken as the fulfillment or hidden source of an earlier one.

We might move infinitely into larger fields of relation. One might suggest, for instance, that Spenser adapts for his central tableau the biblical image of the beloved as an enclosed garden, an orchard of fruit and spice trees (Song of Songs 4.12–15), though in such a way as to retrieve it from the powerful Christian traditions of spiritualizing allegory.[18] We might even see a more direct translation of the Christian mystery of the begetting and birth of incarnate love in Spenser's account of Amoret and Belphebe (the story of whose birth is the explicit occasion for the poet's telling us about the Garden).[19] There are also in the Garden foreshadowings of apocalypse: in the fugitive virgin Chrysogonee, Amoret and Belphebe's mother, who like the "woman clothed with the sunne" of Revelation 12.1 "fled into the wildernesse a space" (III.vi.10); in the image of a beast bound under paradise but threatening to loose itself again; and in the eternal bliss that Adonis enjoys—even perhaps in the millennial periodicity of the soul's sojourn in the Garden after death. The hot-house of the Garden makes odd grafts and hybrids of such recollections, of course, and though Fletcher is right to call canto vi "Spenser's Apocalypse," that episode also asks that we totally revise our notions of what the apocalypse looks like. For the Garden is an apocalypse, as well as a

18. The history of Christian interpretations of the lovers in the Song of Songs as an allegory of Christ's relation to the church or the soul is usefully surveyed by Marvin Pope in his *Anchor Bible: Song of Songs*, 112–32.

19. Recall that the sisters are, like Christ, born painlessly of their virgin mother Chrysogonee following a mysterious (though unannounced) insemination, the divine rays of the sun piercing "into her wombe, where they embayd / With so sweet sence and secret power unspide, / That in her pregnant flesh they shortly fructifide" (III.vi.7). Again, like Christ, these children share "the heritage of all celestiall grace" (III.vi.4), though as twin forms of human love they also stand in lieu of any sublimer myth of supernatural *caritas*. The structure of substitution becomes even more interesting when we recall that Venus also takes Amoret as a substitute for the errant Cupid (naming her "Amoretta" because she stands "in her litle loves stead" [III.vi.28]), just as Belphebe is a stand-in for Diana.

paradise, of the middle, a recapitulation that blurs the margins between the mythic crises in the plot of Christian history to which it alludes rather than providing their final visionary resolution. The poet makes the traditional images of creation, fall, incarnation, sacrifice, resurrection, and apocalypse available to the most extreme and loving deformations of the human imagination, at the same time defending himself against any literalistic transgression of the biblical sources themselves and against any impression that he is naively trying to replace scriptural myths with his own. The paradoxical structures of the Garden of Adonis should rather help us reflect more subtly on how others have developed, used, and apologetically misused the figures of paradise.

In one crucial respect the great, mediate revelations of the Garden are not only not final, they are radically incomplete. For though they provide lessons about time, death, mourning, and even envy, there is little in the place that speaks of the darker, sado-masochistic components of the human psyche in its quests for love, or of the divisiveness of *eros* and erotic fantasy at those points where psychic and social realms collide. In the Garden, as Cheney observes, "the problem of love's wounds . . . has been adroitly, if ominously repressed" (*Spenser's Image of Nature*, 126)—like the castrating boar of winter beneath the bower of Venus and Adonis. Thus invisible and evaded, the painful side of temporal, secular love plays no part in the chaste Amoret's schooling. Hence the Garden does little to prepare either her or the reader for those threats and enchantments encountered in the House of Busyrane, where the restored but weapon-less Cupid glimpsed at the end of canto vi takes up his bow again. From that House she must be freed by an armed virgin who knows something about aggressive postures required in a world where love entails more than the pleasures of generation. And beyond this House, we approach forms of ritual and revelation that belong to an apparently "higher" and less natural order of being than that experienced in the Garden.

Still, it may not quite suffice to circumscribe the Garden by saying that Spenser intended it to represent only a vision of a lower or natural paradise.[20] Certainly this place is only a fraction of the world as the poet knows it. But the sixth canto of Book III shows Spenser perhaps writing better than he knew, or lavishing most attention where he knew he could write best. If the Garden is peopled so thickly with the shadows of Christian redemptive and apocalyptic mythologies, it is

20. Cf. Cheney, *Spenser's Image of Nature*, 118, 127.

perhaps because the incarnation of those mythologies in later books of the poem was itself more problematic. There is indeed no visionary paradise in subsequent episodes of *The Faerie Queene* to set beside the Garden of Adonis, nor any sacred, templar locus that adequately realizes a transcendent state with so much breadth and grandeur—certainly not the dubious courtliness and erotic anxiety of the Temple of Venus, nor even the splendid but much more limited Isis Church or the Court of Mercilla. The only visions remotely comparable are those of the nymphs and Graces on Mount Acidale and of Dame Nature on Arlo Hill, which I will be discussing in Chapter 6. These, however, are more essentially transient, more hedged with a demystifying literary self-consciousness. (I have not forgotten the Heavenly City of Book I, canto x, but Spenser allows himself only the sparest of means in constructing this vision, as I have noted above.) Nowhere else but in the Garden of Adonis has Spenser the poet committed himself to the myth or illusion of a sacred place of pleasure, knowledge, and power with such intensity.

The superflux of imaginative energy invested in the Garden of Adonis at once unifies and fragments our impressions of the myth; the difficulty of trying to come to terms with that energy as such may even allow us to think slightly better of the more extreme Neo-Platonic readings of the episode. Depressing and grotesque as they often can be, the attempts especially of early critics to link this apparently natural paradise to some complexly articulated vision of a cosmic world do after all respond to the hunger for "something more" which emerges in Spenser's allegory. That the poem disallows any such rationalized myths of transcendence is not surprising. Nevertheless, the kinds of distortion they involve may be no greater than those that might come from substituting, as I propose to do, a later myth or perspective of transcendence. Specifically, I want to read in the Garden of Adonis the fable of a splendid and splendidly sublimated narcissism, as great as if not greater than that which we witness on Mount Acidale. According to this interpretation, Spenser's cathexes in his garden fiction would depend on its being a myth of his own poetic mode, the record of his own struggles with time, memory, and language, a vision of his labor in arranging, unfolding, and reclothing the mutable forms or kinds of myth. Though hidden and idealized, the generation of Spenser's poetical character may be the deepest subject of the canto, the redemptive dream of its wounded, embowered visionary. The last section of this chapter offers what can hardly be more than a prolegomenon to such an interpretation (I am more concerned with certain broad links between garden myths and poetics than with the peculiar shape of Spenser's poetic self), but it may yet begin to suggest the difficulty that reading poses.

A Garden of Verses

> Spot more delicious than those Gardens feignd
> Or of reviv'd *Adonis*, or renownd
> *Alcinous*, host of old *Laertes* Son,
> Or that, not Mystic, where the Sapient King
> Held dalliance with his faire *Egyptian* Spouse.

In one of the marvelously irritable footnotes to his "new edition" of *Paradise Lost*, Richard Bentley argues that the above lines from Book IX (439–43) show that Milton's description of Adam and Eve's bower in Eden was tampered with by an unlearned redactor. The Puritan's "not Mystic" is simply an absurdity, while of the first clause he complains,

> There was no such Garden ever existent, or ever *feign'd.* Κηποι Αδώνιδς, *the Gardens of Adonis*, so frequently mentioned by Greek writers, *Plato, Plutarch*, &c., were nothing but portable earthen Pots, with some Lettice or Fennel growing in them. On his yearly Festival, every Woman carried one of them for *Adonis's* Worship; because *Venus* had once laid him in a Lettice Bed. The next Day they were thrown away; for the Herbs were but rais'd about a Week before, and could not last for want of Root. Thence *the Gardens of Adonis* grew to be a Proverb of Contempt, for any fruitless, fading, perishable Affair.[21]

The great classicist does what Milton can hardly have done: he forgets Spenser. However, his error in regard to *Paradise Lost* only underscores the relevance of his words for *The Faerie Queene*, which has not the excuse of literary precedent. Although an essential fact of the Garden is that it contains a multiplicity of places, the main reason for Spenser's having referred to the Garden*s* of Adonis in the "argument" of canto vi (though nowhere else) may have been to elicit some recollection of that class of trivial gardens. Bentley's complaint raises the question of how we are to measure the effect of Spenser's having transformed these movable, talismanic forcing pots into the massive and emphatically "mystic" architecture of the Garden of Adonis. What irony or presumption are involved in the narrativistic explosion

21. Cf. Erasmus, *Adagia* I.i.4, "Adonidis horti," for a similar reading, one that may in fact be Bentley's primary source.

of such an imploded ritual object, and in the poet's apparent reversal of a tradition that took these gardens as emblems for the transient and trashy?

To some degree this episode is simply an extreme example of the unbounded will to mythic transformation, the "complete parodic freedom" that Fletcher sees as characteristic of the Spenserian mode (*Prophetic Moment*, 106). One might compare it to the similarly heroic indecorum of having made the folkloric hero Saint George—whose fantastic legends were exactly the sort that Protestant reformers so strongly deplored—into the Christian knight in Book I. In Book III, canto vi, such parody involves not only a complete inversion of physical and valuative categories, but a mythic literalization, beyond all normative ideas of punning, of the label "*gardens* of Adonis" (as if Spenser's Garden was the "reality" of which the classical pots were merely a travesty). Behind the poet's strategy, of course, is a mythographic tradition that read the wounded youth (if not his material "gardens") as a myth of cosmic, generative power—Adonis being sometimes just a beautiful, elegiac inhabitant of the terrestrial paradise, but often a source of birth, growth, and change identified with the father-sun itself. Still, I want to hold on to the possible perversity of Spenser's choice for a moment and not assume, as Nohrnberg does, that the poet has succeeded in displacing all of the negative associations of the proverbial pots onto the fragile Bower of Bliss (*Analogy*, 494). From this point of view I want to read Spenser's transformations of the tradition in canto vi against two important, if not directly ancestral, texts. Classical and medieval respectively, these will also refine my comments on the Garden as a myth of poetic process.

In that archaically "Egyptian" fable about the invention of writing by the demigod Thoth which closes the *Phaedrus*, Plato observes that those who employ a written discourse instead of dialectical speech are like persons who sow transient gardens of Adonis. Writing, though it appears to be a mode of preserving thought, only plants the seeds of forgetfulness; its empty, external marks provide at best the illusion of permanence:

> That's the strange thing about writing, which makes it truly analogous to painting. The painter's products stand before us as though they were alive: but if you question them, they maintain a most majestic silence. It is the same with written words: they seem to talk to you as though they were intelligent, but if you ask them anything about what they say, from a desire to be instructed, they go on telling you just the same thing for ever. And once a thing is put in writing, the composition, whatever it may

be, drifts all over the place, getting into the hands not only of those who understand it, but equally those who have no business with it. (*Phaedrus* 275D)

This passage links the image of the useless gardens to the lure of painterly mimesis in a way that may remind us more of the Bower of Bliss; certainly it conveys a sense of the dangers of the fixed, iconic word, an entity that feeds the "conceit of wisdom" but is only a dead, repetitive thing, a cipher subject to the "drift" of opinions and misconstructions, of ignorant or faithless misreadings. Against such a view of written language as at once frigid and quickly withering, Plato poses the ideal of a spoken, dialectical form of discourse which "goes together with knowledge, and is written in the soul of the hearer." The rejected process of writing here survives as an internalized metaphor, of course. But for the moment this may be less interesting than the fact that Plato continues to describe the work of dialectic in terms of the temporalized metaphors of farming and gardening, rather than, as in the *Cratylus*, trying to frame an idea of the ways in which language (especially the traditional names of the gods) might yield us some access to early or timeless originals. But Plato also severely distinguishes the barren productions of the forcing pots from the work of the dialectician who "selects a soul of the right type, and in it he plants and sows his words founded on knowledge, words which can defend both themselves and him who planted them, words which instead of remaining barren contain a seed whence new words grow up in new characters; whereby the seed is vouchsafed immortality, and its possessor the fullest measure of blessedness that man can attain unto" (276E–277A).

To leap from Plato to Spenser, one might say that the poet has invented the ground for a marriage between Plato's opposing terms, writing and dialectic, and recovered the rejected gardens as a possible trope for a less corrupt, almost supernaturally generative mode of literary discourse. The fact that the idea of "writing" exists as both a literal and a figurative presence in Plato's explication of dialectic may justify such a marriage or muddling of categories to some degree. Still, what is at stake here is not the bare (and none-too-clear) distinction between writing and voice but broader mythic attitudes toward all forms of language.[22] Hence, while Spenser may have shared some of

22. For some subtle reflections on Plato's account of writing and speech in this section of the *Phaedrus*, see Derrida's essay, "Plato's Pharmacy," in *Dissemination*, 142–55, and *passim*. The general aim of the essay is to show how Socratic dialectic, far from making available a transparent *eidos* or *logos*, continues to depend on the ambivalent, infectious

the philosopher's disdain for such ritual pots insofar as they played a role in popular superstition (a disdain that colors Plato's use of them as an opprobrious figure for the art of writing), he finds in those gardens the best allusive means to open up his own allegory of poetic language into more strongly mythic dimensions. For in Spenser writing can no longer be taken as the dead image or *eidolon* of speech, since his written Garden manages to fulfill all of those functions of dialectical discourse which Plato establishes in his own more restricted, almost Puritan parable about the sowing of thoughtful words. For Spenser's poem also carefully orders and selects the ideas that it clothes and reclothes in imagery; it perpetuates the deep characters of earlier discourses, nourishing their memory even as it calls for acts of imaginative engagement and opens up further spaces for reflective response. If the poem does not quite analytically divide subject and rhetorical mode "according to their kinds" (as Plato suggests), it does give us a complex myth of literary kinds. By the intricate web of revisions, evasions, allusions, and ironies such as I have been analyzing, the Garden and its poet also protect themselves against the random, reductive pressures of a fixating intelligence, whether heretical or orthodox. It shows us an image of erotic and religious mystery which tries to ward off slander, sentimentality, and sacrilegious rationalization (much as Venus hides the "Father of all formes" from both the phallic violence of the boar and from the "skill" of envious Stygian gods). The poem, like Plato's idea of writing, continues to be haunted by a sense of its own vulnerability and fragility. And yet at the center of the Garden, in the image of lovers transformed into flowers by the metamorphic power of Ovidian myth, emblems of a wretched fate "To whom sweet Poets verse hath given endlesse date" (III.vi.45), Spenser can at least for a moment claim the power to grant the seed or soul "the fullest measure of blessedness that man can attain unto."

This ironic, ad hoc allegorization of the Socratic description of dialectic vis-à-vis the Garden of Adonis is still too idealized and open-ended. Certainly the massive and ambiguous elaboration of organic imagery in Spenser's poem plays havoc with the more modest use of similar metaphors in Plato, though for that reason it may keep us

---

magic of sophistic discourse, just as the generative and properly mimetic power attributed to Socratic *speech* cannot wholly be differentiated from the empty, wandering, vulnerable, and yet transgressive forces of *writing*. (Derrida argues that the definition of the "good" term of such oppositions continues to be inscribed by the "bad," both literally and metaphorically.) As should be immediately apparent, all of this is far from irrelevant to Spenser's treatment of both Plato's and Alain de Lille's figures of writing, though such a critique of Platonic discourse is only partially useful in unraveling the metaphoric intricacies of the Garden of Adonis.

from taking the latter too literally. Nevertheless, in order to clarify both the scope and limits of Spenser's redemptive image of the literary garden (his visionary "anthology"), I want to juxtapose to both Plato and Spenser some portions of a late medieval allegory, Alain de Lille's *The Complaint of Nature*. The historical or mythic gardens of Adonis play no part here. Rather, my focus will be on the broad allegorical use of agricultural metaphors to link human language to a more supernatural mode of knowing, and on Spenser's and Alain's differing portraits of the mythic figure of Genius. The interpretation still unfolds in the space of speculative analogy, and often negative analogy at that, but it should nonetheless bring out certain aspects of Spenser's Garden that we might otherwise take for granted.

I will begin with Genius. Spenser rightly gives him a "double nature" and locates him at the threshold of the Garden of Adonis, where he oversees the clothing of the "thousand naked babes" with "sinfull mire." Although Genius functions in pre-Christian myth as a demigod of place, a good or bad demon controlling human fortune and character, or a guardian of dynastic successions, during medieval times Genius becomes most emphatically a god of middles. He is a figure or a power that controls the uncanny passageways of creation, that mediates and rationalizes the gap between what we distinguish as the ideal and the material, the divine and the natural, the soul and the body, the seed and its soil.[23] Genius is also a god of astrological influence and of divine descents, and takes on as well many of the characteristics (and ambivalences) of the Platonic demiurge. Not surprisingly, therefore, Genius becomes a kind of artist-deity who helps explain the metaphysical scope of allegorical representation. In Alain de Lille, he controls the production of those sensible and imaginative *icones* that mediate between the shifting realm of perception and the fixed forms of reason and supernatural authority. The cosmic analogies between ideas of literary representation and natural creation crop up elsewhere in Alain's text: Venus's planting of the *logoi spermatakoi* is illustrated by the image of her divine, phallic reed-pen inscribing animated shapes on the receptive animal-skin parchment of the material world, while the author moralizes about how necessary it is for the writer to obey all of the rules of grammar and rhetoric. But it is nevertheless the figure of Genius which serves to frame Alain's explicit account of allegory. In this case the literary process becomes more the tenor than the vehicle of the extended allegorical

23. Cf. Jane Chance Nitzsche, *The Genius Figure in Antiquity and the Middle Ages*, 42–64.

metaphor, though even here it is difficult to know whether we should emphasize the metaphysical or the literary.

Just as the "descents" of supernatural seeds into the material world can take on creative and degenerative forms, so Genius oversees both "true" representations and those that are fantastic and illusory. In Alain, he is invoked at first as a true scribe, a priest of God, a master of eloquence, even a kind of Orphic poet. Yet his initial appearance makes the work of Genius appear disturbingly ambiguous: "He carried in his right hand a reed of frail papyrus, which never rested from its occupation of writing; and in his left he bore an animal's skin from which a knife had cut and bared the shock of hair, and on this, by means of his compliant pen, he gave to images, which passed from the shadow of a sketch to the truth of very being, the life of their kind. And when these slumbered in the death of deletion, others were called to life in a new rising and birth" (Prose IX, ll. 100–107). Alain also tells us that the left hand frequently took over the work when the right was weary, and that it "forsook the path of true representation with false and limping imagery, and created figures of things, or rather shadowy ghosts of figures, with incomplete depiction" (125–28)—images that can be both corrupt poems and corrupt human minds. Genius is accompanied by both Truth and Falsehood; the one has "sprung from the loving kiss alone of Nature and her son, when the Eternal Mind greeted matter, as it was considering the reflection of forms, and kissed it by the intermediate agency and intervention of an image"—that is, he is the very god of the true *icones*—while the other, seemingly ungenerated, is an envious voyeur who, "secretly spying on the pictures of Truth . . . rudely marred whatever Truth harmoniously formed" (165–66).

The figure of Genius is here the vessel of the writer's ambivalences about the claims of literary artifice, not only as something that leads to false representation but as a means of corruptive magic, as a power that not only mars truth but deforms the soul and attracts the influence of demons. The work of Genius is thus related to the generation of idolatry, the growing of false gods. Yet we must not overestimate the scope of Alain's demystifying skepticism in regard to the powers of art. At least we should see that, insofar as the fragilities, errors, and possible corruptions of both allegorical representation and the created world are linked back to this mediate, demiurgical scribe, the higher metaphysical authorities on which that scribe appears to depend are saved from any such doubt. The contingency and createdness of what are fundamentally doctrinal assertions and emblems, their connection to the wanderings of human power and love—these things are concealed by heaping all of the doubt on the powers of the scribe, priest, and poet Genius. It is indeed the medieval poet, rather than Spenser himself, who really fits Greenblatt's account of Spenser's allegory: it is Alain who "in the face of deep anxiety about the impure claims of art" both renders its createdness explicit and continually refers the reader to a fixed authority beyond the poem which is thereby defended from doubt (*Renaissance Self-Fashioning*, 190). For a post-Reformation poet like Spenser, the processes of literary representation and the hieratic truth of established authority both would have seemed subject to a different sort of skepticism. Allegory might be no less the means of touching the metaphysical world, and yet the privileged medieval image of the scribe copying his work from a sacred, archetypal text, not to mention the projection of that scribal model onto the order of cosmic creation (as in the case of Alain's Venus), could hardly have seemed less than a prideful Scholastic illusion. Even Alain's tactful analysis of the inescapability of allegorical error leaves the authority of such a projection fundamentally untouched.

Though it is an argument of absence, I would think that the most important element in Spenser's use of Genius is his decision to ignore this figure's function as demiurge and allegorical poet, and to cut him off from any relationship (however problematic) to a metaphysical center outside of the cycle of generation in the Garden. The darker side of Genius, together with his priestly functions, is shifted onto that False Genius who proffers an enchanting chalice to travelers at the gate of the garden of idolatry—though even here his association with deceptive writing or iconmaking is absent, as is any suggestion that his magic has such cosmic scope as in Alain. Spenser's move away from the systematic, hierarchical analogies of the medieval poet (a shift one may take as intentional revision of a text Spenser knew, or simply as evidence of an entirely different attitude toward myth, poetry, and authority) does not mean that the Garden is any less a seminary of allegory, a myth of poetic process. The point is that the balance that Spenser strikes between his imagery of natural creation and his depiction of the work of poetry is totally at odds with that struck by the medieval poet. Neither the inscription of Alain's demiurgical Venus, which is itself an image of creative insemination, nor that writing's more explicitly literary extension in the work of Genius finds any analogy in Spenser. Spenser abandons the medieval poet's grand and movingly elaborated figure of creation as scribal copying; and though the basic metaphor of literary art as a form of natural and supernatural creation remains intact, its explicit terms have been more deeply hidden, even repressed, by canto vi's intricately elaborated mythology of growth, death, and rebirth. One might say that the metaphoric tenor (writing or poetry) disappears below the vehicle (the mythic cycle of growth), almost reversing the way that the relationship unfolded in Alain, for whom grammar is more important than nature. While the Garden is made available to the most diverse allegories of poetic process, such allegories cannot coopt or be coopted by a system of hierarchical authority; the figures of creation are less easy to measure according to fixed standards of truth and error, or the iconic types of an established system of analogy. This does not mean that Alain is a barren, dogmatic rationalist. He is, for instance, considerably freer and more fanciful than Spenser in his local play of imagery, more "Gothic" in his moralized grotesques and certainly wilder in his depiction of supernatural creatures like Nature and Genius. He is also more explicit in his criticism of his own allegorical machinery. But it is Spenser, I would say, who knows better what is pragmatically at stake in such a marriage of art and philosophy. The cost of this knowledge, and of the achieved or accepted distance from metaphysical authority, is a reduction of the allegory of poetry to a point of near invisibility.[24]

A reader of an earlier draft of this chapter tells me that so grand a Garden must do more than conceal questions about language and metaphor, or resolve itself into moral and epistemological conundra about the truth and error of fiction (which, by the way, more accurately describes Alain's efforts). But to make the Garden into a place where the poet parabolically reflects on his own writing is neither to deny the physical and metaphysical allegory nor to suggest merely another discrete *level* of allegorical reading. It is rather an attempt to refine our understanding of the project of canto vi as a whole. Especially given the poet's situation as a latecomer in a long tradition of mythmaking, as one who is thus more disenchanted even in his most extravagant idealisms, Spenser needs the Garden to explore those questions about the temporal sources and burdens of poetry

24. The only full-scale reading of canto vi as an allegory of poetic making of which I am aware is Berger's essay, "Spenser's Gardens of Adonis: Force and Form in the Renaissance Imagination." In a remarkable, sustained piece of critical allegorization, Berger argues that the episode shows the poet's work as moving between the deep, eternally reincarnated archetypes of the mind's womblike "Chaos" (placed within or below the Gardens), and the elegant, surface patterns or *topoi* of literary tradition such as one discovers anthologized in the floral bower of Venus and Adonis. This oscillation between archetype and *topos* is fed by a will to vital form which seeks for no valorization by a higher order but plays itself out amidst the lures of an immanent, organizing, dialectical *eros* and an annihilating, reductive *thanatos*.

that were excluded from the more limited critique of mimesis in the Bower of Bliss episode. But such a suggestion should in fact enlarge, or be set in terms of, my prior assertions about the Garden: for example, that it is an early paradise that usurps the place of other forms of transcendence; that it is an apocalypse that preserves rather than destroys the natural, and a vision of supernatural sources that survives being thrown into time, into the warring cycles of *eros* and *thanatos*; that it is a garden that redeems its own fallenness, being at once a lost world and a last, lasting world. For the Garden of Adonis is a point where the more general human and cultural trials of nostalgia dissolve into the specifically poetic ones; the Garden defines a place where the otherwise easy and often deceptive metaphors that link metaphysical, sexual, and poetic creation can find their most strenuous hypothetical home.

6

Enchantment and Disenchantment (Mount Acidale, the Blatant Beast, the Faunus Episode)

The conflict between idolatry and iconoclasm shows up in the Garden of Adonis only in a very abstract way, and I want to return in closing to three episodes of the poem which give it a somewhat more palpable shape. These differ, however, from those passages examined in earlier chapters, though perhaps the difference is one of affect more than anything else. The idolatries of Orgoglio and Busyrane mirror each other insofar as they both represent clearly destructive, usurping forms of imagination, though such a reading cannot be supported by isolating any purer power of disenchantment in Arthur or Britomart. In the passages I shall examine below, on the other hand, the presences or images that are broken may seem more immediately benign, even redemptive in their powers, while the agents of iconoclasm may strike us as being foolish or sacrilegious in themselves. At least the reversal of affect seems clear enough that we can begin by trusting valuative terms such as "sacrilege" to a degree. Still, one of the burdens of the later scenes is that these terms become harder to apply unequivocally. The positive and negative moments of iconoclasm offer too many unsettling parallels, share too many of the same ambivalences, and so break down our typical measures of moral difference. Spenser also tends to muddle the signals of a literary decorum that would allow us to distinguish the authentic from the parodic versions of a certain gesture or image. The result is to make us all the more aware of the ways in which narratives of disenchantment may operate as much in the service of concealment, mystification, and defense as that magic that they are intended (if only mimetically) to dispel. Such an argument seems to follow the poem downward into a general despair about the clarifying capacities of fiction, if not about the stability of truth, and the later books do indeed suggest a collapse of the higher, prophetic ambitions of Book I. Yet I want to attempt to show that the poet's growing ambivalence about his iconoclastic fictions works a gain as well as a loss, allowing him to move into more complex and re-creative forms of rhetoric, into fresher modes of illusion and less constricted postures of self-doubt—stances that may allow him to confront even the darkest of falls with a measure of gaiety and reason.

The Place of Grace

Sir Calidore's vision on Mount Acidale is the climax of Book VI; it occurs in the tenth canto, exactly parallel to Redcrosse Knight's vision of the New Jerusalem from the Mount of Contemplation in the tenth canto of Book I. Spenser's comparison of that earlier mount to Parnassus, the haunt of the "thrise three learned Ladies," the Muses, helps to establish its links to the more classical and pastoral landscape of Acidale, but the differences between the two encounters may strike us more forcibly than the similarities. Whereas Redcrosse was granted his vision after a rigorous sojourn in the House of Holinesse, Calidore's is the fruit of his excursion among pastoral shepherds, which is to say, of his delay and evasion of the quest for the Blatant Beast. Spenser, indeed, speaks of the vision as a partial excuse for the knight's wise refusal to chase after "shadowes vaine / Of courtly favour, fed with light report / Of every blaste" (VI.x.2)—though we might recall that it is just this mean liability of court life, grown large in the rumorous Blatant Beast, that Calidore is needed to control. Having sat down to rest "in the middest" of his race, wandering with the randomness of idle play rather than the directedness of quest, Calidore by accident reaches the ornate, fairy-haunted "pleasuance" of Mount Acidale, the resort of Venus. Where Redcrosse might have encountered Duessa and Orgoglio, Calidore "a troupe of Ladies dauncing found,"

> Full merrily, and making gladfull glee,
> And in the midst a Shepheard piping he did see.
>
> He durst not enter into th'open greene,
> For dread of them unwares to be descryde,
> For breaking of their daunce, if he were seene;
> But in the covert of the wood did byde,
> Beholding all, yet of them unespyde.

> There he did see, that pleased much his sight,
> That even he him selfe his eyes envyde,
> An hundred naked maidens lilly white,
> All raunged in a ring, and dauncing in delight.
>
> All they without were raunged in a ring,
> And daunced round; but in the midst of them
> Three other Ladies did both daunce and sing,
> The whilest the rest them round about did hemme,
> And like a girlond did in compasse stemme:
> And in the middest of those same three, was placed
> Another Damzell, as a precious gemme,
> Amidst a ring most richly well enchaced,
> That with her goodly presence all the rest much graced.
>
> (VI.x.10–12)

These dancers are on the earth rather than in the air, like Redcrosse's vision; Spenser indeed describes them as "thumping th'hollow ground, / That through the woods their Eccho did rebound" (VI.x.10). But they are not for that reason any more solid. Calidore's "breaking of their daunce" and their subsequent disappearance is the crisis but also the secret *telos* of this episode, perhaps in part the poet's attempt to reduce or contain some of the proliferating questions raised by the description of the vision proper. As Berger notes, the ardent precariousness in the staging of the scene actually anticipates the moment of disappearance, and it is on this precariousness that I want to linger before moving to the episode's disillusioning close.[1]

This scene of poetry's visionary source, this celebration of order and love, perhaps owes less to a Dantesque model of celestial dances than to much humbler Irish and English fables about fairies dancing in the woods at night, in circles that were impossible or dangerous for mortals to approach.[2] As in the case of the legend of Saint George or the Garden of Adonis, Spenser is flirting riskily with what some readers must have considered debunked old wives' tales, if not popish superstitions. Though he reclothes the indigenous folklore in much more learned, classical garb, the sense of danger in his choice is reinforced by the poet's treatment of sight and seeing. For while Cali-

1. Cf. Berger, "A Secret Discipline," 70. "[The vision vanishes, but] even without Calidore's intrusion, the descriptive rhythm anticipates this outcome, and one feels that however long Spenser's hidden recreative voice has invoked this vision it is unfolded only now, in the brevity of the present fulfillment."

2. See Humphrey Tonkin, *Spenser's Courteous Pastoral: Book Six of the "Faerie Queene"*, 131–36, on the folklore of fairy dances in Spenser's account of Mount Acidale.

dore's sighting of the supernatural dancers is the culmination of what Frye would call the romance of the centripetal gaze,[3] of the privileged vision or cynosure, Spenser frames the scene by a reminder of the corruptions of the human gaze and allows a suspicion of idolatry to infect our feeling of sacred awe. Colin himself is safely isolated within a world of sound, but Calidore, seeing and yet unseen, is so enthralled by the sight that he is divided from himself by that self-wounding form of seeing which is *invidia*: "that he him selfe his eyes envyde." As alienated voyeur, as a form of what the Geneva Bible calls an "idole shepheard,"[4] Calidore attracts to himself and to the scene as a whole some of the uncertainties which we feel in other accounts of hieratic women of Book VI: Mirabella, the vengeful, self-isolated lady of Petrarchan poetry, surrounded by dead or dying suitors; Serena—Mirabella turned inside out—the helpless victim of savages who view her with a mixture of cannibalism and lust, while she is painted in the painfully gorgeous language of courtly blazon; and Pastorella, the shepherdess placed on a green eminence and surrounded by dancers, who holds out the promise of some gentler mode of erotic attention.[5] But as if to relieve such ambivalent fictions of physical sight—whether they engage the poet or the reader or the quester who shares a space with both—Spenser quickly appeals to a

3. Cf. Frye's comments in *Anatomy of Criticism*, 58, which might by extension help us link the visionary stresses of the Mount Acidale episode to developments in Renaissance theater: "The central episodic theme of the high mimetic is the theme of cynosure or centripetal gaze, which, whether addressed to mistress, friend, or deity, seems to have something about it of the court gazing upon its sovereign, the court-room gazing upon the orator, or the audience gazing upon the actor. For the high mimetic poet is pre-eminently a courtier, a counsellor, a preacher, a public orator or a master of decorum, and the high mimetic is the period in which the settled theatre comes into its own as the chief medium of fictional forms." Spenser's scene on Mount Acidale is the more unsettling and unsettled theater of a courtier, counsellor, preacher, and orator of exile.

4. I am picking up on the pun in the Coverdale and Geneva Bibles' rendering of Zechariah 11.17, part of an attack on false priests and prophets: "O idol(e) shepherd that leaveth the flock." The King James Version is similar: "Woe to the idol shepherd that leaveth the flock." This is more than simply an idiosyncratic spelling, and the pun seems not to have been lost on contemporary preachers (see *OED*, *s.v.*, "idol," II.8). Indeed, "idol shepherd" is in some ways a quite shrewd translation of the original Hebrew text, which refers not so much to what the Revised Standard Version terms a "worthless shepherd," as a "shepherd of worthlessness," where "worthlessness" translates a Hebrew noun often used as a periphrasis for the spiritual vanity of idolatry (cf. Buttrick et al., *Interpreter's Dictionary*, 2:674).

5. Berger lists these scenes of centered females and, seeing them as complex versions of a single idea of harmony, argues that on Mount Acidale the "many embodiments of that single form [are] gathered together through the quest of the imagination, through the reversion of the mind from the scattered particulars of experience to the Idea which is their formal source. Thus on Acidale the center is, so to speak, pushed upward so that it is the apex of a spiral or a mountain top" ("A Secret Discipline," 50).

more radically conceptual, metaphoric mode of seeing. In this case we are asked to see not *what* but *how*, while our attention is displaced from the naked dancers onto a more allusive, reflective, astral dimension, an ideal cosmos of mythic memory:

> Looke how the Crowne, which *Ariadne* wore
> Upon her yvory forehead that same day,
> That *Theseus* her unto his bridale bore,
> When the bold *Centaures* made that bloudy fray,
> With the fierce *Lapithes*, which did them dismay;
> Being now placed in the firmament,
> Through the bright heaven doth her beams display,
> And is unto the starres an ornament,
> Which round about her move in order excellent.
>
> (VI.vi.13)

Here again, however, even the more extreme erotic sublimations are placed against a background of social and sexual violation (proleptic of the savagery that will sweep over the pastoral world at the end of canto x).[6] It is as if the imagery's movement upward also called up or allowed a corresponding intrusion from below. I am not sure that it is sufficient to rationalize the internal conflict by appeal to a Renaissance idea of *concordia discors*, but neither is the problem anything so simple as a return of the repressed. For Spenser's carefully positioned allusion to the violent centaurs serves to heighten as much as to rebuke or infect his more fragile figure of desire. What we may feel as subversive irony is also a mode of inoculation, as if for Spenser to admit the shadow of an ancient violation here might stave off the darker revenges of erotic idolatry or idealization such as we see in the House of Busyrane. That is, such ironies of perspective do not merely undermine the illusory ideal; rather, they become for the poet both infection and defense, even partial (if paradoxical) purifications of the will toward idealization.

A similarly complex play with alternative mythologies is visible in Spenser's treatment of the three Graces, who form the inner circle of the dance. Viewed in retrospect, it may seem that the poet has mobilized all too many possible frames for interpreting their significance: "grace" as the ultimate refinement of human love and courtesy; "Grace" as the incalculable force of divine salvation; the "Graces" as

6. See Cheney, *Spenser's Image of Nature*, 231–35, for a discussion of the intricate ironies present in Spenser's allusion to the marriage of Thetis, and the Battle of the Lapiths and the Centaurs.

analogues for the ambiguous inspiration of poetry, sisters of the "thrise three" Muses of Parnassus.[7] The very word "grace" is put under an extraordinary amount of tension in the text. Spenser uses it frequently as a rhyme word, matched with the equally resonant "place"; it functions variously as proper name and common noun, and occasionally as a verb as well. To show "grace" as simultaneously an agent, a quality, and a mode of action may of course simply be a way of conjuring the very reciprocity and richness of relation that characterize Grace for the poet. And yet there is something stranger at work in the way Spenser liberates the overdetermined referentiality of this word, in his way of suggesting that his complex narrative might find its source or solution in what is after all a radical pun or play of double senses. For his use of "grace" sets at odds as well as in order what we might have assumed were distinct levels of experience or language, driving those different levels together as well as reflecting their fixed, philosophical analogies.[8] The sense of some willful power of reconstruction in the poet's own strategies of description and renaming comes through even more strongly in his way of opening up the closed, classical circle of the Graces to the intrusion of the fourth, making her the new center of the old circle. In all, the episode sets aside a vague, tension-less polysemy for the sake of a more severe kind of poetic substitution, one whose structure might be framed thus: where MacCaffrey finds in the scene on Mount Acidale a point where human love and reciprocity meet with the generosity of God, where *eros* intersects with *agape* (*Spenser's Allegory*, 355), I would read rather a demystifying parody of heavenly Grace as well as a nearly Neo-Platonic theologizing of secular poetry and language, not so much a meeting of *eros* and *agape* as an image of *agape* under the conditions of *eros*, an *eros* made in lieu of *agape*.[9]

7. See Tonkin, *Spenser's Courteous Pastoral,* 124–31 and 248–59, for a more detailed survey of the critical debates over Spenser's depiction of the Graces.

8. I touch rather briefly here on the problem of paronomasia in allegory discussed more at length in Quilligan's *The Language of Allegory: Defining the Genre,* 33–51, and passim. This critic argues that the use of puns to generate and gloss the difficult structures of Spenser's narratives (e.g., the plays on literal and figurative "error" in Book I) is something that characterizes the genre of allegory as a whole. Quilligan's own description of allegorical writing tends to wander between a nearly Realist or Platonic pole, in which words—however ambiguous—seem truly of use in unfolding a solid core of moral or metaphysical truth, and a more Nominalist or skeptical one, in which an allegorical text's fiercely playful "system" of signs holds truth in abeyance, retrieving us from the often narrowing, idolatrous processes of normal naming and intellection.

9. To unpack this telegraphic formula a bit more: I take it that by substituting the Graces for Grace, by depicting these avatars of human love and beauty as unconjurable presences, Spenser is in a strange way situating his vision between Neo-Platonic and more traditional Christian mythologies. For, as I understand it, the unsettling aspect of

As in the case of the apostrophe to Ariadne's crown, I am picturing a situation in which what should be a lower or more purely human order invades the space of a higher, supernatural one, such an invasion yet asking us to reorient our sense of the distinctness, priority, or purity of that higher order. The process both moves toward and defends against idolatry. Spenser's strategy of substitution may be clearer here if read in the light of Philip Sidney's account of the poet's power in the *Defense of Poesie.* The following passage frames itself as an apology for Sidney's earlier, enthusiastic vision of the poet as a second creator, one who becomes almost "another Nature," and who freely ranges within "the Zodiack of his own wit":

> Neither let it be deemed too sawcy a comparison, to ballance the highest point of mans wit, with the efficacie of nature: but rather give right honor to the heavenly maker of that maker, who having made man to his owne likenes, set him beyond and over all the workes of that second nature, which in nothing he sheweth so much as in Poetry; when with the force of a divine breath, he bringeth things foorth far surpassing her doings: with no small arguments to the incredulous of that first accursed fall of *Adam,* since our erected wit maketh us know what perfection is, and yet our infected wil keepeth us from reaching unto it. (*Prose Works,* 3:8–9)

The poet here is not so purely solipsistic as to inspire himself, as is indeed suggested by the idea of his being "lifted up with the vigor of his own invention." Still, Sidney begins by describing the poet's divine in-

---

Renaissance Neo-Platonism lies less in its speculative mysticism or materialistic magic than in its claims that the highest modes of love and knowledge are functions of, and accessible to, a transcendental but still strongly human *eros.* Neo-Platonic *eros,* if it does not exactly usurp the place of a divine *agape* originating in a realm inaccessible to human effort, is nonetheless raised to a position of importance within the economics of salvation such that it may confuse the ideally distinct realms of *eros* and *agape, cupiditas* and *caritas.* It is by following the *via amatoria,* Pico writes, that the soul, purged of earthly affections by the *foco amoroso,* "transforms herself into an angel" (*Commento sopra una canzona de amore composta da Girolamo Benivieni,* I.13; translation mine). Now it may or may not be that Spenser was aware of Ficino's and Pico's accounts of the three Graces as an allegory of the relations between human *eros* and the celestial beauty that was taken to be its end and source—the three goddesses standing for that process of emanation, conversion, and reversion in which the mind, caught by the overflowing of celestial power, is turned from its terrestrial desires and returns to its heavenly origins (cf. Edgar Wind, *Pagan Mysteries in the Renaissance,* 36–44). Certainly Colin's allegorical reading of the Graces (VI.x.23–24) recalls more clearly the moralistic traditions of Stoic allegory. Still, by figuring the Graces as strongly gratuitous presences, inaccessible to the labor of mere human will, he establishes an upward limit to the quest of an intellectual or imaginative *eros,* at the same time as he avoids placing the fulfillment of that quest totally in the hands of a theological or ecclesiastical notion of Grace.

spiration in such a way as to make the elusive, creative force of divine breath nearly coextensive with the poet's own antinatural and supernatural power of making. He defends his own perhaps excessive defense, however, by denying that this might entail any sort of special Grace for the poet, or any peculiar restitution for his all-too-human state of divided power. Sidney does this, strangely enough, by converting the proud claim of inspiration into the best possible argument for man's fallen nature. The advocate of poetry thus reestablishes with a sudden exuberance exactly that gap between human and divine powers which the assertion about inspiration might have tempted him to close, moving from the possible illusion of continuity with a divine source to a skeptical revelation of loss, distance, abjection. Of course, the gesture of asserting human inadequacy—whatever its theological authority—may conceal more complex psychic and rhetorical motives, and Sidney's secret gain here is to have held out (and held onto) the ideal of a divinely inspired poetry while still maintaining a human autonomy for his art.[10] Such a gain is reinforced by the local rhetorical strength of the opposition between "erected wit" and "infected wil," the former positing a residual, if not quite redemptive, power in the faculty that caused the fall. Taking such a problematic text as a frame for examining the encounter on Mount Acidale, we may see Spenser's strategy more clearly. For in lieu of Sidney's explicit, defensive separation of wit and will, Spenser constructs the fragile myth of a Grace and an inspiration that, if they do not redeem the infected will, for a moment at least save the erected wit from an uneasy contemplation of both its early loss and its present power. The force of the allegorical scene lies in the fact that the Graces on Mount Acidale are not just *figures of wit* or of knowing, emblematic signs pointing to unstable metaphysical or psychological presences beyond themselves. We must rather recognize them as *figures of will*, traces of the poet's startling act of substitution.[11] *The vision of the nymphs and Graces is thus a gift which the poet gives himself, as well as a form of perfection given him by another.* The dancers and the crown of Ariadne are like that "song made in lieu of many ornaments," itself a "goodly ornament," which is Spenser's "Epithalamion"—a poem that restitutes the poet's own self-created loss of

10. Sidney's strategy here is but one of the ironic strategies of defense examined in detail by Margaret Ferguson, *Trials of Desire: Renaissance Defenses of Poetry*, 137–62.

11. I am adapting very loosely Harold Bloom's pragmatic distinction between "figures of will" (rhetoric considered as a mode of power and persuasion) and "figures of knowledge" (rhetoric considered as an epistemological problem), worked out at some length in the coda to *Wallace Stevens: The Poems of Our Climate*, 379–388.

other "ornaments," and that becomes the very Grace with which he graces both himself and his bride.[12] On Mount Acidale, without denying the Augustinian skepticism that would insist on the wounds of the fall, which teaches that man and nature are not their own, and that presence is always absence, Spenser hints at a power in his poetry which advances or approaches the things of human love *not as another Nature, but as another Grace.*

I am, of course, turning back onto the poet the closing lines of the episode's climactic stanza, describing Colin's hidden beloved:

> She was to weete that iolly Shepheards lasse,
> Which piped there unto that merry rout,
> That iolly shepheard, which there piped, was
> Poore *Colin Clout* (who knowes not *Colin Clout*?)
> He pypt apace, whilest they him daunst about.
> Pype iolly shepheard, pype thou now apace
> Unto thy love, that made thee low to lout:
> *Thy love is present there with thee in place,*
> *Thy love is there advaunst to be another Grace.*
> (VI.X.16; emphasis mine)

It is the poet here who secretly advances his love and who gives her what presence she has. The closing verses are among the most rhetorically remarkable in the entire poem, and since they are also the last threshold that the reader crosses before Calidore intrudes into the charmed circle, we might pause over them for a moment. In this stanza, Spenser addresses his own earlier pastoral persona, as if this were a necessary prelude to the broader act of mythological substitu-

12. The description of the "goodly band" of dancing Graces and nymphs as a mythic crown which "is unto the starres an ornament" indeed echoes the language of the "Envoi" to Spenser's "Epithalamion":

> Song made in lieu of many ornaments,
> With which my love should duly have bene dect,
> Which cutting off through hasty accidents,
> Ye would not stay your dew time to expect,
> But promist both to recompens,
> Be unto her a goodly ornament,
> And for short time an endlesse moniment.
> (*Poetical Works*, 584)

Though this "apology" seems to blame the "hasty accidents" of the outside world for the loss of any greater, richer ceremony, the impatient agency that initiates that "cutting off" must be read as that of the song itself. The "Envoi" indeed suggests that the poem at once causes and retrospectively masters or recompenses such disjunctions. It presents us with a brief image of the kind of redemptive solipsism such as is unfolded much more complexly in the confrontations with Grace and imagination on Mount Acidale.

tion, namely, making Colin's Lady the Fourth Grace. There is a playful kind of solipsism in Spenser's address to the piper, as if the poet needed to cheer himself on in the act of celebration. But this gesture is pushed to an extreme in the poet's fairly extravagant declaration to Colin that, within the present tense of the poem, "Thy love is present there with thee in place." For to be "in place" is no simple thing within so labyrinthine an allegory, where any site is likely to be a multifaceted *topos*, a texture of conceptual commonplaces, where any temple, grove, or mountaintop is apt to be other than itself, a surface to be fallen through, a where that is also an elsewhere. And yet the inevitable structures of allegorical displacement must be measured here against the poet's willful act of mythic renaming, as well as against the force of his insistence that in spite of everything the erotic object is really "there." We might archly rewrite the penultimate line as "Thy love is present there with thee in trace" (or "in trope"); and yet even so the line retains its imaginative authority, first because any attempt to expose its rhetorical illusions cannot quite come to terms with the poet's strenuous, disenchanted embrace of that illusion, but also because the line after all does place the act of love or grace which is "there" most fully in the poet's act of troping. It is perhaps the precarious pressure of the poet's utterance, and the need retrospectively to frame, isolate, or circumscribe it (even by carefully staging its interruption), that moves the poet suddenly to shift his attention away from Colin and onto the nearly forgotten Calidore:

> Much wondred *Calidore* at this straunge sight,
> Whose like before his eye had never seene,
> And standing long astonished in spright,
> And rapt with pleasaunce, wist not what to weene;
> Whether it were the traine of beauties Queene,
> Or Nymphes, or Faeries, or enchaunted show,
> With which his eyes mote have deluded beene.
> Therefore resolving, what it was, to know,
> Out of the wood he rose, and toward them did go.
>
> But soon as he appeared to their view,
> They vanisht all away out of his sight,
> And cleane were gone, which way he never knew;
> All save the shepheard . . .
>
> (VI.X.17–18)

I spoke of the vision as an "illusion" in the case of Colin and the narrator, but for the latter such illusion exists in the celebratory urgency of the lyric utterance, in the imperative "Pype iolly shepheard," while in Colin's case it entails a solipsistic absorption in the modalities of sound. Both of these situations, especially the hearing of the Shep*heard*, contrast strongly with Calidore's nearly obsessive engagement with sight. For it is the reductive lure of sight, of the egoistic eye that desires knowledge and epistemological certainty about sense, science, and illusion—that desires figures of wit rather than figures of will—which leads Calidore to break in upon the vision, or rather, that which was for him alone a "vision."

The loss is hardly a tragic one, of course; in itself it seems almost inevitable and not a little dreamlike (similar to Britomart's breaking through into the inner chamber of the House of Busyrane). If we follow Guillory, the moment of disappearance may even seem to be a more masterful fiction than the presence of the Graces themselves, the subtlest of the poet's lies in support of the illusion that the gods were ever there to begin with, hence an achieved myth of loss that could satisfy both the poet's desire and his skepticism (*Poetic Authority*, 44). The august persuasiveness, the quickening magic of such fictions of disenchantment lie in Spenser's having so transformed the threats of both idolatry and iconoclasm that we move from a sense of the vision's dangerous fragility and inevitable failure to a feeling that the disappearance might be a kind of redemptive accomplishment. At least such is Berger's argument in his important article on the episode: "The complete self-sufficiency of the second nature, the total inward mastery of experience—this is no triumph at all, only delusion, if it takes itself seriously. For then it would have nothing to do with the poet *now*, a man still faced by life, fortune, malice, Providence. Thus poetry, having triumphed, must dissolve its triumph again and again to show that it is still engaged in the ongoing process of life where experience is not yet ordered" ("A Secret Discipline," 74).

The difficulty of a reading such as this, however, is that it both pitches itself too absolutely against the lure of fantasy and oversimplifies the poetic motives for iconoclasm. Berger's account of disenchantment in Spenser, in the above passage and elsewhere, has been so vivifying and influential that it may be hard for us to measure its idealizations. Yet this exaltation of the Renaissance artist's ironic, self-limiting enterprise may involve as much of a reduction as the idea of a totally self-absorbed, blind visionary poet which Berger seems eager to qualify. At work here, I think, is a somewhat limiting, if passionately felt version of the Freudian reality principle, a concept that informs many of Berger's most innovative essays. One of the difficulties of applying it to the poem, however, is that the intrusion of Calidore on Mount Acidale leaves the different domains of reality and imagination as confused as ever. The poet's fiction of loss, as I have said, is strangely persuasive in itself, but one could argue that the loss does as much to valorize the authentic and fragile magic of these presences as it does retrospectively to expose their status as artifice. Furthermore, to speak of "the ongoing process of life where experience is not yet ordered" occludes the problem that it is exactly "life" and "reality," the reductive and catastrophic *orders* of ongoing political, religious, and psychological experience, of which the poem offers a visionary critique. And it must do so, at least in part, through the polymorphous, dilatory creations of the pleasure principle.

Calidore's transgression of the threshold of vision sets up an apparent contrast between an outside and an inside, a before and an after, a presence and an absence. Yet the interruption is embedded in the romance narrative in such a way that any simple distinctions between fiction and reality, authenticity and inauthenticity, and so on, are set radically in suspension. Insofar as Spenser does dramatize the labor of the reality principle in Calidore, this must come to mean something like literalism or fetishism. Calidore's advance into the circle of the Graces begins in a loss of negative capability; it is somewhat more "illusioned" than disillusioned since it entails an idolatrous attempt to possess or know a vision that he only succeeds in collapsing and to gain a certainty that he only drives further into uncertainty. Calidore thus both makes and breaks the creatures of vision as idolatrous presences, his disenchantment remaining both ironic and inadvertent. His likeness to transgressive questers like Britomart, however strong, may only remind us of how close the latter's encounters bring her to the threshold of idolatry and how unstable is the locus of virtue and power in such moments of iconoclasm.

It is in the necessary loss of firm centers, but also in the determined oscillation between the gestures of the pleasure and the reality principles, that I would locate the importance of Mount Acidale. Thus Spenser is neither quite the Dante of *Purgatorio* 30, granted a vision of Grace as a transformed erotic object, nor Shakespeare's Prospero, confidently breaking and deprecating his own magical powers before his return to the political world. He might be closer to the Dante of *Paradiso* 33, falling from vision with the collapse of his human, fantastic powers of transcription, but Spenser's Colin is hardly Dante's pilgrim, nor is Calidore's failure framed so grandly. Though it may be too ironic an analogue, I would say that the situation of the poet on Mount Acidale—factored into the perspectives of Calidore and

Colin—shares most with that of Petrarch in "The Ascent of Mount Ventoux" (*Rerum familiarum* IV.i). In this founding Renaissance narrative (of questionable historicity, though cast as a true epistolary report), the poet climbs to the top of an actual mountain in Provence. The motives for the ascent are ambiguous, a mixture of nostalgia and intellectual curiosity, but the main thing is that the literal climb becomes the occasion for a variety of meditations on the shape of the poet's moral life. His spatial divagations and delays run parallel with passages of self-accusation and troubled recollection which hinder rather than advance the quest. And having finally gained the summit, the poet presents us with a strange scene of beauty, blank communion, and loss in which the focus is still on the free, enlarged space of the poet's human doubts and the speculative burdens of memory and conscience. Petrarch begins by enjoying both the landscape and his physical presence in it, and there is some justice for scholars taking his view from the top as a crucial moment in the development of a modern, more detachedly aesthetic experience of the physical world. But the text's intensified feeling for the power of sight does not arise from any descriptive achievement. Rather, it emerges retrospectively, when Petrarch turns from the view to his own copy of Augustine's *Confessions*, and reads there only words that rebuke him for seeking illusory grandeurs outside himself. The quest for a summit of vision—though in no way as explicitly "visionary" as Spenser's—thus culminates in a *lost* aesthesis of landscape (framed by suspicions of idolatry) but also in a failed communion with an ancient text. Petrarch is of course self-consciously rehearsing the moment of gratuitous scriptural reading which stirred Augustine's own final conversion (*Confessions* VIII.12). But Augustine's act, motivated by his overhearing sourceless children's voices, is framed as a moment of Grace which allowed a saving identification with the Word of God, an inspired leap into an orthodox *mythos*. In the case of Petrarch, however, the act of reading elicits only a sense of distance and continuing spiritual error, both text and landscape becoming in their different ways empty, useless idols.[13] The narrative thus traces a partial disenchantment with both seeing and reading; in what one critic has called the "crisis of allegory," any attempt by the narrator to conjure correspondences among the present

13. The idol that is the landscape, however, maintains a peculiar autonomy over and against the moral discourse that thus interprets it. For this latter does not move Petrarch from idolatry to true knowledge, from *cupiditas* to *caritas*. Rather, the text that makes idolatry of his seeing remains itself something of a blank, alien realm—chastening his error but in no way offering an opening into a space beyond error. Here one might argue that it is in the interstices and shifts between differing modes of idolatry that we must locate the paradigmatic force of Petrarch's dissenting ascent.

climb and prior journeys or narratives breaks down.[14] The magical rhetoric of allegory yields only disjunctions, negative parallels, textual blanks, while the windy mount, like Mount Acidale, becomes the locus of only the most uncertain form of literary "inspiration," a site of trial which repels as much as it attracts any analogies with Sinai, Patmos, or Parnassus.

It is the power gained by a staged scene of disillusionment, by the denial or putting into question of an inspired contact, which brings Petrarch's text closest to Spenser's. Spenser, indeed, gives us a picture of what the lyric poet in Petrarch might have accomplished on Mount Ventoux, especially insofar as he projects onto Calidore that aspect of Petrarchan poetry which evolves its images in the space of conscious illusion, in the shadowy area of aesthetic and erotic idolatry—an idolatry that, as John Freccero argues, emerges against the background of disenchantment with the Realist, metaphysical allegorizing of the Middle Ages.[15] The encounter on Mount Acidale may be as much a redemptive parody as a simple imitation of the Petrarchan situation, or it may provide a more persuasive illusion of an accessible Grace which might cure the idolatrous excursions of *eros*. And yet, like Petrarch's experience on Mount Ventoux, Spenser's narrative defines most clearly a situation in which the infected will maintains its awkward freedom even in the light of the failures of the erected wit.

Of course, there *is* explicit allegorical knowledge to be had on Mount Acidale. But it exists only because Calidore first shatters Colin's vision, the self-absorbed contemplation of his art and love, and so collapses the fragile gap or space of fictive alienation which allowed the poet to address in such urgent tones his own pastoral persona. The Graces departed, his pipes broken (in despair, but also in a dramatic seconding of Calidore's action), Colin begins to speak in a voice that identifies him more directly with the poet-narrator, explaining to Calidore the significance of the lost vision. The words he speaks are those of a more discursive, secular allegorist, a cultural historian and glosser of emblems who recovers for the reader sterner lessons about virtue, generosity, and courtesy in the political world. But these do not give Calidore quite the positive ontological knowledge of presence which he seems to have been seeking. Colin "dilates" (as Spenser says), in a less stressful, less intensely haunted space, within a temporality that allows him more urbanely to frame words about and images of

14. See Robert Durling, "The Ascent of Mt. Ventoux and the Crisis of Allegory," 21–22 and passim.

15. See Freccero, "The Fig Tree and the Laurel," 38–40.

the Graces, without fearing the stark alternatives of fixation or fragmentation which the vision itself had posed.[16] And yet it is just in this less private, more self-conscious space of comment and praise that the poet finds it suddenly necessary to defend his ideal against the possible discord of courtly envy by placing the previously transcendental lady beneath the sacred feet of the dread Gloriana (VI.x.28). The crisis of allegory is at best only delayed for Spenser and takes on a much darker form than it does in Petrarch; indeed, we might call it not the crisis so much as the revenge of allegory. Despite the poet's preemptive dissolving of the idyll, his second grace or nature continues to be threatened—not so much by the brigands who appear later in canto x as by the Blatant Beast, a demon of envy and allegory who lives not simply in the realm of fixation but in the saving space of dilation and delay, in the unnatural mutability and fecundity of language, in those meanings that human desire lets flow, unfold, and reshape themselves.

The Blatant Beast

The Blatant Beast defines an impasse in the unfolding of Spenser's allegorical quest-romance which brings the six-book *Faerie Queene* to a halt. That the final glimpse we have of the Beast is as a demonic iconoclast, ravaging through corrupt monasteries, should suggest his importance within my own argument, but to fully understand it, that closing must be placed within a broader analysis of the Beast's function in the poem.

This doglike, thousand-headed beast with poisonous tongues (of bears, tigers, and mortal men) and iron teeth emerges at the end of Book V as an agent of Envy and Detraction, who set him on the justicer Arthegall (providing a stark, if evasive, image of the official and unofficial disapproval that followed Lord Grey's harsh rule in Ireland, and that led to his return to England). But the beast becomes truly wounding and virulent only in Book VI, where it wanders

16. On Spenser's use of this key word, cf. Nohrnberg, *Analogy*, 729: "The poet, having lost his pastoral vision, turns to the task of interpreting it to his audience: 'Tho gan that shepheard thus for the dilate' (VI.x.21). The word *dilate* seems unexceptional here, but Spenser uses it only once again in the poem, at the end of the Mutabilitie Cantos, where it turns up as a semi-technical term employed in Nature's explanation of the way in which all mutable things fulfill the law of their being—through dilation. Its use on Mount Acidale thus suggests the way in which Spenser's poem—or Colin's vision—fulfills the law of *its* being: through that delay, or dilation, during which an interpretation is allowed to emerge."

through the pastoral world striking almost randomly at unguarded knights and ladies. The Beast attacks Serena as she wanders "about the fields, as liking led / Her wavering lust after her wandring sight, / To make a garland to adorne her hed, / Without suspect of ill or daungers hidden dred" (VI.iii.23); the three villains Despetto, Decetto, and Defetto also use the Beast to wound Arthur's courtly squire Timias, "To draw him from his deare beloved dame, / Unwares into the daunger of defame" (VI.v.15). In such cases it seems as if the Beast represents not the projected revenges of unacknowledged inward sins (like Sansfoy, Orgoglio, or Lust) but rather the sourceless, unpredictable attacks of envy and slander running wild in a world beyond the control of the victim's self. As such the Beast is the goal and enemy of Calidore, the Knight of Courtesy, that quester who is set to purify the public poetics of social relation and social love. Iconographically, this beast of defamatory noise derives very much from Virgil's *Fama*, or Rumor (*Aeneid* IV.173–97), that inflated monster of public speech which trumpets Dido's romance with Aeneas and which grows uncontrollably, mingling high and low report and metamorphosing even truth into something like a lie.[17] Berger argues that the Beast embodies "the social expression of the malice produced by despair and self-hatred" ("A Secret Discipline," 42), and he usefully connects it with the figure of "Sclaunder" in Book IV:

> Her words were not, as common words are ment,
> T'expresse the meaning of the inward mind,
> But noysome breath, and poysnous spirit sent
> From inward parts, with cancred malice lind,
> And breathed forth with blast of bitter wind;
> Which passing through the eares, would pierce the hart,
> And wound the soule it selfe with griefe unkind:
> For like the stings of Aspes, that kill with smart,
> Her spightfull words did pricke, and wound the inner part.
> (IV.viii.26)

The crucial difficulty here is that we cannot disentangle the source of slander from its aim or victim; indeed, like the self-wounding power of Envy (whose secret thoughts "murder her owne mynd" [V.xii.33]), slander harms the perception of the slanderer as much as it defiles its

17. The Beast is also related to the three-headed Plutonian dog Cerberus and to the many-headed Hydra, who like the Beast itself (in at least one of its two genealogies) are the offspring of Typhaon and Echidna (Hesiod, *Theogony* 311–14; cf. *FQ* VI.vi.9–12). Orgoglio's seven-headed beast is also compared to the Hydra (I.vii.17).

wonted object.[18] Despite the "publicness" of slander, it has an inward poison; it does not express the mind, yet it grows from and strikes at the inward parts—though again Spenser makes it hard to tell whether these belong to the slanderer or the slandered. The empty, foul wind of slander, Spenser suggests, works by breaking down our usual distinctions between surface and depth, inner and outer reality. That is to say, although its venom may appear superficial, slander troubles us especially in that uneasy space between inward desires and the outward forms or images that may variously sustain, define, and even originate those desires.[19] As an extension of envy, it feeds on that separation between subject and object and between desire and expression which is structured into our life in the world and in time. Slander lives in the fluid, negative spaces of discourse that confuse the threshold between the self and the world. Furthermore, the very inevitability of its wounds may suggest the temptations to reduction and violence hovering in the background even of responsible allegorical or satirical discourse such as Spenser's own.

To a culture as invested as that of the Renaissance was in the dynamics of praise, in the power of rhetoric to transfigure both private and public experience, slander might appear not simply as a marginal aberration but as an essential limiting case of language, though also as the revenge of language. The random poison of the Beast may not even depend on something as definable as "malice and self-hatred"; rather, it may be the unspoken underside of praise, prayer, or prophecy, that aspect of the will to define and blame which shifts into the will to divide and accuse. It may be only the repetition of stories without

18. We might point here to Spenser's picture of Envy with her tongue like the sting of an asp and her mouth foaming with poison (v.xii.36), but perhaps even more interesting is Giotto's emblem of *Invidia* in the Arena Chapel: an old woman standing amidst hell fire, with one clawlike hand stretched forth (to snatch or wound?) and the other clasping a moneybag to her side; she has huge ears (to catch tales and slanders), and the snake emerging from her mouth curls back and stings her between the eyes. Here the snake and the slanderous tongue are even more closely identified than in Spenser. Giotto also recalls the poet's play on the question of slander's "sources," his figure suggesting that slander is strangely responsible for (as well as being caused by) the evil eye of envy. (This image appears in Stubblebine, *Giotto: The Arena Chapel Frescoes*, pl. 59.)

19. Cf. W.B. Yeats on the transfiguring power of contempt:

> The finished man among his enemies?—
> How in the name of Heaven can he escape
> That defiling and disfigured shape
> The mirror of malicious eyes
> Casts upon his eyes until at last
> He thinks that shape must be his shape?
> (*Collected Poems*, 266)

ground, cut off from their tellers, yet therefore (like idols) the more able to stick in our minds and mobilize or fixate our desires and fears. Slander and its poison arise at the point where any public or private motives encounter the accidents, inconsistencies, half-truths, and omissions of language. Shakespeare shows us something of this in his picture of how Iago—the victim, scholar, and instigator of jealousy—can take advantage of the common intractability of linguistic reference to do his work. He introduces Othello to the self-born, self-justifying power of the "green-ey'd monster, which doth mock the meat it feeds on" by persuading the naive Moor (so convinced of the simple dichotomies of the moral world and of the unambiguous power of his own eloquence) that none of the words which the two share are transparent, that even words blankly repeated prove unwieldy, duplicitous, and double-edged:

> IAGO: I did not think [Cassio] had been acquainted with her.
> OTHELLO: O, yes, and went between us very oft.
> IAGO: Indeed?
> OTHELLO: Indeed? Ay, indeed! Discern'st thou aught in that?
> Is he not honest?
> IAGO: Honest, my lord?
> OTHELLO: Honest? Ay, honest.
> IAGO: My lord, for aught I know.
> OTHELLO: What dost thou think?
> IAGO: Think, my lord?
> OTHELLO: Think, my lord? By heaven, he echoes me,
> As if there were some monster in his thought,
> Too hideous to be shown. Thou dost mean something . . .
> (III.iii.99–108)

Playing on the Moor's narrowed commitment to meaning, Iago implicates Othello in an empty, almost unutterable iteration of speech which steals words from their speakers, defiles simple meaning, and yet raises the specter of hidden senses which had not even been thought of. The monster so raised, which means nothing rather than something, or the something that is nothing, is a cousin of the Blatant Beast.

Reading more strictly for the "historical" allegory, we can say that Spenser intends the Beast to represent a corrupted and corruptible speech that has its habitation in the public world of his poem's reception. The creature is located in the courtly slanders that brought down Lord Grey, in the vile reception that Spenser thought his own poetry received at the centers of power, in the selfish and indecorous spirit of the public which Spenser describes in "The Teares of the Muses" as mocking, disordering, defiling, and ultimately cutting off the true work of poets.[20] The Beast is thus an analytic allegory of slander and a prophetic satire on its more than natural force. His immense scope suggests a kind of paranoia in the poet (can there have been that many slanderers "out there," after all?). And yet Spenser's strategy may be a way of possessing within his poem something that is an uncertain threat to that poem—though not necessarily in order to delude himself that the Beast can thereby be contained or exorcized. We might thus think of the overinflated Beast as a kind of psychic defense against slander as much as an account of slander's actual power. Spenser's picture of the Beast is, broadly speaking, a piece of apotropaic magic; the act of so representing slander exemplifies Wittgenstein's thought that "the contempt each person feels for me is something I must make my own, an essential and significant part of the world seen from the place where I am" (*Remarks on Frazer's "Golden Bough,"* 11e).

Yet in the case of the Blatant Beast it is hard to place such contempt, or to see whether the poet or another truly owns it. The anxious, wandering power with which Spenser invests the Beast suggests that we may want to ask more closely after the motives, means, and costs of thus constructing such an image of outward contempt. (I do not presume, by the way, that Wittgenstein is unaware of such questions.) We might even ask whether one can possess or make over another's contempt without merely mirroring it, or whether to become "an essential and significant part" of the poet's world the slanderer's contempt must correspond to something already in place there.

What I am getting at is an extension of earlier comments on the dangers latent in aggressive images of evil, and the conceptual violence or slander inherent in the act of choosing an idol to be the victim of an act of iconoclasm. Here I need to go further and frame my analysis of the Blatant Beast in terms of two roughly Freudian questions: In what school does the ego learn its postures of aggression and de-

20. More specifically, the Beast is an agent of men like Lord Burghley, Elizabeth's treasurer and chief advisor, a figure whom Spenser seems to have identified with the narrow, puritanical spirit at court which could read *The Faerie Queene* only as a seductive, erotic romance (cf. IV.proem.1–2), and so cut the poet off from both patronage and fame (Judson, *Life of Spenser,* 153). Spenser satirizes Burghley rather viciously as a self-serving ape in "Mother Hubberds Tale" (*Poetical Works,* 495–508) and also gives him a disturbing, Urizen-like form in one of the dedicatory sonnets to the 1590 *Faerie Queene,* where he appears as the frozen father-god Atlas, upholding the "grave affaires" of the kingdom on his shoulders (*Poetical Works,* 410).

fense? What grounds the ego's introjection of negative or threatening objects of desire? Following through Freud's later hypotheses about an originary complex of sadism and masochism in the ego, one might ask whether the Beast represents not merely a response to an outward threat but also an unfixed violence structured within the poet's self and his poem which is yet directed back against them, a violence that is a constitutive part of the poem's visionary economy. (Such a reading depends, of course, on thinking of the poetic text as a defensive structure, a kind of ego or self in its own right, as well as the self's linguistic expression. Whether or not one accepts this idea as a general possibility, some such hypothesis is required to understand the crisis of slander, which by nature dramatizes the interdependence, however illusory, of the self and its works.) The Beast then could be described as occupying the place of Freud's death instinct, especially as this emerges in the work of some revisionist Freudians as a species of primal envy—like the Beast, a force or instinct of refusal and revenge, an impulse built into the self to defile its objects of desire, a means of outwitting the fear that those objects have always been in danger of being injured or lost.[21] Such a theory posits envy as a delight in disorder and reduction which is yet unavoidably bound up with the expressions of *eros* and turned ambivalently on both the self and the world outside the self. This analogy might illuminate the inevitable way in which Spenser calls up the Beast to shut down his most nostalgic and idealizing of books; it might explain the poet's need always to wound or mar scenes of visionary presence and fulfilled desire with hints of alienation, envy, or idolatry; it might even identify the many-headed Beast as an outgrowth of the extravagance and multiplicity of the poet's narratives, his impulse to trouble all simple centers of purity and authority with ironic mirrors or shadowy doubles. Given that Spenser makes the Beast a poetic and rhetorical more than a clearly psychological entity, the creature would thus represent a power that exists potentially within the poem and its images, rather than merely standing as a symbol for conditions found only in *The Faerie Queene's* intractable audience.

For the Beast is not only loose in the world; it is loose in the word.

21. In his aptly titled book of psychoanalytic essays, *A Game That Must Be Lost*, the British art historian Adrian Stokes writes that "the aggression [of the Death Drive] is immediately bound up with loss also: the destroyed object is often the good object attacked in greed, or in envy, the supreme expression of the desire for object-absence fused with libido, since this persecution by the object issues from its very goodness coveted by the subject" (65). Stokes is here writing very much under the influence of Melanie Klein. I should note that I borrow my question about the ego's schooling from Stokes (55).

Or rather, it grows out of the looseness of words, the capacity of human language for polymorphous, subversive, and yet persuasive babble.[22] The power of the Beast is the power that language takes on in the labyrinth of love, politics, and history. It defines for Spenser an enemy, a sphere of trial, and an inevitable tool. If it does not quite have the tyrannical power of the apocalyptic Beast whose mouth "spake great things and blasphemies" (Revelation 13.5, Geneva Version; cf. *FQ* VI.xii.25), it is all the more unsettling because in accusing it the poet is half accusing himself. For the Beast is ultimately related to the poet's anxious sense of "how doubtfully all Allegories may be construed"; it is the "giant form" of those uncontrollable duplicities, those "gealous opinions and misconstructions" that seem the inevitable shadow of his poetry; it is a force of violation internal to, but also released by, any act of staking out an allegorical vision, especially one with such high spiritual, political, and moral stakes as Spenser's own. Spenser in the opening epistle of his poem defines allegory as a discourse open to slander, but by the end of Book VI he hints more darkly that his iconoclastic allegory shares a space with slander itself.[23]

My argument about the nature of the Beast's poison may be clearer if we look at how Spenser seeks to represent its cure. In Book VI, canto vi, a hermit, himself formerly a knight, heals the obscure wounds of Timias and Serena by telling them to restrain both their will and "outward senses" (vi.7), and at the same time to "shun secresie, and talke in open sight" (VI.vi.14). The regimen, as a way of curing the oddly inward and outward poison of slander, seems aimed at containing both the wanderings of physical desire and the outward "sense" of spoken language, as well as at preventing the growth of poisonous feeling and

22. "Blatant" (sometimes "Blattant") seems to have been Spenser's own coinage and is usually taken to derive from the Latin *blatire*, "to babble." (The OED suggests the possibility of an additional connection with an archaic form of "bleating" which would make the Beast a grotesque relative of those sheep that define the economy of the pastoral world in Book VI.) The invasive power of the Beast perhaps derives from the fact that such "looseness" yet conditions the possibility for the interiority of one's language in the first place, so that the possibility of some distance between self and world, and hence the possibility of desire as such, would seem inextricably bound to whatever the Blatant Beast embodies, most extremely to defilement, to *thanatos*.

23. Cheney, perhaps playfully unfolding Spenser's word "misconstruction," makes the strange joke that this monster of slander is "what today might be called misreading or deconstruction" ("Retrospective Pastoral," 7). The analogy is, I think, precise enough (if not quite fair to the Beast), but one must recognize that the ironies of representation and the errors of reading or desire which such critical stances may imply for Cheney are not purely imposed on the text. The alien enemy is something that the poem yet recognizes as its own; the Beast is *heimlich* as well as *unheimlich*. It represents a disequilibrium that is a permanent feature of the human linguistic situation (though also much more than that), and especially one that infects Spenser's highly articulated, polyvalent, ambivalent, and complexly perspectivizing work.

self-wounding names that the mind nurses in silence. Let us say that it is an attempt to keep hidden thoughts from infecting both desire and speech at once. Ambiguous as such a cure is in itself, it becomes even more confusing when we ask whether it constitutes a likely or literal cure for the poem as a whole—with its unstable forms of secrecy and disclosure, its divagations of desire and praise, its hidden interest in the generative power of alienation and envy. The Hermit movingly expresses the need for "purity of diction." But given the exfoliation of erotic vision and discourse in Book VI, for instance, it is hardly credible that either Calidore or Colin could quite "[his] eies, [his] eares, [his] tongue, [his] talk restraine / From that they most affect, and in due termes containe" (VI.7), as the hermit asks Timias and Serena to do. For there is a sense in which the transgressive idolatry of the knight and the tenuous, celebratory grace of the shepherd continue not only to attract the sounds or wounds of the Blatant Beast but also to feed on the same ambivalences in desire and language which give that creature life. At the end of the poem Calidore seems unable to bind the Beast for more than a short season. Hence, as the narrative moves forward to enclose the poet's own present situation, Spenser himself appears subject to the "venemous despite" and "blamefull blot" of its "wicked tongues," especially as these are embodied in "a mighty Peres displeasure" (VI.xii.41). And yet both the excesses and the defensive moves of Book VI seem strangely calculated to invite such "backbiting," as if the poet wouldn't have it any other way. Hence, Spenser's warning to himself in the last couplet of Book VI may be at best a bitter parody of the Hermit's ascetic teaching: "Therfore do you my rimes keep better measure, / And seeke to please, that now is counted wisemens threasure" (VI.xii.41). Here we have a sign of Spenser's own envy and alienation barely hidden under the mask of wise resignation, and also the traces of an ironic disdain which leave open a space in which the Beast might even take the poet's part.

Spenser hasn't Shakespeare's means to shape the paradoxes of envy and slander into a form of imagination which could work within a wholly human drama. This is perhaps because Spenser is more interested in starker movements of envy proper, the feeling of the subject that would wound the object it lacks, rather than jealousy, that more potentially tragic fear of losing what one already possesses or thought one possessed. But he manages nonetheless to make the dangers of envy terrifying enough, imbuing them both with a religious urgency and with the somewhat less impersonal anxiety of a poet trying to understand the liabilities of his own poetic project. We can see these concerns best, perhaps, in the final vision we have of the Beast—

indeed, the final allegorical encounter of the six-book version of the poem. This is a scene that also will draw us back (with a vengeance) into the major figurative terms of my own critical narrative. For we move at the end of canto xii from the high romance of Pastorella restored by Calidore to her long lost noble parents into an almost apocalyptic piece of ecclesiastical satire in which the Beast becomes a strange myth of iconoclasm:

> Into their cloysters now he broken had,
> Through which the Monckes he chaced here and there,
> And them pursu'd into their dortours sad,
> And searched all their cels and secrets neare;
> In which what filth and ordure did appeare,
> Were yrkesome to report; yet that foule Beast
> Nought sparing them, the more did tosse and teare,
> And ransacke all their dennes from most to least,
> Regarding nought religion, nor their holy heast.
>
> From thence into the sacred Church he broke,
> And robd the Chancell, and the deskes downe threw,
> And Altars fouled, and blasphemy spoke,
> And th'Images for all their goodly hew,
> Did cast to ground, whilest none was them to rew;
> So all confounded and disordered there.
>
> (VI.xii.24–25)

Inverting Calidore's failed attempt to grasp a visionary center, the Beast here seems to expose the empty and corrupt heart of the spiritual order. Indeed, there is a sense in which this last vision rounds off the epic by ironically transporting us back to the center of Book I, where Arthur in canto viii broke through into the bloody, idolatrous sanctuary of Orgoglio in order to save the imprisoned type of true Holiness and Christian faith. And yet in Book VI the Beast seems to engender, feed upon, and perpetuate the very corruption it would cure; the pretense is reformation but the practice is deformation.[24] The sacrileges of the Beast thus recall precisely the work of Orgoglio's seven-headed beast, who also defiled a church and pulled down its holy ornaments. If the later monster seems considerably more strange to us, it is because we see in it a fundamental impulse of the Protestant imagination mirroring so closely the Reformation's own picture of what its corrupt Roman enemy looked like.

24. This last phrase is taken from a sermon of George Sandys which criticizes the abuses of the queen's "surveyors" (quoted by Kermode, *Shakespeare, Spenser, Donne,* 46).

But the Beast at this point in Spenser's romance is more than a satire on radical Protestantism (as Jonson thought) or an image of the general distrust of authority which the religious troubles of the sixteenth century could release. The poet knew the relics of Henry VIII's "dissolution" of the monastaries, with its uneasy mixture of political, economic, and religious motives.[25] But if Spenser, writing in the 1590s, complicated his myth of slander with an image of the physical and spiritual violence that half a century earlier had founded the church of the Faerie Queen, it was to remythologize that violence and the ruins it caused for his own purposes. The depiction of the Beast at the end of Book VI is more like a final act of conscience, a gesture filled with both anxiety and presumption. The Beast almost literalizes Spenser's awareness of the complexly iconoclastic motive that runs through his own work (including the impulse to prophetic slander that gives life to Book I) but that here seems to destroy the work. To find a place for such a Beast within his own poetic temple entails more than a modest poetic skepticism. If the passing vision of dancing nymphs and Graces is the poet's best image of imaginative faith—however much he achieves that image through an ironic recapturing of loss—the Beast is the type of faithlessness and disenchantment become obsessive. He is the poet's confession and catharsis of that aspect of desire which perfects itself in the devaluation, the despoiling, the destruction of desire's objects. He is the demonic triumph of reform preempting even the elegiac triumphs of time. Again, besides being an image of an external force that presses in on the fragile world of the poem, the Beast is an imaginative violence from within, an interior enemy that answers darkly to Colin's interior paramour. The monster that grows within the necessary space between ourselves and our images is as apparently gratuitous in its advent as those presences that attend the singer on Mount Acidale; it is

25. See Chapter 1, n. 20. It may or may not be worthwhile to note that in 1582 Spenser leased lands in County Kildare which contained the ruins of a Franciscan friary, New Abbey, and which had "an old waste town adjoining" (Judson, *Life of Spenser*, 103). Spenser's engagement with the complex poetry of ruins, in both its elegiac and apocalyptic aspects, goes back to his earliest translations in *The Theatre for Worldlings* and his splendid rendering of Du Bellay's *Les Antiquitez de Rome* (*Poetical Works*, 606–8 and 509–14, respectively). To focus on the idea of ruins from the perspective of iconoclasm, however, may raise fresh questions about the ways that active violence may intersect with entropy or decay, and the ways that the shapes of ruin may be variously figured as failure or triumph, something inherited or something achieved. It might be interesting to try pushing back to the sixteenth century an analysis of the myths, philosophy, and phenomenology of ruins such as Thomas MacFarland attempts in *Romanticism and the Forms of Ruin: Wordsworth, Coleridge, and the Modalities of Fragmentation*, 3–55 and passim.

equally the product of the poet's "love." But the Beast is also, alas, considerably less transient than those dancers. Nor will Spenser at this moment allow himself to form the image of an Arthur who might defeat this catastrophic version of what has been called Spenser's "inescapable romance." That Calidore succeeds even partly may be mainly a result of the difficult lessons of Acidale. Having heard Colin's words about grace and discipline, he may also have acquired a sense of the imaginative tact that is needed to live in a world where magic and its passing away, desire and its destruction, idolatry and iconoclasm, are inextricably folded together.

The Triumphs of Hobgoblin

Book VI closes with a diffused, apocalyptic monster that is hurled into the present world, and that finds there no final enemy. The poet's last words in that book suggest a cold, poised resignation, an abandonment of a poetic career. Though it is dangerous to simplify such complex gestures, one might say that the loss of vision on Mount Acidale somehow entails the secret quest of the Blatant Beast, the two events leaving us with a broken poem in a broken world. All the more remarkable, then, that Spenser recovers his voice so strikingly in the Mutabilitie Cantos. Though that poem hardly evades the mutual entanglements of idolatry and iconoclasm, it maps out a space in which the poet can maintain less chilling attitudes of disillusionment and can find a critical irony that sustains some real gaiety. Through these Spenser wins back, if only in parable, some measure of reconciliation between his poem and his world.[26]

My main focus in this section is on the Faunus episode, that digressive etiological fable at the end of the first of the cantos in which the poet explains why Arlo Hill, the site of the trial of the titaness Mutabilitie, came to be abandoned by the gods that inhabited it—the responsibility falling on a comical faun who combines aspects of both Calidore and the Blatant Beast. In order to frame my commentary, however, I need first to sketch out a few ideas about Book VII as a whole.

26. I have taken it as a working assumption that the Mutabilitie Cantos are Spenser's attempt to find a form of ending fit for a poem that is preternaturally anxious about the forms and figures of ending, but that otherwise could have achieved no closure besides mere truncation. They are an attempt to come to terms with the personal, literary, and theological burden of ending, to save both ending and endlessness from the infectious iconoclasm of the Blatant Beast. Setting aside the strictly circumstantial and probably insoluble mystery of their late publication in 1609, I would say that the force of the cantos lies in the fact that we must read them simultaneously as a closed, autonomous epyllion and a fragment or fraction of an incomplete seventh book.

Two points define for me the stress and strangeness of the book, though neither are much spoken of in the available criticism.[27] The first is harder to argue, since it depends on construing the meanings of the story in ways that reverse the poet's more explicit thematic signals. The account of Mutabilitie's rebellion against what she takes to be the illegitimate rule of the Olympian gods, her claims to power over both sublunary and celestial worlds, the conversion of cosmic battle into legal trial under the eyes of Dame Nature, and the titaness's subsequent defeat when the evidence of cyclical, patterned change is presented—all of this suggests that we should read Book VII as a philosophical allegory that seeks mimetically to contain the threat of unbounded, violent, disorderly flux. Yet I would suggest that, to make full sense of some of the poet's strange ironies, we must see that the threat he is fighting off lies as much in order itself—especially order as a facet of human life lived in time—as in disorder or change.

It is the unchangeable facts of the past as much as the uncontrollable accidents of the present which account for the tragedies of human fortune and desire; faith in the fixed idols of anteriority, whether personal or social, serves as well as the ruins of past authorities and times to disorder the choices and powers of present life. In our movements toward an uncertain future, the urge to embrace a usurping order that, one imagines, may change things utterly, can in the end engender greater trouble than the simple loss of stable goals or ordered harmonies. Order itself then—or the will to order, stability, division, equality, closure—may indeed be more effectively catastrophic than whatever is named by idealized myths of unbounded change, decay, entropy, or chaos. The Mutabilitie Cantos tend to repress any direct image of the threatening work of order and defensively project its opposite in the ultimately less disturbing fantasy of the rebellious titaness. The logical emptiness in the arguments of this abstract enemy makes her all the easier to defeat and strengthens Nature's own beautiful and authoritative sophistries, especially those that tell us that all changeable things "by their change their being doe dilate: / And turning to themselves at length againe, / Doe worke their owne perfection so by fate: / Then over them Change doth not rule and raigne; / But they raigne over change, and doe their states maintaine" (VII.vii.58). But the darker wisdom of Spenser's poem is that this will to self-fulfillment can be crossed with a will to self-an-

27. Among more conservative readings, perhaps the best is that of S.P. Zitner, contained in the introduction to his edition of the Mutabilitie Cantos. This critic pays very careful but undogmatic attention to Spenser's fundamentally Boethian theories of time, change, and form, and brings out some of the more idiosyncratic facets of Book VII's narrative and allusive mode.

nihilation. One may then wonder whether Nature's subsequent warning to the ambitious titaness—that she seeks her own decay by trying to fulfill her desire for place and rule—is not something more than a clever joke at the expense of a fragile personification of change unwisely seeking reification. For in human, if not in allegorical agents, the gentle unfoldings of being may end up in repetition or stasis, just as the will to perfect an arbitrary desire may end up in skewed or partial forms of fulfillment or lead to the imposing of that desire as a tyrannical, divisive fatality. Such possibilities may help explain why the poet, invoking a "Sabaoths sight" in the concluding stanzas of Book VII, makes that image of eternal rest at once inevitable and strangely inaccessible. He projects such a rest beyond all human types, as if to remind us that the discourse that would lay hold of apocalyptic vision in any less tentative a fashion would most likely collapse into false prophecy and idolatry. A similar desire to hold lightly onto the blank superiority of order over change may even account for the odd, Lucianic irony that plays over the narrative, making a mockery of both established authority *and* the forces that rebel against it.

My second point is related to this last and concerns the status of the Mutabilitie Cantos as a form of substitute mythology. I have already pointed to one example of such substitution in the way that Mutabilitie herself is introduced as a metonymic evasion of any more explicit myth of the fall, since she is described as the cause of our growing into death instead of life rather than as the effect of creation or crime. On a larger scale, one could say that Book VII is a last vision written "in lieu of" the Book of Revelation.[28] Like the Garden of Adonis, it provides us with a strongly secular apocalypse, or, rather, an apocalypse of the secular. The trial of the titaness issues in a last judgment that tries to locate some sufficient form of restitution, balance, and justice within rather than beyond the cycles of time (even if it does not quite succeed); it also offers an eschatological vision that breaks down the reductively dualistic perspectives or cloven fictions which usually characterize eschatological writing, in particular, as I mentioned above, the coarsely contrastive projection of a demonic en-

28. The only critic in whom I find any anticipation of this reading, however sketchy, is Nohrnberg. Commenting on the disappearance of Nature at the end of canto vii, he adds: "It is time to put away expectations of some noisier or more tangible apocalypse. Almost without allowing us to know it, Spenser has his vision, and its crisis is closed. The argument of the Mutabilitie Cantos will allow of nothing more definitive, and neither will *The Faerie Queene.* That self-balancing progression of becoming and decline and replenishment, through which all of Being is regularly perpetuated throughout Spenser's long poem, rightly issues, not in an apocalyptic cataclysm, but in an apocalyptic homeostasis" (*Analogy,* 86).

emy as a way of establishing the greater purity of one's own stance. If Spenser's epic unfolds its most overt version of the biblical apocalypse in its very first book, it then closes with an apocalyptic invention that can be said to take the place of any other final vision. Admittedly, there is a gesture toward some more orthodox vision of apocalypse at the end of Book VII, once the cyclical pageant of the seasons has dissolved. Still, it is only a gesture, and we must take seriously Spenser's refusal to fill out any vision of a new heaven and new earth according to the lineaments of Scripture, as well as his refusal to claim that that final image might show a providential order which is intelligibly at work in history. Spenser reduces, schematizes, but also demystifies the dream of Saint John the Divine; neither prophecy, promise, or threat, it becomes largely the shrill cry of the self that longs for an abstracted glimpse of simple rest and changelessness. "If faith is indeed a refuge here, it is a lonely and bitter one. For the poet has no sight of God or of that hearsay Sabbath. He invokes and he waits, but he affirms only the reality of the Titaness" (Greene, *Descent from Heaven*, 323).

As a first step toward developing both of these altered perspectives, I propose to read the Faunus episode as an ironic replacement for that crucial phrase of apocalyptic which occupies itself with the marking and casting out of idolatry. In this reading Faunus is no intrusive Caliban but a prophetic iconoclast. This interpretation of course contradicts the surface evidence that Faunus, in suborning a handmaid of Diana and spying on the naked goddess as she bathes, is caught and cursed for violating a truly sacred presence. The narrative occasion for the inset fable, that of explaining how the Irish hill on which Mutabilitie's trial is held became so barren and wild, also suggests a parallel between the desacralizing of Arlo Hill and the loss of Eden. Likewise, various details of Spenser's story—Faunus's gifts of cherries and apples to the beguiled Molanna, as well as traditional allegorizations of the source myth of Actaeon—seem to identify the faun with the temper Satan. The evident comedy of Faunus's attempt to get a glimpse of Diana has been noted, of course, but few critics doubt the basically criminal nature of his act or the justice of Diana's punishment (though it is just this punishment that is called into question in Ovid's original version of the Actaeon story [*Metamorphoses* III.253–54]). Yet we need to view Faunus's place within the mythological economy of the Mutabilitie Cantos as a whole, and there he plays a more heroic, if still ambivalent, part.

Faunus banishes from the landscape of Arlo Hill not simply a particular pagan divinity but also a mode of mythic fable. As Richard

Ringler has shown in detail, Spenser, despite the generally Ovidian tone of the episode, pointedly stops short of realizing the fiction of metamorphosis ("The Faunus Episode," 292). Alluding to the story of Actaeon, Spenser reports that the unfortunate hunter had indeed been devoured by his hounds, but only "in Hunters hew" (VII.vi.45); the nymph Molanna is punished by being overwhelmed with stones, but she survives as the river we presume she always was; and Faunus himself, instead of being slain, gelded, or transformed, is simply chased across the landscape wrapped in the skins of a deer. Spenser is not, of course, getting rid of the literal belief in metamorphosis, which itself is hardly Ovidian. But he *is* evading the easy fictions of transformation, the habitual depiction of the gods of the landscape, the ironic patterns of punishment, all of which form the literary machinery of Ovid's quite urbane, secularized mythmaking. And he does this, it seems to me, not so much to prove that he is more disenchanted than Ovid as to prepare for the more strenuous and evanescent forms of magic that appear in the vision of Nature and the pageant of the months in canto vii.[29]

It is possible, of course, that Spenser's strategy brings to the surface a more hidden anxiety about the Ovidian tradition. Massey's discussions of the demented literalization of figurative language imposed by the fictions of metamorphosis (*The Gaping Pig*, 26–33), and Harold Skulsky's suggestions as to the epistemological uncertainty generated by the endless, grotesque, and often arbitrary tranformations of Ovid's poem (*Metamorphosis: The Mind in Exile*, 24–61), both indicate directions in which one might pursue this line of argument. My own accounts of both idolatry and iconoclasm show the space these phenomena share with metamorphosis, as well. What Spenser retains from Ovid, however, is his habit of parodying etiological myth. For as a fable of iconoclasm, the Faunus episode presents us not so much with sacred history as with an etiology of disenchantment, a myth of demythologization. It tells a story not of the origins of nature or the gods but of the degradation of both. While it echoes the myth of the fall, its ironizing of Edenic loss sets in questionable light not only myths of divine origins but myths of human failure as well. Its deli-

29. Berger, reading in Book VII a comic allegory of literary history, speaks of the process of "desymbolization" and "depersonification" by which mythological figures like Mutabilitie and the other gods lose their wonted integrity, a process "in which the referent breaks free from its containing symbolic form. Thus released, it is open to new forms and to new life in later times. This process is already underway as we move from the aggressive pagan individuals of canto vi to the impersonal concord of forces and functions shining more clearly through the figures and emblems of canto vii" ("Archaism and Evolution in Retrospect," 163).

cately self-conscious ironies suggest the ways in which such myths may at best be rationalizations, by means of a fiction of loss, of a difficult situation in the present, and so inevitably a function of nostalgia for an idealized past. The Faunus episode then, instead of asking us to read *through* the puzzling allegorical surface to some ground in scriptural myth, forces us to see how that surface itself reframes the idea of a fall, even as it manages to reinforce the strongly deromanticized nature of the sacred site. Arlo Hill, like Mount Acidale and Mount Ventoux, becomes most haunted in its very warding off of analogies to other sacred hills. This historical height near Spenser's Irish home thus becomes at once more familiar and more strange, no *omphalos* but a place where fiction, myth, and history uneasily cross.

Thus to define the poetic status of Arlo Hill, however, is not the same as showing Faunus himself to be the avatar of the poet's own creatively disenchanting quest, a figure through whom the poet can repossess the blankness of the Irish landscape as more of an imaginative achievement than a curse. One might begin to support such a reading by looking at Faunus's analogies with other characters both within and without *The Faerie Queene*. For example, Faunus, like Britomart and Calidore, violates an apparently sacred place and yet stands as a distanced witness to superhuman presence. Even more interestingly, the Actaeon-like faun recalls the distraught love goddess Venus who comes upon Diana bathing while searching for her lost son Cupid (III.vi.17–19). In all of these cases, the intruding viewer's "interest" in the scene is by no means easy to dismiss as simply idolatrous or corrupt. Nohrnberg's detailed discussion (*Analogy*, 730f.) of the pastoral magician Colin as a composite of the sylvan Pan and his father Hermes—interpreter and imp, thief and psychopomp—could be extended in large part to the guileful faun as well. Indeed, Faunus is really closer than Colin Clout to Gabriel Harvey's famous description of Spenser's poem as "*Hobgoblin* runne away with the Garland from *Apollo*." We could add to this list several fragmentary but quite clear hints of a Christ-like vocation in Faunus, both in his work as ironic subverter of pagan divinity and in his unusual patience at suffering mockery and beating at the hands of Diana's nymphs. (The identification is perhaps reinforced by Spenser's repeated use of the word "foolish" to describe the faun in his lowly, absurd, and transgressive aspects, recalling Erasmus's complex variations on the ideas of human and Christian foolishness in the *Moriae encomium*.)

But such an accumulation of analogy, even when aptly ironic, only fills in part of the picture. One may lose sight of the way in which the poet fragments, juxtaposes, and sometimes suppresses such resemblances, the different "sources" being at times "checkt and changed from [their] nature trew, / By others opposition or obliquid view" (VII.vii.54). Hence one must retreat at least briefly from the all too pleasant excursions of analogy into the more strenuous dislocations of close reading. Here then is Faunus watching Diana from his covert, caught like Mutabilitie in the desire to "see that mortall eyes have never seene" (VII.vi.32):

> There *Faunus* saw that pleased much his eye,
> And made his hart to tickle in his brest,
> That for great ioy of some-what he did spy,
> He could him not containe in silent rest;
> But breaking forth in laughter, loud profest
> His foolish thought. A foolish *Faune* indeed,
> That couldst not hold thy selfe so hidden blest,
> But wouldest needs thine owne conceit areed.
> Babblers unworthy been of so divine a meed.
> (VII.vi.46)

Faunus is at this moment the mythological source of the Lucianic humor that haunts the entire Mutabilitie Cantos, such as is elicited even by the theomachic conflicts of earlier stanzas, where the titaness challenges the power of Jove at the circle of the moon, the threshold of the celestial world, only to have a kind of divine squabbling ensue.[30] The above lines, indeed, anticipate within the poem the laughter that may rise in the reader when, in the next stanza but one, the goddess Diana is compared to an angry "huswife" shaking and threatening a pest that has fouled her creaming pans. Faunus himself, however, seems laughing not so much at the domesticity as at the human nakedness, and especially the sexual nature of pagan divinity. His open laugh indeed strangely reverses the sense of shame and secrecy felt by Adam and Eve upon opening their eyes to their own nakedness. The "some-what" that he spies with so much joy, though not necessarily with desire, is clearly the goddess's genitalia, but the modest, perhaps even prurient evasiveness of Spenser's word—which restores a verbal covering where there is no visual one—does suggest ironies that point beyond a merely physiological demystification of pagan divinity. "Some-what," for all its apparent blandness, may take on an odd reso-

30. The mixture of apocalyptic and satirical elements in Book VII may reflect a deeper generic affinity. Martin Hengel, *Judaism and Hellenism*, 84, suggests that the use of diatribe and satire in late classical literature, and such satiric types as "letters of the gods," "testaments," and journeys to heaven and the underworld may have had some influence on the eclectic creations of late Jewish and early Christian apocalyptic.

nance of its own, especially when we recall the association of sexual organs with the topography of secret/sacred centers like the Garden of Adonis. I do not mean to suggest that Spenser is happily mocking an ancient image of chastity in the service of a more urbane and sexualized ideal of *eros*, or that the half-human faun is himself not cast as a rather crude form of male sexual seeing or priapic peering. Still, the faun's transgressive laughter, more engagingly mysterious than the goddess herself, wholly problematizes the relation of the eye and its object; the laugh raises questions that unsettle any normative distinctions we might make between what would be sacred and what profane contemplation, what enchantment and what disenchantment, what idolatry and what iconoclasm.

Before going further with my analysis, I want to propose a somewhat unusual "genealogy" for Faunus's laughter. As in the case of my comparison of Mount Acidale to Mount Ventoux, I am interested in a similarity of stance rather than in a definite source, even though here the text is one that Spenser must have known quite well: Boccaccio's *Genealogy of the Pagan Gods.* The passage I have in mind follows from the complex proem to that work, and we will need to pause for a moment over this introductory movement. In the proem, Boccaccio describes himself as a scholarly quester, descending into the darkened landscape of the past and reassembling the fragments of classical fable into a single, renewed body, like Aesculapius restoring the torn *corpus* of Hippolytus.[31] This quest, we must observe, is shadowed by a sense of possible failure and by the fear of envious detractors; there is also a sense of guilt at the violence involved in his reconstructions and interpretations, at the dismemberment that accompanies the act of remembering, as well as a lingering consciousness of the fact that he is still moving within a world of false gods or idols (especially given Boccaccio's lack of interest in the more orthodox accommodations of medieval moral allegory).[32] The landscape of the ancient gods thus proves both sacred and profane, while the work of the poetic theologian becomes an uneasy meditation on the errors and absences of mythographic history as well as on its authentic sources.[33]

31. On the sources of this mythology and its relevance for Renaissance theories of literary history, see A. Bartlett Giamatti, "Hippolytus among the Exiles: The Romance of Early Humanism" (*Exile and Change*, 12–32).

32. On the defense of poetry and interpretation undertaken by the proem and the fourteenth book of Boccaccio's *Genealogy*, see the pointed observations in Ferguson, *Trials of Desire*, 166–68 and 182–83.

33. Boccaccio's famous chiasmus, "Dunque bene appare, non solamente la poesía essere teologia, ma ancora la teologia essere poesia" (*Comento alla Divina Commedia*, 1:43), frames an ideal identification of poet and theologian, but it may also suggest

The proem culminates in an intricate account of the father god Demogorgon, a chthonic deity that, as Boccaccio may have known, owed its literary existence to a medieval scribal error.[34] He at least knew that the god had no place in any major classical texts, even though he claims that the ancients placed Demogorgon first in their own genealogies "for the sake of a beginning"—adding that it was really the terror of his name which silenced the later authors. Boccaccio's almost certainly comic parable on the problematic authority of classical myth is filled out even more clearly in the opening scene of Book I of his encyclopedia, where Boccaccio presents us with a grotesque theophany of the god:

> With greatest majesty of darkness, just when I had described that [genealogical] tree, the oldest grandfather of all the pagan gods, Demogorgon, terrifying by his very name, wrapped in clouds and mist, appeared before me as I was crossing through the bowels of the earth. He was dressed in a sort of mossy pallor, damp and dishevelled, sending forth a fetid and earthy odor, and, declaring rather by the words of others than by his own mouth that he was the father of their unhappy pre-eminence, he stood before me, the contriver of a new work. I confess that I began to laugh when, looking at him, I remembered the madness of the ancients who thought him first and uncreated, the eternal father of all things, and living in the bowels of the earth. (*Genealogy* I.11c; translation mine)[35]

It is altogether remarkable that Boccaccio should stage such a scene of mocked fatherhood at the threshold of his own book of genealogies. Demogorgon is presented as the debunked progenitor of an idolatrous literary mythology; and yet, as a creature of fantasy and a figuration of nostalgia, it may be that the god represents a genuine temptation and threat (especially since the poet's quest must cross into the space where the god himself dwells). The very grotesqueness of the apparition suggests a residue of anxiety in the confrontation. Hence, though Demogorgon is hardly as great a demon of earth and imagination as the catastrophic Orgoglio, Boccaccio feels a need both to conjure and to exorcise him. In this not quite Vichian divination of Demogorgon, the most startling moment is the poet's dramatized memory of his own laughter. For to such an uncertain necromancer

---

something about the uneasy breakdown of differences between the two vocations that troubles Boccaccio's attempts at both reading and rewriting the narratives of classical myth.

34. On this matter see Maurice Castelain, "Demogorgon ou le barbarisme déifié," and Nohrnberg, *Analogy*, 104, n. 38.

35. I am grateful to the late Robert Fitzgerald for his advice on this rendering.

as Boccaccio, invoking the demystifying testimony of ancient, ghostly voices, that laugh is both defensive and freshening; it neither quite slanders nor quite sanctifies; it is an enlightened but not coldly sardonic response. Boccaccio's laugh defines rather a regenerating ambivalence in which he who is laughing is, oddly enough, also laughed at or ironized.[36]

Boccaccio's laughter is echoed and intensified in Faunus's. Though the latter resounds at the end rather than at the opening of his mythographic project, Spenser's scene of voyeurism and laughter betrays the same comic fascination with archaic divinity. And though Boccaccio's more nearly Oedipal mockery is replaced in Spenser by an attack on the divine authority of a chaste, queenly goddess, the English poet's retrospective fable achieves a similarly complex lesson about the founding skepticism that places the poet in his spiritual and literary landscape.

But if Spenser *is* the faun, he is more fully exposed to his own mockery than Boccaccio appears to be; the gestures of mockery, that is, are themselves regarded with a greater degree of ambivalence. For we must remember that it is the faun's laugh, not the act of still, silent watching itself, that the poet appears to condemn and that leads to Faunus's punishment. What indicts the wood god is the breaking from rest into motion, from hidden to open, from silence into song. And yet this burden must not keep us from recognizing the laugh's peculiar efficacy. As has often been pointed out, the poet's emphasis on the faun's "silent rest" and entranced sight foreshadows the fragmentary closing of Book VII, where the poet invokes a vision of the reality which stands behind the ever changing, unresting world of Nature, a vision of all things settled "upon the pillours of Eternity" (VII.viii.2). Though the poet seems eager to place this vision beyond all possible images or figures of desire, it is yet mirrored in the faun's "hidden blest" stance of wordless watching. But having noticed the analogy, we must recognize that such watching can at best be read as a parodic prolepsis of Sabbath sight and may even constitute a shrewd warning against the regressive impulses underlying any sort of vision-

36. I am drawing here on Mikhail Bakhtin's intriguing typology of medieval and Renaissance laughter in *Rabelais and his World*, 59–144, in particular his description of Rabelaisian laughter as a defensive and yet liberating gesture, a motion that at once asserts and denies, that both buries and revives the object of ridicule. Such laughter ideally frees those who laugh from the violence of both religious superstition and political authority, even while it exposes them to their own irony. Bakhtin, however, associates such laughter with the organized disorder and the publically sanctioned gestures of medieval festival, whereas Boccaccio's and Faunus's laughs seem to project more obscurely private motives.

ary longing. If the sight that the genial narrator calls "so divine a meed" is after all a kind of mute idolatry, then the intrusive laughter professed so loudly may not be as criminal as it first appears.

Faunus's laugh is indeed the original speech—or the poet's best image of it—that invades the uncertain space infantile voyeurism shares with the desire for apocalyptic vision, breaking the tendency of both to self-absorbed or tyrannical silence. It is hardly a numinous primal word, a prophetic god-cry, a creative *logos*, or a transparent Adamic name. It is strictly speaking "no language," without any illusions of referentiality or ideological effectiveness. Yet Faunus's laughter has the risk and freshness of a human voice, the voice of one who announces his private delights and desires, though neither strictly to himself nor to any calculated audience. Both less and more than human, the demigod is a version of the poet who "areeds his own conceit"—his own poetic figures and continued allegory of praise as well as his own egotism. That laughter may even be the poet's dreamed revenge against the personal and political constraints that led him into bitter, chastened silence at the end of Book VI.

In the opening verses of "The Fall of Hyperion," John Keats wrote that

> . . . Poesy alone can tell her dreams,
> With the fine spell of words alone can save
> Imagination from the sable charm
> And dumb enchantment.
>
> (*Poetical Works*, 403)

Faunus's laugh is anything but a "fine spell of words," and yet it is a brilliant trope for the troubling magic of Spenser's own poetic idiom, which seeks to disenchant even the dumb enchantment possible in the sounds of language itself. Faunus is a form of the poet at his most exuberant and ambivalent, a figure mocked and mocking, idolatrous and iconoclastic. Thinking of Spenser—for whom every word of desire or praise was a necessary risk, a betrayal of private thought to public chaos; who dilated, distanced, and qualified every divinizing image half a dozen ways and yet was still pursued by the fear of envy and slander—we may recognize that the words that condemn Faunus are strangely directed at the poet himself: "Babblers unworthy been of so divine a meed." The babbler may suffer the fate of Echo and have the expression of his or her desires caught up within nonsense or the alienating repetition of anterior utterance. His poems may wander into or invite the noise, *rumor*, babble, or bleating of the sacrilegious Blatant Beast, the language of desire fulfilling itself in postures of envy rather than grace. Yet Faunus, the poet as Hobgoblin running away with the laurel from Apollo, is also a cousin of that Spenser figured by Raleigh as a "celestiall theife," a more triumphant invader of sacred presence who cast out another chaste poetic goddess from her tomblike temple.[37] Hermetic and Promethean at once, Faunus is a creature who tells the prophetic secrets of the gods, even if those secrets tell us that "Here there are no gods."

37. Raleigh's dedicatory sonnet, "A Vision upon this conceipt of the *Faery Queene*," mythologizes the poet's literary ambitions in a scene in which the Faerie Queen intrudes into a shrine that holds "the grave, where *Laura* lay," stealing away the graces and the "living fame" that attend Petrarchan poetry, while "Oblivion laid him downe on *Lauras* herse: / Hereat the hardest stones were seene to bleed, / And grones of buried ghosts the heavens did perse. / Where *Homers* spright did tremble all for griefe, / And curst th'accesse of that celestiall theife" (Spenser, *Poetical Works*, 409)—this last line suggesting that Spenser's poem overgoes classical epic as well as earlier Renaissance erotic poetry.

Coda:
The Veil of Idolatry

The goddess Nature descends in the second of the Cantos of Mutabilitie, as if to replace the departed Diana and to restore to flourishing life the vacated, chaotic landscape of Arlo Hill. Her function is to judge the titaness whose own transgressions of divine authority are parodied in the exuberant violations of Faunus—as if their memory made Arlo the most appropriate site of trial. Having refreshed the barren landscape of his present exile by giving it a demystifying and mythic past, Spenser can risk conjuring up—if only as a visitor—the figure that Ernst Robert Curtius called "one of the last religious experiences of the late-pagan world" (*European Literature*, 107). Nature seems to present us with a final *imago dei* for *The Faerie Queene*. As the mythological form of God's manifestations within the phenomenal world, she seems to command or at least comprehend the flux of appearances which Mutabilitie claims as her own; as in Alain de Lille (an author whom we cannot be sure if Spenser knew directly, though he had read Chaucer's references to him), Nature is also a goddess of poetic mediations, a divination of the desire that allegorical imagery refer to higher truths as well as a possible image of the hieratic authority that might control allegory's exfoliations. Hence it is appropriate that what absorbs the poet's attention, as it must absorb ours, is the veil that covers her face:

> That some doe say was so by skill devized,
> To hide the terror of her uncouth hew,
> From mortall eyes that should be sore agrized:
> For that her face did like a Lion shew,

> That eye of wight could not indure to view:
> But others tell that it so beautious was,
> And round about such beames of splendor threw,
> That it the Sunne a thousand times did pass,
> Ne could be seene, but like an image in a glass.
>
> That well may seemen true: for, well I weene
> That this same day, when she on *Arlo* sat,
> Her garment was so bright and wondrous sheene,
> That my fraile wit cannot devise to what
> It to compare, nor find like stuffe to that,
> As those three sacred *Saints*, though else most wise,
> Yet on mount *Thabor* quite their wits forgat,
> When they their glorious Lord in strange disguise
> Transfigur'd sawe; his garments so did daze their eyes.
> (VII.vii.6–7)

To try and explicate the poet's allusions here may end up both darkening and illuminating the description. I must be schematic for the present. Nature in her blinding veil is implicitly likened to the transfigured Christ, and yet strictly speaking this latter image only enters the text as a dis-simile, a testimony to the poet's inability to find "like stuffe" to which to compare the veil. Spenser's recollection of this peculiar moment in the Gospels does manage to raise the stakes of the vision, framing the account of Nature typologically, even as it implicitly transfigures the poet-witness, but the allusion in the end offers us no clear ground by which to rationalize the parallel between the two divinities. That Nature's face or veil appears "like an image in a glasse" may put us in mind of the figure of redemptive vision in 2 Corinthians 3.18: "We all beholde as in a mirrour the glorie of the Lord with open face, and are changed into that same image" (Geneva Version)—but Spenser's emphasis on the essential obscurity of the face is closer to the pattern of 1 Corinthians 13.12, which starkly opposes vision "through a glasse darkely" to the promised encounter "face to face." Indeed, here the mediating, defensive veil is itself only to be glimpsed as if in a mirror, such that *both* hidden face and covering veil may recall the petrifying gaze of Medusa, which had to be gazed at deflected in the shield of Perseus. In addition to the ambivalent recollections of the Gorgon, however, we may find even more unsettling echoes. For whatever other types Spenser mobilizes within his overloaded text, the profoundest source for his image of a blindingly veiled lawgiver handing down judgments on a hillside is Paul's uncanny and largely un-Mosaic Moses, a figure whose shining veil composes the New Testament's central metaphor for spiritual and textual idolatry. Both the poem and its critics have repressed this questionable image of sacred presence (much as the goddess Nature herself had forbidden the Stygian gods to show themselves at the trial on Arlo Hill "for horror of their count'naunce ill" [VII.vii.3]), and we cannot quite be sure what it means to drag that image into the light here. We might want to say that, naturalized, eroticized, framed by self-conscious literary paradox and placed within the context of other sovereign females in Spenser's poem, the Pauline image has begun to steal back for itself some of its original force as a type of mediated revelation. It would thus be another version of Spenser's divination of idolatry, his way of reappropriating and even redeeming the most dangerous shapes of magic and enchantment. But this would mean that the poet has so turned typological tradition on its head that we can hardly distinguish the types of revelation from the types of idolatry.

The irony wrought by calling up Moses or the Medusa from the poem's allusive underworld seems to me a necessary one, but again the gesture of recovery throws me into doubt. For there is a tendency in critics, whether they read the face of Nature piously or ironically, to overestimate what the vision of that goddess can tell us about Spenser's sense of his poem's epistemology, theology, and authority. Hence, whether we take it as a final unfolding of the paradoxes of idolatry, or even as a final allegory of the poem's endlessly ambiguous relation to truth and representation, a moment of radical skepticism and self-consciousness, we should be careful of lingering too long over so fragile an illusion of closure. For its very fascinating confusion may itself constitute a subtle kind of trap. At least I would suggest that, at this point in the critical history of the Mutabilitie Cantos, any reading of the goddess will open up considerably less interesting questions than those raised by looking at the pageant that follows her appearance. It is this pageant, after all, so often taken for granted by critics, that occupies most of the final canto. Hence at the risk of some awkwardness I want to close by examining a few of its stanzas in detail. For it is in these stanzas that the mysteries of a deity transfigured "in strange disguise" are unfolded, perhaps even displaced by the apparitions of a mythicized world continually "chang'd by strange disguise" (VII.vii.18), a world that poses difficulties which push beyond even those of the tightly knit paradoxes we find in Nature's veil.

In the pageant—or, rather, in the parade of witnesses to Mutabilitie's claim to rule both nature and divinity—we *may* find the emblematic evidence of order in mutability which Nature sees there, especially in Spenser's complex mingling of zodiacal symbols with traditional signs of seasonal labor and the liturgical calendar.[1] But more difficult to lay hold of is what one might call the narrative's phantasmagoria or visionary texture, those inflections of the poet's writing which both free and intensify our fascination with the mythic images and give to Spenser's allusions both a certain whimsicality and a fateful urgency. Throughout the pageant, we see the domain of the poetry itself emerging as the main realm in which the wise, iconoclastic author can claim to "rule over the stars," as he says in *A View.* The once banished astral gods reappear, but they are now a little harder to see, framed within a subtler grammar of allusion and illusion:

> Then came hot *Iuly* boyling like to fire,
> That all his garments he had cast away:
> Upon a Lyon raging yet with ire
> He boldly rode and made him to obay:
> It was the beast that whylome did forray
> The Nemaean forrest, till th'*Amphytrionide*
> Him slew, and with his hide did him array;
> Behinde his back a sithe, and by his side
> Under his belt he bore a sickle circling wide.
> (VII.vii.36)

In this as in other stanzas there is large precedent for Spenser's alignment of human and zodiacal emblems.[2] But whereas on Gothic calendars or cathedral portals the constellations are depicted in distinct compartments and commonly placed above the icons of the natural or cultural year, Spenser has forced them into the same space; moreover he has made the starry creatures into mounts that are guided by the seasons of labor. By poising these images against fragments of associated fable, Spenser further violates the structured logic of the medieval emblems and suggests so many strange threads of mythic relation that one hardly knows where to begin tracing them. For example, by connecting the image of burning July shedding its garments with a recollection of Hercules' lion-skin cape, Spenser may force us to recall another episode from that hero's history: his unwitting putting on of a mantle poisoned with the blood of his slain enemy, the centaur Nessus, a garment that his bride had supposed would win his love but that instead drove him to self-cremation. What makes this allusion so fascinating is that the image of Hercules' tragic

1. On this subject, see Sherman Hawkins, "Mutabilitie and the Cycle of the Months," in *Form and Convention in the Poetry of Edmund Spenser*, 76–102.

2. See, for example, the bas-reliefs on the portal of Amiens Cathedral, reproduced in Emile Mâle, *The Gothic Image: Religious Art in France of the Thirteenth Century*, 69–75.

death here becomes a shadowy figure for (in a sense, interprets) our commonplace relation to seasonal weather, even as it is further associated with the peaceable machinery of harvest (though the sickle's iconographic links to Death and Time may return us to a more sober frame). The text's subtle intertwinings of human, natural, and supernatural realms are worthy of the later Ruskin. It hardly serves to call Spenser's description syncretistic. We might try to show how it reflects Nature's argument about the place of order in a world of change, but that would have to mean that the process by which all created things turn "to themselves at length againe" has here been fused with, even subordinated to, the severe dilations of analogy and the intricate turnings of metaphor.

Spenser juxtaposes and reworks some ancient emblems even more powerfully in the final stanza of the pageant proper:

> And after all came *Life*, and lastly *Death*;
> *Death* with most grim and griesly visage seene,
> Yet is he nought but parting of the breath;
> Ne ought to see, but like a shade to weene,
> Unbodied, unsoul'd, unheard, unseene.
> But *Life* was like a faire young lusty boy,
> Such as they faine *Dan Cupid* to have beene,
> Full of delightfull health and lively ioy,
> Deckt all with flowres, and wings of gold fit to employ.
> (VII.vii.46)

Death appears in the masque as a sort of crude personification. But his "visage seene" is rapidly dissolved, his dark presence emptied out by a series of spare, negative translations. Indeed, we might say that some portion of the negativity of death as the cutting off of life has been displaced into the gestures of a critical consciousness which strike at the poetic and psychological rationale of the *image* of Death, which expose the "grim and griesly" face as a projection of human anxieties, an empty cultural idol. Spenser then allows a myth of death to die, but he does not replace those primitive terrors with any simple moral or theological reassurance. Indeed, in lines that are plainly intended to be a demystifying description of death as unbodied, unsouled, and unsensed (rather than senseless and soulless) we may only find ourselves faced with a deeper feeling of opacity and terror.

Into this blank and wholly uncanny space, however, the image of Life as Cupid enters with unaccountable freshness. This effect is partly a simple function of the chiastic structure of the descriptions: Death enters and is named *after* Life in the first line of the stanza, as if by a natural or fatal sequence; its oppressive power is further emphasized by the repetitions at the end and opening of contiguous verses (". . . and lastly *Death; / Death* with most grim"). But the lines that follow describe the two in the reverse of their original order. Death is thus denied any illusion of finality, while Life gains for itself an illusion of recovery. Moreover, the last four lines try to push beyond the strict questions of being and appearance such as hedged the earlier description of Death. The poet is now content with the freer, fictive identifications of things that are "like" or "as they faine," and that frame the description of Life as the god of idolatry and love—his "wings of gold fit to employ" here set to work in all the strenuous uselessness of the imagination. It is left to the reader to decide whether such a recovery is loss or gain.

By linking the evidence of the pageant together with earlier accounts of the chaotic changes of the elements and the scandalous metamorphoses of the Olympian Gods, Mutabilitie hopes that she will have proved her right to rule. But she is swiftly countered by the arguments of Nature about all things working their own perfection by fate, ruling over change and maintaining their states. Warned, "thy decay thou seekst by thy desire" (VII.vii.59), the goddess of change is put down by a combination of logical conundrum and pun: by appealing to a more abstracted, if no less mythicized ideal of "change," the poet can suddenly refine the titaness out of existence by a sentence that allows her no identity as either militant rebel or eloquent plaintiff. All of this was carefully contrived in the setting up of the conflict, of course, and it is somewhat surprising that critics find it so splendid a triumph. For we may justifiably feel that Nature's clever argument that Change cannot rule without destroying her part in that order which legitimates rule is just a little too pat. The fact that Nature herself disappears so hastily after her utterance (with little of the pathos felt on Mount Acidale) may be more than anything else a way of keeping us and everyone else at the trial from lingering over the real inadequacy of her words. For the species of turning and entropy, relation and disorder which we glimpse in the masque suggest shapes of change that cannot quite be compassed by Nature's comforting metaphysics. Insofar as the pageant tells us something about the workings of Spenser's poetry, Nature's retreat also suggests that there is no time left for this or any other sort of refined, reflective mythmaking, nor any space remaining in which *The Faerie Queene*, as opposed to life or nature, might enlarge and perfect its being. Her words may in retrospect seem mainly to convey the desperate wish for the continuity and perfection of a text that the poet knows must come to an "untimely" end. To cut off the unfoldings of such a graceful poetry may also block the wanderings and wounds of the Blatant Beast, but this may be small consolation.

At the end of a very different visionary epic, Blake's *The Four Zoas*, we find words that echo the entire tradition of Protestant iconoclasm: "The dark Religions are departed & sweet Science reigns" (*Complete Poetry and Prose*, 407). Spenser, for whatever reasons, neither attempted nor could he master so extreme a rhetoric. The apocalyptic present tense belongs only to his giants and enchanters. The authoritative rule of order over change is asserted only for a space, and Book VII closes, though less desperately than Book VI, by leaving the temporal world to its shifting illusions and images, and turning instead to a projected sight that, for all the poem knows, is "visionless entire":

> Then gin I thinke on that which Nature sayd,
> Of that same time when no more *Change* shall be,
> But stedfast rest of all things firmely stayd
> Upon the pillours of Eternity,
> That is contrayr to *Mutabilitie:*
> For, all that moveth, doth in *Change* delight:
> But thence-forth all shall rest eternally
> With Him that is the God of Sabbaoth hight:
> O that great Sabbaoth God, graunt me that Sabaoths sight.
> (VII.viii.2)

The conceptual and emotive force of the final gesture will always remain elusive. But if we are to comprehend it at all, we must see how disillusioned, how disenchanted the spare and intricate phantasms of the final pageant already are, and how self-wounding a reduction it is for Spenser to call them "flowring pride" and "love of things so vaine" (VII.viii.1). In dismissing the world, the poet turns not only from idolatry but also from the subtlest agon of his own iconoclasm.

Works Cited

Alighieri, Dante. *Literary Criticism of Dante Alighieri.* Ed. and trans. Robert S. Haller. Lincoln: Univ. of Nebraska Press, 1973.

Alpers, Paul J. *The Poetry of "The Faerie Queene."* Princeton: Princeton Univ. Press, 1967.

Aptekar, Jane. *Icons of Justice: Iconography and Thematic Imagery in Book V of "The Faerie Queene."* New York: Columbia Univ. Press, 1967.

Auerbach, Erich. *Scenes from the Drama of European Literature.* New York: Meridian Books, 1959.

Augustine. *On Christian Doctrine.* Trans. D. W. Robertson, Jr. Indianapolis: Bobbs-Merrill, 1958.

——. *The City of God.* Trans. Henry Bettenson and ed. David Knowles. New York: Penguin, 1972.

Bacon, Francis. *Works.* 14 vols. Ed. James Spedding, Robert Leslie Ellis, Douglas Heath, 1857–74. Rpt. New York: Garrett Press, 1968.

Bakhtin, Mikhail. *Rabelais and His World.* Trans. Helene Iswolsky. Cambridge, Mass.: M.I.T. Press, 1968.

Barfield, Owen. *Saving the Appearances: A Study in Idolatry.* New York: Harcourt Brace Jovanovich, n.d.

Barth, Markus, trans. and ed. *The Anchor Bible: Ephesians.* 2 vols. Garden City: Doubleday, 1974.

Battenhouse, Roy W. *Marlow's 'Tamburlaine': A Study in Renaissance Moral Philosophy.* Nashville: Vanderbilt Univ. Press, 1941.

Bender, John. *Spenser and Literary Pictorialism.* Princeton: Princeton Univ. Press, 1972.

Benjamin, Walter. *The Origin of German Tragic Drama.* 1928. Trans. John Osborne. London: New Left Books, 1977.

Bentley, Richard, ed. *Milton's "Paradise Lost": A New Edition.* London, 1732.

Berger, Harry, Jr. *The Allegorical Temper: Vision and Reality in Book II of Spenser's "Faerie Queene."* New Haven: Yale Univ. Press, 1957.

———. "A Secret Discipline: *The Faerie Queene,* Book VI." In *Form and Convention in the Poetry of Edmund Spenser,* ed. William Nelson, 35–75. New York: Columbia Univ. Press, 1961.

———. "Spenser's Gardens of Adonis: Force and Form in the Renaissance Imagination." *University of Toronto Quarterly* 30(1961):128–49.

———. "Spenser's *Faerie Queene,* Book I: Prelude to Interpretation." *Southern Review* (University of Adelaide) 2 (1966):18–49.

———. "*The Mutabilitie Cantos*: Archaism and Evolution in Retrospect." In *Spenser: A Collection of Critical Essays,* ed. Harry Berger, Jr., 146–76. Englewood Cliffs, N.J.: Prentice-Hall, 1968.

Bernheimer, Richard. *Wild Men in the Middle Ages: A Study in Art, Sentiment, and Demonology.* Cambridge, Mass.: Harvard Univ. Press, 1952.

———. *The Nature of Representation: A Phenomenological Inquiry.* Ed. H.W. Janson. New York: New York Univ. Press, 1961.

Bevan, Edwyn. *Holy Images: An Inquiry into Idolatry and Image-Worship in Ancient Paganism and in Christianity.* London: Allen and Unwin, 1940.

Blake, William. *Complete Poetry and Prose.* Ed. David Erdman. Rev. ed. Berkeley and Los Angeles: Univ. of California Press, 1982.

Bloom, Harold. *A Map of Misreading.* New York: Oxford Univ. Press, 1975.

———. *Wallace Stevens: The Poems of Our Climate.* Ithaca: Cornell Univ. Press, 1976.

Boccaccio, Giovanni. *Genealogy of the Pagan Gods. (Genealogie deorum gentilium libri).* 2 vols. Ed. Vincenzo Romano. Bari, 1951.

———. *Il comento alla Divina Commedia.* 3 vols. Ed. Domenico Guerri. Bari, 1918.

Boman, Thorleif. *Hebrew Thought Compared with Greek.* 1954. Trans. Jules L. Moreau. New York: Norton, 1970.

Bowker, John. *The Targums and Rabbinic Literature: An Introduction to Jewish Interpretations of Scripture.* Cambridge: Cambridge Univ. Press, 1979.

Brown, Huntington, ed. *The Tale of Gargantua and King Arthur.* Attributed to François Girault. Cambridge, Mass.: Harvard Univ. Press, 1932.

Brown, Peter. *Augustine of Hippo.* Berkeley and Los Angeles: Univ. of California Press, 1967.

———. *The Cult of the Saints: Its Rise and Function in Latin Christianity.* Chicago: Univ. of Chicago Press, 1981.

Buber, Martin. *The Prophetic Faith.* 1949. New York: Harper & Row, 1960.

Bultmann, Rudolf. *Theology of the New Testament.* 1948–53. 2 vols. Trans. Kendrick Grobel. New York: Scribner's, 1951–55.

Burckhardt, Jacob. *The Civilization of the Renaissance in Italy.* 1860. Trans. Benjamin Nelson and Charles Trinkaus. 2 vols. New York: Harper & Row, 1958.

Burke, Kenneth. *A Rhetoric of Motives.* New York: Prentice-Hall, 1952.

———. *The Rhetoric of Religion: Studies in Logology.* Boston: Beacon Press, 1961.

———. *The Philosophy of Literary Form: Studies in Symbolic Action.* Berkeley and Los Angeles: Univ. of California Press, 1973.

Butler, E. M. *The Myth of the Magus.* Cambridge: Cambridge Univ. Press, 1948.

Buttrick, George, et al. *Interpreter's Dictionary of the Bible.* 4 vols. Nashville: Abingdon Press, 1962.

Calvin, John. *Institutes of the Christian Religion.* 2 vols. Trans. Henry Beveridge. Edinburgh, 1845.

Cassirer, Ernst. *The Individual and the Cosmos in Renaissance Philosophy.* 1927. Trans. Mario Domandi. Philadelphia: Univ. of Pennsylvania Press, 1972.

Castelain, Maurice. "Demogorgon ou le barbarisme déifié." *Bulletin de L'Association Guillaume Budé* 36(1932):22–39.

Cave, Terence. *The Cornucopian Text: Problems of Writing in the French Renaissance.* London: Oxford Univ. Press, 1979.

Cheney, Donald. *Spenser's Image of Nature: Wild Man and Shepherd in "The Faerie Queene."* New Haven: Yale Univ. Press, 1966.

——. "Spenser's Hermaphrodite and the 1590 *Faerie Queene.*" *PMLA* 87 (1972):192–200.

——. "Retrospective Pastoral: The Returns of Colin Clout." Paper read at the Modern Language Association Convention, New York, 29 December 1981.

Childs, Brevard. *Myth and Reality in the Old Testament.* 2d ed. London: SCM Press, 1962.

——. *The Book of Exodus: A Critical, Theological Commentary.* Philadelphia: Westminster Press, 1974.

Clark, Francis. *The Eucharistic Sacrifice and the Reformation.* London: The Newman Press, 1960.

Cohn, Norman. *The Pursuit of the Millennium: Revolutionary Millenarians and Mystical Anarchists of the Middle Ages.* Rev. ed. New York: Oxford Univ. Press, 1970.

Colie, Rosalie. *Paradoxia Epidemica: The Renaissance Tradition of Paradox.* Princeton: Princeton Univ. Press, 1966.

——. *The Resources of Kind: Genre-Theory in the Renaissance.* Berkeley and Los Angeles: Univ. of California Press, 1973.

Comes, Natalis. *Mythologiae.* Venice, 1567.

Comito, Terry. *The Idea of the Garden in the Renaissance.* New Brunswick: Rutgers Univ. Press, 1978.

Crew, Phyllis Mack. *Calvinist Preaching and Iconoclasm in the Netherlands: 1544–1569.* Cambridge: Cambridge Univ. Press, 1978.

Curtius, Ernst Robert. *European Literature and the Latin Middle Ages.* 1948. Trans. Willard R. Trask. Princeton: Princeton Univ. Press, 1973.

Cusanus. See Nicholas of Cusa.

Daniélou, Jean. *From Shadows to Reality: Studies in the Biblical Typology of the Fathers.* 1958. Trans. Wulfstan Hibbert. London: Burnes and Oates, 1960.

De Lille, Alain. *The Complaint of Nature.* Trans. Douglas M. Moffat. Yale Studies in English 36. New York: Henry Holt & Co., 1908.

Derrida, Jacques. *Dissemination.* 1972. Trans. Barbara Johnson. Chicago: Univ. of Chicago Press, 1981.
Detienne, Marcel. *The Gardens of Adonis: Spices in Greek Mythology.* 1972. Trans. Janet Lloyd. New Jersey: Humanities Press, 1977.
Dodds, E. R. *The Greeks and the Irrational.* Berkeley and Los Angeles: Univ. of California Press, 1951.
Du Bellay, Joachim. *The Defense and Illustration of the French Language.* Trans. G. M. Turquet. London: Dent, 1939.
Durling, Robert. "The Ascent of Mt. Ventoux and the Crisis of Allegory." *Italian Quarterly* 18(1974):7–28.
Ebeling, Gerhard. *Luther: An Introduction to His Thought.* 1964. Trans. R. A. Wilson. Philadelphia: Fortress Press, 1972.
Eliade, Mircea. *Patterns in Comparative Religion.* 1958. Trans. Rosemary Sheed. Cleveland: Meridian Books, 1963.
Ellrodt, Robert. *Neoplatonism in the Poetry of Edmund Spenser.* Travaux d'Humanisme et Renaissance xxxv. Geneva: E. Droz, 1960.
Farrer, Austin. *A Rebirth of Images: The Making of St. John's Apocalypse.* London: Dacre Press, 1949.
Ferguson, Margaret. *Trials of Desire: Renaissance Defenses of Poetry.* New Haven: Yale Univ. Press, 1983.
Fletcher, Angus. *Allegory: The Theory of a Symbolic Mode.* Ithaca: Cornell Univ. Press, 1964.
——. *The Prophetic Moment: An Essay on Spenser.* Chicago: Univ. of Chicago Press, 1971.
——. "'Positive Negation': Threshold, Sequence, and Personification in Coleridge." In *New Perspectives on Coleridge and Wordsworth,* ed. Geoffrey Hartman, 133–64. New York: Columbia Univ. Press, 1972.
Foucault, Michel. *Madness and Civilization: A History of Insanity in the Age of Reason.* 1961. Trans. Richard Howard. New York: Random House, 1965.
Fowler, Alistair. *Triumphal Forms: Structural Patterns in Elizabethan Poetry.* Cambridge: Cambridge Univ. Press, 1970.
——. *Spenser and the Numbers of Time.* New York: Barnes & Noble, 1964.
Frankfort, Henri, et al. *The Intellectual Adventure of Ancient Man: An Essay on Speculative Thought in the Ancient Near East.* Chicago: Univ. of Chicago Press, 1946.
Franklin, Julian H. *Jean Bodin and the Sixteenth-Century Revolution in the Methodology of Law and History.* New York: Columbia Univ. Press, 1963.
Freccero, John. "Medusa: The Letter and the Spirit." *Yearbook of Italian Studies* (1972):1–18.
——. "The Fig Tree and the Laurel: Petrarch's Poetics." *Diacritics* 5 (1975):34–40.
Freedman, H., and Maurice Simon, eds. and trans., *The Midrash Rabbah.* 13 vols. London: Soncino Press, 1961.
Freud, Sigmund. *Standard Edition of the Complete Psychological Works.* Ed. and trans. James Strachey et al. 24 vols. London: Hogarth Press, 1955.

Friedrich, Carl Joachim. *The Philosophy of Law in Historical Perspective.* 2d ed. Chicago: Univ. of Chicago Press, 1963.

Frye, Northrop. *Anatomy of Criticism: Four Essays.* Princeton: Princeton Univ. Press, 1957.

——. *Fables of Identity: Studies in Poetic Mythology.* New York: Harcourt, Brace, & World, 1963.

——. *The Secular Scripture: A Study of the Structure of Romance.* Cambridge, Mass.: Harvard Univ. Press, 1976.

Giamatti, A. Bartlett. *Exile and Change in Renaissance Literature.* New Haven: Yale Univ. Press, 1984.

Girard, René. *Violence and the Sacred.* 1972. Trans. Patrick Gregory. Baltimore: The Johns Hopkins Univ. Press, 1977.

Goldberg, Jonathan. *Endlesse Worke: Spenser and the Structures of Discourse.* Baltimore: The Johns Hopkins Univ. Press, 1981.

——. *James I and the Politics of Literature: Jonson, Shakespeare, Donne, and Their Contemporaries.* Baltimore: The Johns Hopkins Univ. Press, 1983.

Golding, Arthur, trans. *Ovid's "Metamorphoses."* Ed. John Frederick Nims. New York: Macmillan, 1965.

Gordon, D. J. *The Renaissance Imagination: Essays and Lectures.* Ed. Stephen Orgel. Berkeley and Los Angeles: Univ. of California Press, 1975.

Graves, Robert. *The Greek Myths.* 2 vols. New York: George Braziller, 1957.

Gray, M. M. "The Influence of Spenser's Irish Experiences on *The Faerie Queene.*" *Review of English Studies* 6(1930):412–28.

Greenblatt, Stephen. *Renaissance Self-Fashioning: From More to Shakespeare.* Chicago: Univ. of Chicago Press, 1980.

——. "Murdering Peasants: Status, Genre, and the Representation of Rebellion." *Representations* 1(1983):1–30.

Greene, Thomas M. *The Descent from Heaven: A Study in Epic Continuity.* New Haven: Yale Univ. Press, 1963.

——. *The Light in Troy: Imitation and Discovery in Renaissance Poetry.* New Haven: Yale Univ. Press, 1982.

Grennan, Eamon. "Language and Politics: A Note on Some Metaphors in Spenser's *A View of the Present State of Ireland.*" *Spenser Studies* 3 (1982): 99–110.

Guillory, John. *Poetic Authority: Spenser, Milton, and Literary History.* New York: Columbia Univ. Press, 1983.

Hamilton, A. C., ed. *Essential Articles for the Study of Edmund Spenser.* Hamden, Conn.: Archon, 1972.

——, ed. *The Faerie Queene.* Annotated English Poets Series. London: Longman, 1977.

Hankins, John E. *Source and Meaning in Spenser's Allegory: A Study of* The Faerie *Queene.* London: Oxford Univ. Press, 1971.

Hartlaub, G. F. *Zauber des Spiegels: Gesichte und Bedeutung des Spiegels in der Kunst.* Munich: R. Piper, 1951.

Hathaway, Baxter. *The Age of Criticism: The Late Renaissance in Italy.* Ithaca: Cornell Univ. Press, 1962.

Havelock, Eric A. *Preface to Plato.* Cambridge, Mass.: Harvard Univ. Press, 1963.

Hawkins, Sherman. "Mutabilitie and the Cycle of the Months." In *Form and Convention in the Poetry of Edmund Spenser,* ed. William Nelson, 76–102. New York: Columbia Univ. Press, 1961.

Hazlitt, William. *Selected Essays.* Ed. Geoffrey Keynes. London: Nonesuch, 1930.

Hengel, Martin. *Judaism and Hellenism: Studies in their Encounter in Palestine during the Early Hellenistic Period.* 1968. 2 vols. Trans. John Bowden. Philadelphia: Fortress Press, 1974.

Heninger, S. K., Jr. "The Orgoglio Episode in *The Faerie Queene.*" In *Essential Articles,* ed. A. C. Hamilton, 125–38. Hamden, Conn.: Archon, 1972.

Hersman, Anne. *Studies in Greek Allegorical Interpretation.* Chicago: Blue Sky Press, 1906.

Hieatt, A. Kent."Scudamour's Practice of *Maistrye* upon Amoret." In *Essential Articles,* ed. A.C. Hamilton, 199–201. Hamden, Conn.: Archon, 1972.

Hollander, Anne. *Seeing through Clothes.* New York: Viking Press, 1978.

Honig, Edwin. *Dark Conceit: The Making of Allegory.* Providence: Brown Univ. Press, 1959.

Hope, A. D. *The Cave and the Spring: Essays on Poetry.* Chicago: Univ. of Chicago Press, 1965.

Hyde, Thomas. "Love's Pageants: The Figure of Cupid in the Poetry of Edmund Spenser." Ph.D. diss., Yale Univ., 1978.

Jauss, Hans Robert. *Aesthetic Experience and Literary Hermeneutics.* 1977. Trans. Michael Shaw. Minneapolis: Univ. of Minnesota Press, 1982.

Jewel, John. *An Apology for the Church of England.* Ed. J. E. Booty. Charlottesville: Folger Shakespeare Library and Univ. Press of Virginia, 1963.

Jonas, Hans. *The Gnostic Religion: The Message of the Alien God and the Beginnings of Christianity.* 2d ed., rev. Boston: Beacon Press, 1963.

Judson, Alexander C. *The Life of Edmund Spenser.* Baltimore: The Johns Hopkins Univ. Press, 1945.

Kafka, Franz. *The Great Wall of China: Stories and Reflections.* 1936. Trans. Willa and Edwin Muir. New York: Schocken, 1946.

Kaufmann, Yehezekel. *The Religion of Israel: From its Beginnings to the Babylonian Exile.* 1937–56. Trans. and abr. Moshe Greenberg. New York: Schocken Books, 1972.

Keats, John. *Poetical Works.* Ed. H. W. Garrod. London: Oxford Univ. Press, 1956.

Kermode, Frank. *The Sense of an Ending: Studies in the Theory of Fiction.* New York: Oxford Univ. Press, 1967.

——. *Shakespeare, Spenser, Donne: Renaissance Essays.* London: Routledge & Kegan Paul, 1971.

Kerrigan, William. "The Articulation of the Ego in the English Renaissance." In *The Literary Freud: Mechanisms of Defense and the Poetic Will,* Psychiatry and the Humanities, vol. 4, ed. Joseph H. Smith, 261–308. New Haven: Yale Univ. Press, 1980.

Kitzinger, Ernst. "The Cult of Images in the Age before Iconoclasm." *Dumbarton Oaks Papers* 8(1954):83–150.

Klein, Melanie. *Our Adult World and Other Essays.* New York: Basic Books, 1960.

Knight, G. Wilson. "The Spenserian Fluidity." In *The Burning Oracle,* 1939. Rpt. and rev. in *Poets of Action,* 1–17. London: Methuen, 1967.

Kris, Ernst, and Otto Kurz. *Legend, Myth, and Magic in the Image of the Artist: A Historical Experiment.* 1934. New Haven: Yale Univ. Press, 1979.

Lacan, Jacques. *Écrits: A Selection.* 1966. Trans. Alan Sheridan. London: Tavistock, 1977.

Ladner, Gerhart B. "The Concept of the Image in the Greek Fathers and the Byzantine Iconoclastic Controversy." *Dumbarton Oaks Papers* 7(1953):1–34.

——. *The Idea of Reform: Its Impact on Christian Thought and Action in the Age of the Fathers.* Cambridge, Mass.: Harvard Univ. Press, 1959.

Lewis, C. S. *The Allegory of Love: A Study in Medieval Tradition.* London: Oxford Univ. Press, 1936.

——. *Spenser's Images of Life.* Ed. Alistair Fowler. Cambridge: Cambridge Univ. Press, 1967.

Longfellow, Henry Wadsworth. *Complete Poetical Works.* Boston: Houghton-Mifflin, 1886.

MacCaffrey, Isabel G. *Spenser's Allegory: The Anatomy of Imagination.* Princeton: Princeton Univ. Press, 1976.

MacFarland, Thomas. *Romanticism and the Forms of Ruin: Wordsworth, Coleridge, and the Modalities of Fragmentation.* Princeton: Princeton Univ. Press, 1981.

MacLachlan, Hugh. "'In the Person of Prince Arthur': Spenserian *Magnificence* and the Ciceronian Tradition." *University of Toronto Quarterly* 46 (1976):125–46.

Mâle, Émile. *The Gothic Image: Religious Art in France of the Thirteenth Century.* 1898. Trans. Dora Nussey. New York: Harper & Row, 1958.

Malinowski, Bronislaw. *The Language of Magic and Gardening.* Vol. 2 of *Coral Gardens and Their Magic.* Bloomington: Indiana Univ. Press, 1965.

Manley, Lawrence. *Convention: 1500–1750.* Cambridge, Mass.: Harvard Univ. Press, 1980.

Marks, Herbert. "The Double Cave: Biblical Naming and Poetic Etymology." Paper read at the English Institute, Cambridge, Massachusetts, 30 August 1984.

——. "Pauline Typology and Revisionary Criticism." *Journal of the American Academy of Religion* 52(1984):71–92.

Markus, R. A. "St. Augustine on Signs." *Phronesis* 2(1957):60–83.

Marlowe, Christopher. *Complete Plays.* Ed. Irving Ribner. New York: Odyssey Press, 1963.

Massey, Irving. *The Gaping Pig: Literature and Metamorphosis.* Berkeley and Los Angeles: Univ. of California Press, 1976.

Milton, John. *Poetical Works.* Ed. Helen Darbishire. London: Oxford Univ. Press, 1958.

Montaigne, Michel de. *Essays*. Trans. John Florio. 3 vols. London: Dent, 1910.
Nelson, William. *The Poetry of Edmund Spenser: A Study*. New York: Columbia Univ. Press, 1963.
Nicholas of Cusa. *Of Learned Ignorance*. Trans. Germain Heron. New Haven: Yale Univ. Press, 1954.
Nietzsche, Friedrich. *The Twilight of the Idols*. 1888. In *The Portable Nietzsche*, trans. Walter Kaufmann, 463–563. New York: Viking Press, 1968.
——. *Daybreak: Thoughts on the Prejudices of Morality*. 1881. Trans. R. J. Hollingdale. Cambridge: Cambridge Univ. Press, 1982.
Nitzsche, Jane Chance. *The Genius Figure in Antiquity and the Middle Ages*. New York: Columbia Univ. Press, 1972.
Nohrnberg, James. *The Analogy of "The Faerie Queene."* Princeton: Princeton Univ. Press, 1976.
Noth, Martin. *Numbers: A Commentary*. Philadelphia: Westminster Press, 1968.
Orgel, Stephen. *The Jonsonian Masque*. Cambridge, Mass.: Harvard Univ. Press, 1965.
Otway-Ruthven, A. J. *A History of Medieval Ireland*. London: Ernest Benn, 1968.
Ozment, Stephen. *The Age of Reform, 1250–1550: An Intellectual and Religious History of Late Medieval and Reformation Europe*. New Haven: Yale Univ. Press, 1980.
Panofsky, Erwin. *Studies in Iconology: Humanistic Themes in the Art of the Renaissance*. New York: Harper & Row, 1972.
Parker, Patricia A. *Inescapable Romance: Studies in the Poetics of a Mode*. Princeton: Princeton Univ. Press, 1979.
Pelikan, Jaroslav. *Luther the Expositor: An Introduction to the Reformer's Exegetical Writings*. St. Louis: Concordia Publishing, 1959.
——. *The Emergence of the Catholic Tradition (100-600)*. Vol. 1 of *The Christian Tradition: A History of the Development of Doctrine*. Chicago: Univ. of Chicago Press, 1971.
Petrarch, Francesco. *Rerum familiarum libri, I-VIII*. Trans. Aldo S. Bernardo. Albany: State Univ. of New York Press, 1975.
Phillips, John. *The Reformation of Images: Destruction of Art in England, 1535–1660*. Berkeley and Los Angeles: Univ. of California Press, 1973.
Pico della Mirandola, Giovanni. *Commento sopra una canzona de amore composta da Girolamo Benivieni*. In *De Hominis Dignitate, Heptaplus, De Ente et Uno, e Scritti Vari*, ed. Eugenio Garin. Florence: Valecchi, 1942.
Plato. *Phaedrus*. Trans. R. Hackforth. Cambridge: Cambridge Univ. Press, 1972.
Pocock, J.G.A. *The Machiavellian Moment: Florentine Political Thought and the Atlantic Republican Tradition*. Princeton: Princeton Univ. Press, 1975.
Pope, Marvin H., trans. and ed. *The Anchor Bible: Song of Songs*. Garden City: Doubleday, 1977.
Preus, James Samuel. *From Shadow to Promise: Old Testament Interpretation from Augustine to the Young Luther*. Cambridge, Mass.: Harvard Univ. Press, 1969.

Puttenham, George. *The Arte of English Poesie.* Ed. Edward Arber. London: A. Constable and Col., 1906.
Quilligan, Maureen. *The Language of Allegory: Defining the Genre.* Ithaca: Cornell Univ. Press, 1979.
——. *Milton's Spenser: The Politics of Reading.* Ithaca: Cornell Univ. Press, 1983.
Raleigh, Sir Walter. *The History of the World.* Ed. and abr. C. A. Patrides. Philadelphia: Temple Univ. Press, 1971.
Rathborne, Isabel E. *The Meaning of Spenser's Fairyland.* New York: Columbia Univ. Press, 1937.
Reynolds, Henry. *Mythomystes.* 1632. Rpt. Menston, Yorkshire: Scolar Press, 1972.
Ricoeur, Paul. *The Symbolism of Evil.* 1967. Trans. Emerson Buchanan. Boston: Beacon Press, 1969.
——. *Freud and Philosophy: An Essay on Interpretation.* Trans. Denis Savage. New Haven: Yale Univ. Press, 1970.
Ringler, Richard N. "The Faunus Episode." In *Essential Articles,* ed. A. C. Hamilton, 289–98. Hamden, Conn.: Archon, 1972.
Ripa, Cesare. *Iconologia.* Rome, 1593.
Roche, Thomas P. *The Kindly Flame: A Study of the Third and Fourth Books of Spenser's "Faerie Queene."* Princeton: Princeton Univ. Press, 1964.
Ruskin, John. *Works.* 39 vols. Ed. E. T. Cook and Alexander Wedderburn. London: George Allen, 1903–10.
Schneidau, Herbert N. *Sacred Discontent: The Bible and Western Tradition.* Berkeley and Los Angeles: Univ. of California Press, 1977.
Schneweis, Emil. *Angels and Demons According to Lactantius.* Washington, D.C.: Catholic Univ. of America Press, 1944.
Scholem, Gershom. *Major Trends in Jewish Mysticism.* New York: Schocken, 1946.
——. *The Messianic Idea in Judaism.* New York: Schocken, 1971.
——. *Kabbalah.* New York: Quadrangle, 1974.
Seidel, Michael. *Satiric Inheritance: Rabelais to Sterne.* Princeton: Princeton Univ. Press, 1979.
Shakespeare, William. *The Complete Works.* Ed. Alfred Harbage et al. Baltimore: Penguin, 1969.
Shroeder, John W. "Spenser's Erotic Drama: The Orgoglio Episode." *ELH* 29 (1962):140–59.
Sidney, Sir Philip. *Prose Works.* 4 vols. Ed. Albert Feuillerat. Cambridge: Cambridge Univ. Press, 1912.
Siebers, Tobin. *The Mirror of Medusa.* Berkeley and Los Angeles: Univ. of California Press, 1983.
Skulsky, Harold. *Metamorphosis: The Mind in Exile.* Cambridge, Mass.: Harvard Univ. Press, 1981.
Snell, Bruno. *The Discovery of the Mind: The Greek Origins of Human Thought.* 1948. Trans. T. G. Rosenmeyer. Cambridge, Mass.: Harvard Univ. Press, 1953.

Speiser, E. A., trans. and ed. *The Anchor Bible: Genesis.* Garden City: Doubleday, 1964.

Spenser, Edmund. *Poetical Works.* Ed. J. C. Smith and E. de Selincourt. London: Oxford Univ. Press, 1912.

——. *A View of the Present State of Ireland.* Ed. W. L. Renwick. Oxford: Clarendon Press, 1970.

Starobinski, Jean. "The Struggle with Legion: A Literary Analysis of Mark 5:1–20." *New Literary History* 4(1973):331–56.

Steinberg, Leo. "The Metaphors of Love and Birth in Michelangelo's *Pietàs.*" In *Studies in Erotic Art,* ed. Theodore Bowie and Cornelia V. Christenson, 231–85. New York: Basic Books, 1970.

Stevens, Wallace. *Collected Poems.* New York: Alfred A. Knopf, 1942.

Stokes, Adrian. *A Game That Must Be Lost.* Cheshire: Carcanet Press, 1973.

Stubblebine, James. *Giotto: The Arena Chapel Frescoes.* New York: Norton, 1969.

Sylvester, Joshuah. *Complete Works.* Ed. Alexander Grosart. 2 vols. Edinburgh, 1880.

Todorov, Tzvetan. *The Poetics of Prose.* 1971. Trans. Richard Howard. Ithaca: Cornell Univ. Press, 1977.

Tonkin, Humphrey. *Spenser's Courteous Pastoral: Book Six of the "Faerie Queene."* Oxford: Oxford Univ. Press, 1972.

Tuve, Rosemond. *Allegorical Imagery: Some Medieval Books and Their Posterity.* Princeton: Princeton Univ. Press, 1966.

Tyndale, William. *The Work of William Tindale.* Ed. S. L. Greenslade. London: Blackie & Son, 1910.

Upton, John. *Spenser's Faerie Queene.* 2 vols. London: R & J Thompson, 1758.

Vico, Giambattista. *The New Science.* Trans. Thomas Goddard Bergin and Max Harold Fisch. Rev. ed. Ithaca: Cornell Univ. Press, 1968.

von Rad, Gerhard. *Old Testament Theology.* 1957. 2 vols. Trans. D.M.G. Stalker. New York: Harper & Row, 1962.

Walker, D. P. *Spiritual and Demonic Magic from Ficino to Campanella.* London: Warburg Institute, 1958.

Waters, D. Douglas. *Duessa as Theological Satire.* Columbia: Univ. of Missouri Press, 1970.

Welsford, Enid. *The Court Masque: A Study of the Relationship between Poetry and the Revels.* Cambridge: Cambridge Univ. Press, 1927.

Whitbread, Leslie George, trans. *Fulgentius the Mythographer.* Columbus: Ohio State Univ. Press, 1971.

White, Hayden. "The Forms of Wildness: Archaeology of an Idea." In *The Wild Man Within: An Image in Western Thought from the Renaissance to Romanticism,* ed. Edward Dudley and Maximillian Novak, 3–38. Pittsburgh: Univ. of Pittsburgh Press, 1972.

Williams, Arnold. *The Common Expositor: An Account of the Commentaries on Genesis, 1527-1633.* Chapel Hill: Univ. of North Carolina Press, 1948.

Wind, Edgar. *Pagan Mysteries in the Renaissance.* New York: Norton, 1968.

Wittgenstein, Ludwig. *Remarks on Frazer's "Golden Bough."* 1967. Trans. A. C. Miles. Ed. Rush Rhees. Atlantic Highlands: Humanities Press, 1979

Wittreich, Joseph Anthony, Jr. *Visionary Poetics: Milton's Tradition and His Legacy.* San Marino: Huntington Library, 1979.

Yates, Frances A. *Giordano Bruno and the Hermetic Tradition.* Chicago: Univ. of Chicago Press, 1964.

——. *Astraea: The Imperial Theme in the Sixteenth Century.* London: Routledge & Kegan Paul, 1975.

Yeats, William Butler. *Essays and Introductions.* New York: Macmillan, 1961.

——. *Collected Poems.* London: Macmillan, 1961.

Ziolkowski, Theodore. *Disenchanted Images: A Literary Iconology.* Princeton: Princeton Univ. Press, 1977.

Zitner, S. P., ed. *The Mutabilitie Cantos.* London: Nelson, 1968.

Index

Library of Congress Cataloging in Publication Data

Gross, Kenneth.
Spenserian poetics.

Bibliography: p.
Includes index.
1. Spenser, Edmund, 1552?–1599. Faerie queene.
2. Idols and images in literature. 3. Iconoclasm in literature. 4. Magic in literature. 5. Gods in literature. I. Title.
PR2358.G76 1985 821'.3 85-47701
ISBN 0-8041-1805-4